RESPONSE TO LITERATURE

WILLIAM J. GRACE
Fordham University

RESPONSE TO LITERATURE

McGRAW-HILL BOOK COMPANY
New York • St. Louis • San Francisco
Toronto • London • Sydney

RESPONSE TO LITERATURE

Library of Congress Catalog Card Number 64–8616

PREFACE

This book assumes that a genuine response to literature engages our whole being—our emotions and imagination as well as our critical faculties. To the extent that literature trains the imagination, exercises the intellect, and matures the emotions, it is a shaping force in our lives; it provides the values and locates the terms on which we must meet the actual challenges of life.

As a basic introduction to prose fiction and nonfiction, poetry, drama, and literary criticism, this book attempts to guide the student toward the essential things that the study of literature is meant to provide. The book is concerned largely with fundamentals of literary analysis and appreciation. It does not assume any immediate or sweeping changes in the way we academically assess the results of literary study. It provides definitions of the vital literary terms a student should know in order to make the fruits of literary study as rich as possible and to write critical essays and examinations with maximum effectiveness. It also presents the key terms of the new criticism and the new scholarship which are now filtering through all levels. Such material is developed partly in the text proper and partly in the full-dress glossary of common terms. Discussion questions have been included at the end of each chapter. Footnotes and suggestions for further reading, however, have been placed at the back of the book in order to keep the text as clear and uncluttered as possible. The text is flexible and lends itself to a variety of existing needs, whether as a companion text for use with anthologies or selected paperbacks in literature courses or as a basic text in courses in literary criticism.

At every point, the text is meant to balance a sense of inner freedom with objective norms, so that the student's approach to literature is initially concerned with the sincerity of his own reactions.

These reactions may be far from perfect or "right," but their sincerity will give him a chance really to grow rather than to parrot the findings of others. This honesty, whether naïve or sophisticated, is central to any growth in his response to literature, for the student must finally find his own way through the vast sea of utterance that we call literature. The great artist in literature has already shown the way. Constantly imposing an inner unity on diverse, conflicting, dynamic, and sometimes apparently inchoate forces in his own material, the artist finally gives us a testament which we know is to be treasured and constantly reexamined. It is this sense of literature, going far beyond any classroom, which we deeply desire the reader to share.

WILLIAM J. GRACE

CONTENTS

PREFACE v

PART ONE

WHAT IS LITERATURE? 1

A Book 2

What Is Literature? 5

Relationship of Literature to Culture 7

Literature and Psychological Growth 8

Responsibility of Literature to Truth 9

Holding the Mirror Up to Nature 11

Literature and Contemplation 13

Elements of the Beautiful 14

Perceiving the Beautiful 16

Tension in a Work of Art 20

The Question about the Moral Value of Literature 22

Literature and Symbolism 29

Archetype and Myth 36

Illustration: An Archetypal Poem 39

Literature and Human Values 41

Literature's Role of Integration 42

Discussion Questions 48

PART TWO

RESPONSE TO POETRY 51

Art Asks for Response 52

Response to Poetry 53

Characteristics of Poetry 55

Intuition 56

Imagination 58

Synthesis 59

Mental Association 61

The Inspiring Power of Poetry 64

Levels of Meaning 68

Illustration: Levels of Meaning in *Paradise Lost* 73

Poetic Mood 79
Poetry, Rhythm, Meter 83
Content and Form 91
The Artist's Intention 93
Rhetoric and Pure Poetry 94
Discussion Questions 97

PART THREE
RESPONSE TO PROSE 99

Response to Prose 100
Narrative: From Public Hero to Private Analysis; from Epic to Novel 102
Illustration: Ancient and Modern Odysseys 104
The Epic Narrative 105
The Realistic Novel 107
The Naturalistic Novel 108
A Change in Emphasis 109
Later Developments of the Novel 110
Modern Theories of Fiction 113
Narrative as Showing Rather Than as Telling 114
The Role of Convention 116
The Great Scene in Narrative 118
Illustration: The Death of Anna Karenina 119
Pity and Fear 123
Humor 124
Illustration: Humor in Gogol's *Dead Souls* 126
Illustration: Humor in Strachey's *Queen Victoria* 129
Satire 131
Illustration: Satire in Zamiatin's *We* 132
Prose as Personality and Reflection 135
The Short Story 139
Range and Versatility of the Short Story 143
New Art Forms in the Short Story 148
Illustration: Art Form in James Joyce's "The Dead" 149
Discussion Questions 152

PART FOUR
RESPONSE TO DRAMA 155

Response to Drama 156
Illustration: Action of *Antigone* 157

Aristotelian Principles 162
Dramatic Action 163
Illustration: Dramatic Analysis of *Riders to the Sea* 165
The Emotional Power of Tragedy 167
The World of Comedy 171
The Problem of Tragicomedy 174
Other Forms of Drama 176
Expressionism in the Theater 176
The Theater of the Absurd 178
Discussion Questions

PART FIVE
THE CRITICISM OF LITERATURE 183

Approach to Criticism 184
The Critic: Judge or Interpreter? 185
The Dual Character of Criticism 188
Moral Criticism 190
Vividness In Criticism 191
Criticism and Literary Labels 191
The Reader as Critic 192
Criticism of Specific Types 193
Illustration: Criticism of a Poem 194
Discussion Questions

EPILOGUE
THE POWER OF THE IMAGINATION 203
Discussion Questions 210

GLOSSARY OF COMMON TERMS 211
NOTES 276
BIBLIOGRAPHY 285
INDEX 291

PART ONE

What Is Literature?

. . . yet the majority of men will always require
humane letters; and so much the more,
as they have the more and greater results of science
to relate to the need in man for conduct,
and to the need in him for beauty.

MATTHEW ARNOLD

. . . and with a tale, forsooth,
he cometh unto you,
with a tale which holdeth children from play,
and old men from the chimney-corner.

SIR PHILIP SIDNEY

A BOOK

To have a new book in your hand is in itself an adventure. To what new world, to what new experience will you be taken? What half-felt, half-expressed ideas and intuitions do you now find eloquently expressed for you—matters that you knew about but could not quite realize? How often in a new book do you find the completion of your own thoughts? And how often do you find astonishingly new and important things to think about for the first time?

A book is excitement. This is the primary thing you have a right to expect, before there is any question of courses, scholarship, points of departure, and "bull sessions" about life and its problems. And it is this excitement that should always underlie any advanced study of literature. Sometimes you may come across a teacher to whom literature has become a great mass of facts and of arid and bewildering relationships. The world of literature becomes like a mountain of sawdust, apparently hardly worth the trouble of shoveling it—for the stuff simply sifts back into the same unconquerable shifting mess. Where love, enthusiasm, vitality should be, we have smog, tedium, a sort of chain-gang work on an endless road. This relationship to literature is like that of a married couple who try to maintain their relationship by ceaseless activity when love no longer exists.

A great book deserves attention and love in return for what it gives us. Just as in human relationships we cannot rush from person to person, giving no one a real concern or sympathy, and expect fruitful relationships, so it is with books. Just as in life it is better to deepen and strengthen a few relationships than to acquire a passing acquaintance with everyone in the world, so it is with books. But to achieve this is a kind of art, an art with which this book is concerned.

Literature has aspects at least as complex as those of any human personality we may know. It can arouse every conceivable kind of emotion in us, often several emotions at once. It can appeal to our evaluating ability, to our critical intelligence, by humor, irony, satire. It can move us to the deepest kind of sympathy through pathos and tragedy. It can delight us by the beautiful and restful world of dream and fantasy. It can plunge us into the powerful and turbulent world of the imagination. It helps us to love, to sympathize, to hate properly (for there is a proper way to hate), to tolerate and to reject, to realize the realities of the known and of the unknown. It often gives us an insight into truth, and it often gives us the key to how to search for truth. A great book can be open-ended as in the case of Plato's *Dialogues* or Shakespeare's *Hamlet,* leaving us with an unanswered problem we are grateful to know about even if we do not have a present solution. A book can also be dynamite blasting us into awareness of something important that we have ignored.

As our knowledge of books increases—real knowledge of books gained by care and attention, not a promiscuous and cursory acquaintance with books—we become increasingly aware of what is meant by *tradition.* A great figure or symbol of the imagination germinates in the minds of others besides its original inventor, is born and reborn. Consider the image of Helen of Troy. She was already invested with curiosity, mystery, and dignity when Homer wrote about her. She already had a heroic, a legendary quality. In one sense, it was foolish for the Greeks and Trojans to fight a major war over a woman, yet Helen manages to stand for what men live for, what motivates them in the face of disaster and catastrophe—home, love, beauty. All this, in spite of the fact that Helen does not have a morally strong character. But she stands for something universal in woman, even in a curious way for the sense of honor, and interestingly enough, for a kind of ambiguity and fragility even in man's finest hour. There is a moment in Homer's *Iliad* when the opposing warriors come together and try to get to the heart of the matter, Helen's role in the war. They have their moment of rationality, but it is brief and the war continues. But somehow in this complex psychological situation, though it is regrettable that men cannot always act rationally, the warriors maintain their nobility, and Helen herself is far more than a simple seductress. If wars have to be fought, there is something basically human, personal, and yet universal about fighting for the love of a woman—irrational, maybe, but not petty or trivial in human terms, as the possession of a military base or of a mining area of strategic raw materials might seem.

Helen's attractiveness is reborn in the minds of other men besides Homer. Of the many instances, we may cite two that are widely known. For Christopher Marlowe, Helen becomes the legendary image of all that is beautiful, that inspires men to run into the heart of danger:

I will be Paris, and for love of thee,
Instead of Troy, shall Wertenberg be sacked;
And I will combat with weak Menelaus,
And wear thy colors on my plumed crest.

(*The Tragical History of Doctor Faustus,* XIV, 100–103)

Helen is the motivation to courage and the reward of conflict:

O, thou art fairer than the evening air
Clad in the beauty of a thousand stars.

(XIV, 106–107)

For Edgar Allan Poe, Helen has become the symbol of all that is enchanting, enticing in the classical tradition:

Helen, thy beauty is to me
Like those Nicaean barks of yore,
That gently, o'er a perfumed sea,
The weary wayworn wanderer bore
To his own native shore.

On desperate seas long wont to roam,
Thy hyacinth hair, thy classic face,
Thy Naiad airs, have brought me home
To the glory that was Greece
And the grandeur that was Rome.

("To Helen")

If a Marlowe or a Poe is moved to excited expression by Homer's image of Helen, think of the excitement of Keats on first reading Chapman's translation of Homer's work. Herein is expressed the great emotion of a great reader of a great work. This is the sort of primal reaction that great literature is intended for:

Much have I travell'd in the realms of gold,
And many goodly states and kingdoms seen;
Round many western islands have I been
Which bards in fealty to Apollo hold.
Oft of one wide expanse had I been told

That deep-brow'd Homer ruled as his demesne;
Yet did I never breathe its pure serene
Till I heard Chapman speak out loud and bold:
Then felt I like some watcher of the skies
When a new planet swims into his ken;
Or like stout Cortez when with eagle eyes
He star'd at the Pacific—and all his men
Look'd at each other with a wild surmise
Silent, upon a peak in Darien.

("On First Looking into Chapman's Homer")

Nothing can be substituted for this sense of immediacy, of excitement in greeting literature. There are many things useful to know about literature, as we shall show in the following pages, but the primary thing is to experience literature so that it means something important in terms of the reader's own life. New knowledge about literature, to be fruitful, must add to this sense of excitement, of wonder.

WHAT IS LITERATURE?

Before one embarks on a serious study of a subject, it is helpful to stand aside and get the long view of it, to see it in perspective—in its largest terms as well as in its details.

So we have a right to ask, "What *is* literature?" And in discovering an answer, we touch upon many other things, because literature is almost coextensive with life itself.

Literature is, first of all, a creative work of art, an object that an artist makes. It is not merely an idea, a theory, a system of thought, although ideas, theories, and systems of thought enter into it. As an object made by an artist, it has two main purposes.

First, a creative work expresses the truth of experience in terms of "beauty to be contemplated." Beauty is meant to be contemplated and, in this sense, a creative work helps to meet the human need for contemplation.

Secondly, a creative work meets the human necessity for a means of communicating ideas of intellectual and social significance. In this sense, a creative work indicates what the artist thought, and also, through its germinative power, it is the source of new ideas in the future, forming a living tradition.

The material out of which the human artist creates is experience of life. That is why Aristotle defines art as *mimesis,* or a heightened imitation of experience.[1]

Because the artist cannot be haphazard in gathering materials for the making of his art, he brings choice and a system of values to bear on the multiplicity of experience. In this sense, a creative work because it is selective is also a *criticism* of life.

In its criticism of life, literature explains, in terms of the concrete, the values of general ideas and theories that socially influence various ages. In order to know what the prevailing values of any given society are, it is necessary to discover that society's view of the nature of man. Literature helps us to evaluate such essential ideas. It is a focal point where leading concepts from other studies (philosophy, history, science) are expressed in terms of concrete experience.

According to Aristotle's *The Poetics,* art (including the art of literature) is a heightened or selective imitation of life or experience. It is not merely a report of experience. It is experience viewed and assessed by a beholder. All art is, in this sense, a *mimesis.* One art differs from another in the medium it employs for the purpose of imitation.[2] Music, a no less sensitive, but more restricted, form of art than that of literature, is concerned with sound. Literature embraces aspects of many of the other arts, including those of music. Aristotle relates art to experience directly by viewing art as a legitimate and selective expression of experience.

In the study of literature, therefore, all that makes for *understanding* as distinct from mere information is important. As Mortimer Adler says, "It is as wasteful to read a great book solely for information as to use a fountain pen for digging worms."[3]

The function of literature is to make a heightened or selective imitation of life through the medium of literary art. The value of literature depends partly upon the degree to which the imitation of life is heightened or selected. Consequently, where there is little selection (for emphasis results from selection) we merely have in a work an unemphatic transcription of actual fact. Such a work would find a fairly low place in the hierarchy of literary values, for the value of the imitation must depend, among other things, upon the degree to which it is heightened or selected. And this, in turn, depends upon the depth of the artist's thought and upon the artist's ability to recreate his thought in the actual making of a work of art.

The importance of literature in relation to the life of the reader may be simply stated by saying that literature concentrates our impression of certain areas of human experience. We have in literature a suitable medium for clarifying the meaning of experience and thus organizing our own reactions, actual and potential, to the experience of life.

It seems reasonable that we should read literature not only to appreciate it as an art, to recognize its beauty of form, but also to gain experience, a vicarious or imaginative experience that has an analogy to reality.

"Vicarious" is a word etymologically derived from a Latin word meaning "in place of." Literature gives us a special knowledge of life that is not identical with that of real experience but provides a profitable supplement in terms of intellectual and critical values. It is actually possible for a well-read person to make a mature evaluation of life without having had a great deal of direct experience.

RELATIONSHIP OF LITERATURE TO CULTURE

Educational institutions have made a point of emphasizing literature as a *cultural* study. Culture in this sense should be understood as something more important than group *mores* or social convention. The word "culture" has a wide connotation, but it always implies the embodiment of the fruits of thought in actual living. One can easily distinguish, for example, between the truly cultured person, the person who renders his life harmonious with his thought, and that person who is informed but not cultured, whose life is unrelated to his thought, whose life does not embody the fruits of thinking.

Literature brings the test of experience to a wide range of ideas drawn from different fields of study. Literature in itself embodies actual material from wide and different fields. In order to gather and supplement those fruits of thought needed for a deepened culture, a person must go to literature. Philosophy, history, and science, invaluable in themselves, are nevertheless not sufficient to present the fruits of thought and experience of life with which a cultured person should be familiar.

Literature and Psychological Growth

Aristotle laid down the principle that we imitate unconsciously or consciously what we admire. There is some justification in saying that, if we come to admire what has been best thought and expressed concerning life (this is the highest literature), we also should personally develop similar powers of thought and even of expression. From our very admiration, from the very fact of a growing sensitivity, we should come to embody in actual life the fruits of thought that we have acquired from literature. The concept of the hero in Homer or Virgil, in Tasso, Ariosto, or Spenser is closely associated with imitation, for it assumes that, through reading about a perfect prince or leader, we shall come to express similar values in our own lives.[4]

Some philosophers have argued that a sense of morality is not innate, that we have to learn all knowledge on the natural level through the use of the senses. Morality has to be taught and learned like any other branch of knowledge. Good moral teaching, like all other teaching, has to keep in mind the principle of "imitation."

A creative work is also a means to psychological health through its emotional impact both for the artist who creates and for the audience who enjoys the creation. By *catharsis* Aristotle suggests an increase of health in the soul through the fruitful expression of the emotions in the aesthetic experience. Sigmund Freud, in his concept of sublimation, or the "raising up" of instinctual urges to a higher "threshold," offers a similar idea to that of Aristotle's.[5] To the observations of these two men a religious observer would add another: emotional response to creative work leads to increased contemplation of beauty on the level of direct experience and makes contemplation on the religious level more possible.

How useful is a creative work? It is not of immediate use in a narrow sense, in terms of dollars and products. But if one could think of what is demanded by the transcendent spiritual nature of man, of his need to practice contemplation, nothing could be more useful than the beautiful. Since a creative work is beautiful, it is the material of contemplation, therefore useful in the highest sense.

Responsibility of Literature to Truth

When we assume that literature is responsible to truth, we mean those deeper levels of truth that are essential to a rational concept of the nature of man. We mean the truth of experience. It is possible for all literature—not merely literature from the Hebraic-Christian tradition—to portray the nature of man convincingly on the *natural* level. Even where literature appreciably fails in this matter, it may still have considerable value for the student of ideas and of historical perspective. But literature is defective from the point of view of its intrinsic worth if it does not present a true picture of the nature of man, in terms of the truth of his experience.

This does not mean that literature must not conflict with factual or scientific truth. The truth of art is not that of science. Even art that we have come to regard as representational—a portrait, for example—actually depends upon the acceptance of certain illusions (we may call them conventions). We assume in a portrait, for example, that two dimensions (length and breadth) are the equivalent of three (length, breadth, and *depth*). We are so accustomed from childhood to certain artistic conventions or illusions that we never question them. When we come to an unfamiliar medium such as abstract art, however, we may be at a loss because of a lack of familiarity with a new set of conventions or illusions necessary to understanding such art.

Violations of scientific truth simply do not matter because of the nature of artistic illusion. Samuel Taylor Coleridge understood rightly that art works through illusion when he spoke of the "willing suspension of disbelief" as a prerequisite for the enjoyment of art.[6]

Violations of factual or scientific truth in art might be compared to a game in the sense that an audience watching a man take a rabbit out of a hat will accept a deception that it knows is not a lie. The order of art is not the order of immediate experience. But it does not follow that because art is different from the immediate order of experience that is therefore free to lack truth in the universal sense and on the deepest levels. Any assumption that is *organic* to a work of art and at the same time denies and vitiates human experience on the deeper levels irreparably lowers the value of such art. Occasional statements about life and death and general experience that are fallacious do not necessarily mar a work of art to any great degree, but when they are *basic* to the whole imitation that an artist has to offer of life, we can legitimately object that the art lacks greatness because it lacks truth. We may say paradoxically that we are entitled to criticize an artist adversely if within the terms of the illusion of art he gives us *an illusioned view of life.*

It does not matter, for example, that the voyage the Ancient Mariner takes in Coleridge's poem could not be duplicated by the most ambitious travel agency. We are not likely to see ice, mast-high, as green as emerald nor will the water burn with witches' oils. We are not likely to meet with the Specter Woman or even water snakes. The truth of *The Rime of the Ancient Mariner* does not consist in these matters, but in the social and ethical values symbolized in its concepts of providence and repentance.

Art is concerned not with the immediate order of experience but with experience imitated in a work of art. Art and experience are not identical. This is a simple statement, but how often it needs to be repeated! Many ethical and critical confusions arise from the disregard of this essential fact. It would be unfair criticism, for example, to say that the author of *A Tree Grows in Brooklyn* lied because she presented an incident as taking place in Greenpoint, Brooklyn, when it did not *in fact* occur there. What is relevant is not whether such an incident actually occurred but whether such an incident *could* conceivably occur. An artist is not concerned with what actually happened but with what may happen. In fact Aristotle thinks of poetry (by which he does not mean verse but creative art generally) as more philosophical and universal than history (which *is* concerned with the authenticity of fact) because poetry deals with what *may be* rather than with what *has been:*

> The distinction between historian and poet is not in the one writing prose and the other verse—you might put the work of Herodotus into verse, and it would still be a species of history; it consists really in this, that the one describes the thing that has been, and the other a kind of thing that might be. Hence poetry is something more philosophic and of greater import than history, since its statements are of the nature rather of universals, whereas those of history are singulars.[7]

HOLDING THE MIRROR UP TO NATURE

Hamlet spoke of the need of holding the mirror up to nature—"to show virtue her own feature, scorn her own image, and the very age and body of the time his form and pressure."[8] *Hamlet* itself is a study of interior states of mind and is, in this way, a work of art close to our own time where criticism has extended the concept of nature to include the inner psyche of the artist.

What is meant by "holding the mirror up to nature"? One critic points out an extremely relevant statement about this principle. "The poem itself is not a mirror. It does not merely reproduce a shadow of nature; it causes nature to be reflected in its containing form."[9] Actually what the artists present is an analogy (a correspondence, a partial similarity) with external nature. The mirror does not merely reflect external nature. Nature also includes a man's intelligence, his feelings, even himself seeing himself seeing! Dr. Samuel Johnson interpreted the phrase to mean "just representations of *general* nature," not passing elements of the contemporary scene.[10]

Much in the interpretation of literature depends upon the evaluation of this mirror-reflector. Plato thought it incurably defective, incapable of yielding a flawless and accurate image of reality. Aristotle, on the other hand, thought of a work of art as an object of its own kind and as an end in itself. The tendency in modern criticism is to extend the Aristotelian concept—a work of art is "heterocosm or 'second nature,' the overflow from a fountain, the music of a wind-harp, a growing plant—which would avoid some of the troublesome implications of the mirror."[11] Particularly strong in the Romantic era was the emphasis on the mirror as a reflector of the artist's mind, as in Percy Bysshe Shelley's "poet hidden in the light of thought":

Like a poet hidden
In the light of thought,
Singing hymns unbidden,
Till the world is wrought
To sympathy with hopes and fears it heeded not.

("To a Skylark," 36–40)

In considering literature as mirroring experience (where "experience" carries the sense of vicarious), we must not think of literature as presenting some sort of statistical norm. In so far as it reflects society, it may indicate only some special segment of it. Medieval narrative literature, for example, is largely one of the aristocracy, which partly accounts for the prevalence of certain themes, such as that of courtly love, which affected only a minority of the people of that time. More especially, as we shall show later in discussing literature as an art of conflict, literature tends to emphasize extraordinary rather than routine acts. Shakespeare, for example, presents a much higher statistical average of killings than would occur in real life. Many today speak adversely of violence in television, failing to call to mind the violence in Greek or Shakespearean drama. The question is not one of violence in itself, but of how violence is subordinated to a much higher, unifying purpose. Is the violence meaningful within the work of art or merely pointlessly sensational?

In great works of art, the values absorbing the violence are so great that one hardly ever suspects that a *Hamlet* or an *Agamemnon* is violent. It is, therefore, instructive to see, in a detached reportorial way, what constitutes the raw material of some great literary themes. A *Life* magazine writer describes below the facts about the great House of Atreus. Seen by themselves, the macabre details build up to the point of the absurd, become almost grotesquely comic. Yet when this violence has been transformed into major works of art by the Greek tragedians, one thinks only of illumination and profundity, emotional and intellectual. But can one say that the bare outlines of the story hold the mirror up to nature?

The legend begins with Pelops, who crossed the sea from Asia Minor to win the hand of the Greek princess Hippodamia. It was a dangerous quest because her father, King Oenomaus, challenged every suitor to a chariot race. If the suitor won, he won the princess. If he lost, he lost his life. Pelops accepted the challenge, won the race, married Hippodamia, and took over the kingdom. But he owed his victory to a crime. Before the race began he had bribed the king's charioteer to pull out the pins that secured the wheels to the king's chariot. Just as the king was overtaking Pelops, the wheels flew off and the king, tangled in the reins, was dragged to death behind his horses. When the charioteer later demanded his reward—half the kingdom and one night in the arms of Hippodamia—Pelops pushed him into the sea, where he drowned. But as he was dying, the man pronounced a curse on Pelops and all his

> breed. The curse began to take its toll in the next generation. Pelops' two sons, Atreus and Thyestes, quarreled over the kingdom of Mycenae. Atreus' wife took Thyestes as her lover and plotted to help him seize the throne. In spite of the conspirators, Atreus, with the help of Zeus, became king. When he had learned of the plot, Atreus devised a horrible revenge. He hacked his brother's children to bits and served them to him in a cannibal meal. Thyestes reeled back, kicked over the table, vomited and dashed out, screaming more curses on the House of Atreus.
>
> At Delphi the oracle revealed to Thyestes that he could avenge himself only by committing an unnatural outrage. His avenger, said the oracle, would be a son whom he must beget on his own daughter, his only surviving child. Thyestes seized the girl and raped her. She bore Aegisthus, who grew up to murder his uncle, Atreus, and establish the aged Thyestes on the throne of Mycenae.
>
> But Atreus' renowned sons, Agamemnon and Menelaus, soon drove Thyestes out again. Agamemnon took over Mycenae and Menelaus became ruler of Sparta. But the curse still held. Menelaus' beautiful wife, Helen, was abducted by Prince Paris of Troy. Agamemnon mobilized an expedition to bring her back. In obedience to the oracle, he added another crime to the family record. At Aulis he sacrificed his own daughter, Iphigenia, to obtain favorable winds for his fleet.
>
> During Agamemnon's long absence at Troy, Aegisthus, son of Thyestes, thirsting for revenge, came slinking back to Mycenae, seduced Agamemnon's strong-willed queen, Clytemnestra, and arrogantly lorded it over the city. When Agamemnon returned triumphant from Troy, it was only to meet a shameful death at the hand of the two lovers, who butchered him with an ax in his bath.[12]

And, of course, more is to follow. Orestes, with the help of his sister, Electra, kills his father's murderers, Clytemnestra, his own mother, and Aegisthus. In turn, Orestes is hounded by the Furies to the ends of the earth. The point, of course, is that modern times cannot improve on ancient tales of violence, and that violence never remains as violence in great literature.

LITERATURE AND CONTEMPLATION

Much as this fact seems to conflict with some of the prevailing habits of our national culture, man's nature is concerned with contemplation as well as with activity. A philosopher who has frequently written on art and literature states:

> Art prepares the human race for contemplation, the spiritual joy of which surpasses every other joy and seems to be the end of all human activities. For what useful purpose do servile work and trade serve, except to provide the body with the necessities of life so that it may be in a state fit for contemplation? What is the use of the moral virtues and prudence if not to procure the tranquility of the passions and interior peace which contemplation needs? To what end the whole government of civil life, if not to assure the exterior peace necessary to contemplation?[13]

Art is meant for contemplation. Art is meant to be beautiful. Beauty is meant for contemplation. And philosophers have stressed the relationship between the contemplative faculty and the ability to see the beautiful.

The beautiful is something we contemplate for its own sake, not for some intermediate end. The beautiful is often useful in the narrow sense, but it is not for the sake of being useful that it is beautiful.

Beauty is as necessary for the soul as food is for the body. We do not speak nearly enough of man's need for beauty.

ELEMENTS OF THE BEAUTIFUL

While a transcendent or universal value is to be found in the beautiful, no less important is the concrete and the unique aspect of the beautiful. It is particularly this concrete individuality that is so hard to define.

Gerard Manley Hopkins, the Jesuit poet who has greatly influenced modern letters, was particularly sensitive to the individuated aspect of the beautiful, particularly in the application of his favorite words, *instress* and *inscape*. Instress is "in effect for Hopkins the hand of God upon his creation."[14] "Inscape . . . was an insight, by Divine Grace, into the ultimate reality of seeing the 'pattern, air, melody' in things from, as it were, God's side."[15]

From the point of view of a Hopkins, we come to know God, to experience instress through knowledge of the concrete, the individuated. The keener our understanding of concrete individuality, the keener our perception of the transcendent and the universal. Man's knowledge is not purely intuitive, it is not angelic; it is also dependent upon the perception of matter. "The highest of human 'intuitions' are not innate, *infused*. . . . They require a mediated contact with matter through the senses, however brief, to set the soul aflash."[16] Human intuition, while not a material principle, is dependent upon perception of the material world for its activity.

In literature what is called the image may roughly be paralleled with the matter upon which the soul makes a "mediated contact" and penetrates the world of intuition. Notice, for example, how the concrete image of leaves serves to set the imagination aflash in the following passages, and how leaves become universalized as symbols.

Thus a Homeric speaker instresses the sadness of men as they abide the recurring experience of death, seen only in the light of natural experience:

> Great hearted Tydeides, why enquirest thou of my generation? Even as are the generations of leaves such as those likewise of men; the leaves that be the wind scattereth on the earth, and the forest buddeth and putteth forth more again, when the season of spring is at hand; so of the generations of men one putteth forth and another ceaseth.[17]

Glancing over the pages of a Milton or a Homer, you will come across complex images in which the transcendent and the immanent, the universal and the individuated, are fused to suggest vastness and grandeur. Thus Milton "mediates" with the same image:

> . . . *he stood and called*
> *His legions, angel forms, who lay entranced*
> *Thick as autumnal leaves that strew the brooks*
> *In Vallombrosa, where the Etrurian shades*
> *High over-arched embower. . . .*
>
> (*Paradise Lost*, I, 300 304)

John Ruskin in his essay "Of the Pathetic Fallacy" particularly stressed the greatness of the poetry that combined two levels of reality, the transcendent and the individuated, without any loss of the distinctness between them.

> When Dante describes the spirits falling from the bank of Acheron "as dead leaves flutter from a bough," he gives the most perfect image possible of their utter lightness, feebleness, passiveness, and scattering agony of despair, without, however, for an instant losing his own clear conception that *these* are souls, and *those* are leaves; he makes no confusion of the one with the other.[18]

As much as we might study or learn, vast areas of knowledge remain beyond our immediate comprehension, areas which seem to us, perhaps, like great sweeps of the ocean or of the skies or of the depths of the interstellar spaces. The artist's act of creation often gives us insights and intuitions into this world of mystery. Such areas of knowledge, while they may be not completely assimilable by our conscious intelligence, can at least be made "companionable" to us by literature. Literature, because it touches the transcendent world, taps these vast areas of meaning. At the same time, because it is wedded to the concrete and the individuated, it expresses itself in symbols whereby a specific form created by the artist carries overtones and transcendentals of meaning not subject to merely logical penetration.

PERCEIVING THE BEAUTIFUL

While we all have a sense of the beautiful in varying degrees, normally we find it difficult to supply a scheme that will determine whether a given object is beautiful. We may feel that it is all a matter of one's opinion, that standards are almost impossible to set up.

But there are some useful guidelines even if these do not meet every conceivable objection.

What are some practical considerations for determining the beautiful?

We should exclude at once from consideration here those "Great Books" that were meant primarily as scientific documents or technical works. These are great productions of the human mind, but their primary purpose is analysis and information. They are great because of their impact on subsequent thought. Such works may not even provide sound thought or information; they may be important solely because of their social repercussions. Machiavelli's *The Prince* may be a great work in this sense. It is certainly not a great book in the sense that *Paradise Lost* is.

Two key words help us to understand the beautiful. They are "function" and "being."

When we look at something as a function we see it as subservient to an end outside itself. When one regards the being of a thing, one looks at it in and for itself. A personnel manager about to engage a telephone operator looks at a girl entirely in regard to her qualifications and suitability for her job. A lover looking at the same girl sees her from the point of view of her being. He is delighted that she just is; if she can answer the telephone, that is an added accomplishment, but quite unessential.

What we love must seem beautiful to us. To love something means to desire it; we cannot desire what seems repulsive to us (the ugly).

Beauty creates love; but love also deepens our perception of beauty.

Beauty is not relative in the sense that it is merely the creation of the beholder's mind. Beauty is in the object whether we perceive it or not. But our appreciation of beauty is relative in the sense that we are not all equally perceptive. Tastes may be the result of convention or environment rather than of actual perception. We may not give the object the time or attention it deserves. That we cannot agree on the existence of beauty or the degree of beauty in a given object in no way invalidates the objective fact of beauty.

Certain principles have received a good deal of attention in recent years through the influence of James Joyce *(A Portrait of the Artist as a Young Man)* and others.[19] Although Joyce does not cover everything, he offers some workable principles that permit subtleties of discernment and analysis.

According to Joyce, we perceive the beautiful by noticing three characteristics: (1) integrity, (2) harmony, (3) individuation.

What is implied by these terms?

By integrity is meant unity, oneness. It means an organic unity, not a mere collection of parts. The beautiful object must have all that is essential to it. An antique Greek statue may be missing a limb, but if in its totality it was beautiful, it still remains beautiful though in a lesser degree than if it were undamaged. But take the type of monstrosity one sometimes sees at auctions—a contraption that is at once and at the same time a clock, a radio, a hatrack, and a lamp: this must be ugly because it is a mere collection of unrelated items with no organic unity containing them. All these items that separately considered may have some sort of unity cannot join in forming a beautiful work, because the unity containing them is impossible to conceive. They merely remain a collection of parts improperly joined together.

By harmony is meant the proper proportion and relationships of the parts to one another and to the integrity of the whole work of art. A simple harmony, as in decorative art, is easy enough to understand. But most works in the literary field are examples of what may be called an art of conflict rather than an art of contemplation. Although all art is distinguished by tension, in that all parts of a work of art are not static but intensely alive, nevertheless some art is primarily contemplative, like Fra Angelico's paintings or some medieval lyrics. But most literary works of art are examples of an art of conflict—the short story, the novel, the epic, the play; in these you cannot find the simple harmonies with which you may too easily and too exclusively associate the beautiful.

An art of conflict means that something besides the good, the true, and the beautiful must be presented in terms of heightened imitation. It is a traditional axiom that the good cannot conflict with the good, the true with the true, and so on. Therefore, you cannot have an art of conflict without presenting the evil, the untrue, the ugly. This fact bears an important influence on the relationship of art to morality, as we shall show later.

In an art of conflict we must think of a higher and more complex harmony that can assimilate, resolve, and transcend material that in itself may be asymmetrical, even ugly and evil.

Dante presents Hell. Would *The Divine Comedy* be more beautiful without it? Considered cut off, as a thing by itself, the *Inferno* might be regarded as repulsive. But no one has a right in looking at a work of art to regard a part as cut off, or unorganically related to the whole. Without the *Inferno,* Dante would lack the contrast by which to assert the beauty and transcendence of Paradise.

It is true that the evil and the ugly are presented in *The Divine Comedy*. But first of all it should be remembered that they are presented under conditions of aesthetic distance, or heightened imitation, so that they are not exactly the same forces as in real life. Second, they are assimilated and transcended by the total purpose of the work of art, its *integrity*. It is this integrity that one ultimately contemplates. This integrity is an organism, and it is purely a forced and rationalistic measure to consider its separate parts divorced from the total lifegiving stream of meaning. So considered, some elements might be considered ugly, but such a consideration ignores the whole meaning of a work of art as a totality.

It remains to speak of individuation. A work of beauty has a certain uniqueness. One beautiful work is not interchangeable with any other, like mass-manufactured items. Literature is an art in particular which reflects a distinct object, a distinct point of view. If we were to consider the typical cover girls on our national magazines, we would see certain approaches to beauty in terms of regularity and harmony, but something is seriously lacking—individuality, individuation. They lack what Joyce called "quidditas" ("whatness").[20] We might say they lack "itness." And this is true of a good deal of routine popular writing. It is proficient, even slick, but individuality, personality are lacking. It is obvious that beautiful objects are specifically different, for individuality is an element of beauty. The miniature intensity of a violet is a very different beauty from that of the rich grandeur of the rose.[21] A lyric by Robert Herrick is one type of beauty, *The Brothers Karamazov* quite another. A great work of art is unique. Great works of art may have a common share of the qualities that make for greatness, but each work is different in terms of the individuating principle of the beautiful. There are, of course, general resemblances in works of art just as there are in human persons. But as a human person, for example, I am not merely the repetition of a pattern—*the human person*. I am distinct and unique. I am not just like anyone else. I could argue that God as the artist created me as a single, specific work of his art in the broadest sense of the word. I share a common bond of humanity, it is true, but the formal cause of my being is not general but specific and unique. I am like other people; I am also quite different from them. So with art itself.

The form of art, then, should not be viewed as a mechanical pattern into which concepts can be canalized. One should seek in art "inner," or "organic," form as distinct from "surface," or "mechanical," form. Organic form arises from the individuated act of creation, whereas surface form is common to all art. Coleridge puts the matter in this light: "The form is mechanic, when on any given material we impress a predetermined form, not necessarily arising out of the properties of the material; as when to a mass of wet clay we give whatever shape we wish to retain when hardened. The organic form, on the other hand, is innate; it shapes, as it develops, itself from within, and the fullness of its development is one and the same with the perfection of its outward form. Such as the life is, such is the form."[22] It would seem wise in applying "beautiful" to any object to keep in mind the distinctions between organic and surface forms. A work of organic beauty would certainly rank higher than one of mere surface beauty. A work could be conceivably classified as beautiful on the basis of organic form alone. Surface form in itself, however, would not be a sufficient basis to speak assuredly of "beauty." We enter a kind of gray area here.

One might consider the thought content, let us say, of a poem by Alexander Pope as somewhat trivial or trite and yet admire the technical regularity of his lines, the "sense of difficulty overcome," that is present in them. On the other hand, surface form is most perfect when it is *consonant* with its organic material. We must be careful not to overrate abstract forms. Metrical regularity, for example, would not be consonant with the organic material of a Walt Whitman poem. His surface form is at least as appropriate to what he has to say as Pope's surface technique is to his material.

TENSION IN A WORK OF ART

When we say that a work of art is meant for contemplation, we do not imply in any way that the work of art is static. Often one thinks of great works of art as possessing a kind of permanence, an immobility. But, more properly, what a work of art possesses is balance, a bringing together and harmonizing of various dynamicisms. Works of art are distinguished by tension, all that is opposed to flaccidity and limpness. Balance and tension go together. Balance gives a sense of the permanent, the stable. Tension reminds one that the forces in a work of art are all intensely alive. Tension that is the result of a balance of forces gives a work of art its value no less than a tennis racket or a violin string.

We think easily enough of tension in the short story, the novel, the drama. But it is no less characteristic of other forms of art that are more quiet and reflective. Coleridge, in speaking of the imaginative power, says that it reveals itself

> . . . in the balance or reconciliation of opposite or discordant qualities: of sameness with difference; of the general with the concrete; the idea with the image; the individual with the representative; the sense of novelty and frankness, with old and familiar objects; a more than usual state of emotion, with more than usual order; judgment ever awake and steady self-possession, with enthusiasm and feeling, profound or vehement.[23]

It is not always easy to pin down the exact tensions you would find, let us say, in specimens of poetry. Such tensions depend upon mental association and the psychological factors entering such association. But, frequently, a little analysis will indicate a tension ending in the balance or reconciliation of opposite qualities. Consider these lines from William Wordsworth:

The silence that is in the starry sky
The sleep that is among the lonely hills.

("Song at the Feast of Brougham Castle," 163–164)

At first you might say that no lines could suggest more complete relaxation, more complete escape. But there are overtones of other elements (and opposed elements) besides those of silence and sleep. The "starry sky" suggests a clarity, an expansion, a vitality that creates an opposition to silence. The phrase "lonely hills" provides an opposed overtone to "sleep." Sleep may be a symbol of escape, it is true, but the ideas of loneliness suggests the need to "escape from escape" back to the society of men.

Sometimes this tension is much more obvious, as in statements that are clearly in terms of contrast, ironic or dramatic, as in the famous lines from Chaucer's "Knight's Tale":

What is this world? What asketh men to have?
Now with his love, now in his colde grave
Allone, withouten any companye.

(1919–1921)

It might be said that every work of art is the theater of contrast and struggle, the drama of this synthesis and harmony. In major works, such as *Antigone* or *Hamlet,* the tensions are on a cosmic level, in which great spiritual deeps and calms are in violent contrast to the turbulent confusion of the surface storms of fate and chance and accident.

The tension that derives from a balance of forces often results from bringing together, as in simile and metaphor, associations that are remote or opposed to one another. Tension includes many kinds of reconciliation of discordant qualities: of literal meaning and metaphorical meaning, of formal and informal language and rhythm, of the abstract and concrete, and so on. The harmony of beauty is thus intimately connected with tension, or Coleridge's "reconciliation of discordant qualities."

THE QUESTION ABOUT THE MORAL VALUE OF LITERATURE

Two traditional and conflicting views of the social and moral effects of art stem from Aristotle and Plato. Aristotle follows a philosophy of realism, Plato of idealism. These two views may be roughly contrasted on the basis of the part the material world plays in the two philosophical systems.

Plato, as interpreted in the history of literature, is distinguished by an antimaterial bias. The tradition claiming Plato as its source did not regard the material world as a tribute to the Creator, something beautiful in itself which, through its beauty, indicates the operative presence of God in the world. Rather this tradition regarded the physical, sensuously perceived world as a veil hiding us from the transcendent beauty. The material world retards rather than aids vision. In *The Republic* Plato argues that the world of sense is an imperfect imitation of the order of divine ideas. An artist in making a work of art makes an imitation of what is already an imperfect imitation of the order of divine ideas. Plato, partly led by the logic of this position, partly influenced by the fact that the poets of his time purveyed religious ideas which he deplored, is obliged somewhat reluctantly to decree the banishment of artists from *The Republic*.[24]

Plato recognized the fact that art exercised a social and moral influence, but he considered that influence bad. For that reason he banished artists. He is in direct contrast to Aristotle, who considers art necessary to the psychological health of society.

Why does Plato ignore the values implied by the idea of *catharsis,* of emotional expression? Because, in brief, he believes that man should seek for spiritual perfection and should not be concerned with the expression or exploitation of his emotions. Plato does not sufficiently recognize the necessity for emotional and psychological growth.

It is relevant here to consider the fact that Plato in *The Republic* was outlining a totalitarian society, in which all the citizen's energies and purposes were absorbed by the state. Plato envisioned a society in which everyone was selected and trained to serve the state to the best of his ability. A community of women bore children to approved citizen stock. At the age of seven these children were removed from their mothers and trained according to their abilities to become guardians (members of the philosopher class from which the ruler came), soldiers, or artisans. No one was to have any life apart from the state. Of course Plato's totalitarianism was comparatively enlightened; the ruler was supremely well educated and motivated by the highest ethical principles. But Plato unconsciously foresaw what always takes place in totalitarian society—the banishment of the artist. Hitler inaugurated his regime by a great book burning, and the Soviets tend to tolerate an artist only in so far as he is a propagandist for their political juggernaut. The reason that a totalitarian society cannot tolerate an artist is to be found in the fact that an artist tries to tell us what experience is really like, what life actually is. This personal testament may prove highly embarrassing to the ruler who is seeking to impose a rationalistic blueprint on society. If reality does not conform to the blueprint, well then, from the totalitarian point of view, reality must be suppressed along with the artist who expresses it.

Aristotle, in contrast to Plato, has a keener understanding of the psychological values of art. In one section of *The Poetics* he speaks of *catharsis.* The term, taken from medicine, literally meant a purgation or cleansing. Applied by analogy to art, Aristotle's term means a cleansing or purgation of the emotions through their fruitful release in the aesthetic experience. This idea is, in a sense, analogous to Freud's thesis of sublimation, the assumption that certain basic and instinctual drives are released and transformed through art in a way that makes them socially constructive.

Aristotle uses the word "catharsis" in speaking of tragedy:

> A tragedy, then, is the imitation of an action that is serious and also, as having magnitude, complete in itself; in language with pleasurable accessories, each kind brought in separately in the parts of the work; in a dramatic form, not in a narrative form; with incidents arousing pity and fear, wherewith to accomplish its catharsis of such emotions.[25]

This concept of catharsis is pivotal in any discussion of the moral value of art.

We know that art does not belong to the order of immediate experience. For example, I should enjoy a performance of Shakespeare's *Hamlet*. It should be a deep and meaningful experience for me. Yet if I enjoyed such events in real life, I would justifiably be classified as psychopathic.

Even as great a thinker as St. Augustine does not seem sufficiently aware of the difference between the order of immediate reality and the order of art, which is a heightened imitation of such reality. In the *Confessions* St. Augustine argues that the emotions enjoyed in the drama are unhealthy.

> How is it that a man wants to be made sad by the sight of tragic sufferings that he could not bear in his own person? Yet the spectator does want to feel sorrow and it is actually his feeling of sorrow that he enjoys. Surely this is the most wretched lunacy?
>
> For the more a man feels suffering in himself the more he is moved by the sight of them on the stage. Now when a man suffers himself, it is called misery, when he suffers in the suffering of another, it is called pity. But how can the unreal sufferings of the stage possibly move pity? The spectator is not moved to aid the sufferer but merely to be sorry for him; and the more the author of these fictions makes the audience grieve, the better they like him.[26]

St. Augustine thinks of a spectator as a man who welcomes misery in the world so that he may have the pleasure of pitying it.

> Only in the impossible event of good-will being malevolent, could a man who is truly and sincerely filled with pity, desire that there should be miserable people for him to pity. There is a kind of compassionate sorrow that is good, but there is no kind that we should rejoice to feel.[27]

Here again is the basic problem. Is the sorrow felt, let us say, on seeing *Hamlet,* a sorrow which St. Augustine would call pleasurable, the *same* kind of sorrow that one would feel on the death of a friend, which would be extremely painful? A new dimension is present here which contrasts aesthetic emotion with direct emotion.

What Mortimer Adler points out in *Art and Prudence* in regard to Bossuet applies here. He says that Bossuet does not

> . . . distinguish the manner in which natural things excite our passions, with the consequence of relief through natural action, from the way in which imitations excite our passions artificially and artificially relieve them to effect purgation.[28]

The crux of the problem in regard to catharsis is the estimate one makes of the present moral position of man in the temporal order. It is also relevant whether we regard man as exclusively spiritual, unhappily trapped by matter, or whether we regard him essentially as both body and soul and, consequently, also as a psychological being. Adler points out in *Art and Prudence* that Plato's views would have relevancy if man were in a perfected condition. In heaven the truth of our experience need not be expressed in works of art. But since man is not perfected, but is seeking perfection, art is an instrument that helps to this end.

> But no man is perfectly rational, which means that every man has disordered passions to a greater or less degree. Every man needs to learn the discipline of submitting passions to reason. But just as the passions in every man are in varying stages of violence and uncontrol, so the reason of every man is in varying stages of weakness and undevelopment. It is in this situation, in which all men find themselves, that the arts and other imitation perform their valuable political and moral function.[29]

In summary, then, it may be said that the moral responsibility of art primarily lies in the proper education of our emotions and that the method of art is a special method. But we are still left with one problem: granted that art in a general sense performs a moral service, can we have particular works of art that are immoral, or does the definition of a work of art preclude immorality?

It is amazing how few of the great works of art, whether in literature, painting, or sculpture have ever been seriously thought to be immoral.

Although a perverted sense of values can be expressed with great technical skill so that a work may be a borderline case in the catalogues of masterpieces, most works of art that have been questioned on moral grounds have been misinterpreted, either through the narrowness of the critic or through the limited *mores* of a particular social period. Shakespeare was forbidden during the Puritan regime in England, and one of the popes had to have Michelangelo's figures in the Sistine Chapel reclothed.

Common sense is necessary here.

Most misunderstandings about art and morality arise from a misunderstanding about the art of conflict (discussed under "Perceiving the Beautiful"), an insistence on an eccentric version of what morality should be, or a restriction of art to subjects suitable to the least common denominator of audiences, the child audience, on mistaken grounds of prudence.

The problem of presenting evil in art (necessary to an art of conflict) has special difficulties. Sin has a certain kind of attractiveness (there are many kinds of sin, of course, besides sexual license); otherwise we would not yield to temptation. In order to convey the meaning of sin and evil—a meaning which also includes attractiveness—the artist must not create a source of temptation for the beholder. This demands that the order of direct experience yield to aesthetic transformation, to aesthetic distance from the order of immediate experience. Aesthetic distance or the *selective* process in the *mimesis* evaluates the true nature of evil at the same time that it presents evil. The philosopher Jacques Maritain, in speaking of the novelist's art, puts the problem in this way:

> The essential question is not to know if a novelist can or cannot paint a particular aspect of evil. The essential question is to know at what height he places himself to make this painting, and if his heart and his art is pure enough, and strong enough, to make it without connivance.[30]

We should be careful not to condemn a work of art as immoral because of its subject matter. The presentation of evil does not in itself constitute immorality. Always to be kept in mind is the distinction between the evil which the artist imitates and the viewpoint (herein connivance is found or not found) he brings to bear upon the evil he represents. It does not follow that a mimesis of sin and evil in a work of art implies that an artist approves of them or that he intends the reader to approve of them. Immorality in a work of art becomes evident only when an artist "glorifies" evil and suggests it as a suitable pattern for human conduct. A moral work of art may present evil no less realistically than an immoral work, in no less detail, but the moral work of art, in contrast to the immoral work, implies an adverse criticism of such evil. Such criticism need not be explicit; it is sufficent that it is implicit.

In summary, we may say that the morality of a work of art does not depend upon the raw material it handles but upon the way this material is subject to a heightened imitation and upon the purpose this imitation serves. Anything that may be considered legitimately a part of human experience (this would include suffering, death, sin, tragedy) is a matter suitable for an artist's handling.

It is true, of course, that certain kinds of material carry with them special dangers and difficulties. Currently, the arguments for and against censorship are misstated. Some works are condemned by zealots on grounds that could just as well apply to the Greeks, Dante, Chaucer, and Shakespeare. Other works, like the comics and Mickey Spillane, are defended in the name of Freud on grounds that would make Freud turn in his grave. The current argument for letting everything go is based on the assumption that if we murder and commit mayhem imaginatively we are less likely to do it in actual life. We are "released," but that is not what Freud or Aristotle meant. If this were so, we would be faced with the ridiculous alternative that if we read about noble and heroic people we should be less inclined toward doing good! The emotions excited by art are aroused not in terms of abstract murder or licentiousness but by a complex situation of conflict in which we respond to moral principles, in the presentation of which violence is incidental. When we "respond" to *Othello,* we respond not merely to a murder but to the whole play in which the murder is an *incident.*

In dealing with the immature, prudence is necessary. An artist, like a teacher, has a responsibility to be prudent. A teacher, for example, should not assign literature for which his students are emotionally and intellectually unprepared. But in this matter, a careful distinction should be made between literature that should not be allowed to fall into the hands of the immature and literature that is immoral in itself. We should not, for example, determine the morality of literature by the norm, let us say, of what is fit for young children. The audience for literature, from the point of view of a norm, should be an adult audience of reasonable education and critical capacity. College students, particularly in view of the fact that they are studying under guidance, fall into this class.

Care should be taken in any allegation that a literary work of art causes scandal. Scandal may be taken where none is offered in the case of readers who are excessively suggestible or who possess a false conscience. Such readers might find even the Scriptures themselves immoral. Nor should a special problem of individual morality be confused with the problem of general morality. Milton makes a good point about censorship conducted for the benefit of the abnormal individual in his *Aeropagitica:*

> And again, if it be true that a wise man, like a good refiner, can gather gold out of the drossiest volume, and that a fool will be a fool with the best book, yea or without a book, there is no reason that we should deprive a wise man of any advantage to his wisdom, while we seek to restrain from a fool that which being restrained will be no hindrance to his folly.[31]

The test for the morality of literature should be its inner integrity, that is, the honest effort of the artist to follow the truth of experience, even though he may be mistaken in some of his ideas and interpretations. It is obvious that the purpose of literature should be opposed to meretriciousness (falseness, from the Latin, *meretrix,* a prostitute) whether of the sensational or sentimental variety.[32]

In considering the immorality of art we should bear in mind the complete moral code. One teacher before introducing Dante to a class in a large southern university asked what the students considered to be the chief sins in their community. The teacher's object was to introduce the students, by way of comparison, to Dante's complete and complex definition of sin. The students' reply to the teacher's questionnaire was practically unanimous: the two chief sins in their communities were "sex and radicalism." Very few students could think of anything else. Today a book may implicitly or explicitly glorify any of the seven deadly sins, but it is not considered immoral unless it treats sex. Defrauding laborers of their just wages, a sin sometimes incidental to making Pollyanna's or Horatio Alger's fortunes,[33] is one of the sins that call to heaven for vengeance. Yet in sentimentalized literature the sin of avarice is often identified through a series of mental equations with virtue and "success." Seldom, however, is there any hue and cry about a book of this kind. Obviously, if we are going to be either fair or consistent, our moral sense should be inclusive; we should not concentrate merely on pet sins for condemnation.

Misjudgments about the moral values of a work of literature are likely to be more frequent with new works than with the established classics that are the core of a school program. As a general policy, our aim should be to enjoy books rather than to condemn them. It might well be argued that the only person who makes a good censor is the person who doesn't wish to censor.

LITERATURE AND SYMBOLISM

Many misunderstandings about the function of literature, on moral, psychological, and other levels, arise from not knowing what is meant by symbolism in literature. Because readers are often accustomed to viewing a book only in terms of its narrative line, its information, they miss its symbolic meaning. The symbol is one part of an orchestration of symbols that, in their totality, give the unitive impression of a great work. The symbol offers an analogy for something undefined, not directly stated, but yet part of a literary work of art. The death of Anna Karenina in Tolstoi's novel does not tell us only about the death of a person called Anna Karenina (herself a fictional character—therefore, a symbol in Tolstoi's inclusive presentation of his world); it also tells us about love, hatred, compassion, nihilism, about God and the general plight of man. A novelist once said, before explaining a book to others, "I wait for them to explain it to me. To explain it first is to limit its sense; for if we know what we wished to say, we do not know if we have said only that. One always says more than that. And my interest is what I have put into the work without knowing it."[34] According to this novelist, the artist should expect his book to be "revealed" to him by the readers. Many unconscious factors, of course, enter into a work of art; in fact, the psychologist Jung regards the symbol as shared by artist and audience as unitive of the conscious and unconscious. Contrary to this, in the thought of the English critic Cyril Connolly, the recipe for creative work, as distinct from legal and philosophical language, includes *suggestion* as well as statement. Connolly has said that the perfect use of language "is that in which every word carries the meaning that it is intended to, no less and no more."[35] This is very good advice for drawing up a contract, but not for writing *Anna Karenina* or *Hamlet.*

But it may be objected that the word "symbol" is itself confusing and elusive. What do we mean by symbol and symbolic language?

We sometimes overlook the fact that art achieves its purpose by means of conventions—symbols. Suppose we have a table in front of us. Why do we call it a table? Because it is in itself essentially a table, or because it corresponds in some way to an *idea* of a table we have in our minds? If we were to read the tenth book of Plato's *Republic,* we would be told that we call this object in front of us *a* table, because it is an imitation in material form of an idea we have in our minds—*the* table. Actually, we might describe the object in front of us as a collection of pieces of wood. If we had a very powerful microscope, we might actually see what the scientists tell us is present: a vast world—perhaps infinite in the sense of being indefinitely divisible—of protons, electrons, and neutrons as vast and as complicated as the mightly stellar system that we can behold above our heads. In this sense it may well be argued that we call the object in front of us *a* table, merely to indicate the function or *use* to which we put it, rather than to say what it is essentially. It serves a purpose I have in mind—"the table purpose." If I make a drawing of the table, the drawing is even more symbolic, for then I make lines on a flat surface that symbolize a table—a table which, in fact, is not a flat surface, but three-dimensional (length, breadth, and depth)—and these lines are an abstract matter for the human intelligence in the same way that an equation in algebra is. The drawing is even more "symbolic" than the table. Of course, both the table and the drawing have their own reality or being.

It is important to understand the function of the intelligence in understanding a symbol, which might be called a sign that, through mutual agreement or convention, stands for a transcendent meaning. I talk to you. What am I really doing? On one level, I am merely making sounds. Scientifically, we could measure the type and variety of the sound waves. After they have hit your nervous system through your sense of hearing, you accept these sounds as symbols of meaning. Your intelligence acts upon these sounds and you see them as *meaning-bearing* sounds. The sounds that I make with my diaphragm and throat are symbols as complicated and as wonderful as anything you will find in the higher calculus. Fortunately, of course, they are more familiar to us.

Symbolism is habitual to us. Even ordinary courtesies—like shaking hands or removing one's hat—are symbolic actions. The action has meaning only as a sign or symbol of a value that is not explicit or obvious but is understood through convention and experience.

In art, symbols may occasionally offer added difficulty or subtlety, but basically they are not unfamiliar to us. Symbols—images—are used to convey *overtones* of meaning which are implicit. The shaking of hands is a simple physical act. Its overtone of meaning is the universal and abstract idea of friendship. In writing, the artist chooses his word symbols not merely to express an actual, outward fact but also an inner, transcendent meaning. Thus, you might walk along the shore and notice the seagulls and you might make a mental note, such as, "I have heard the seagulls singing, each to each." But T. S. Eliot, in "The Love Song of J. Alfred Prufrock," uses a special word symbol, "mermaids," to signify the imaginative vision that has disappeared from the life of Prufrock—an actual bird would not suggest this overtone. "Mermaids" rather than "seagulls" provide better symbols of his meaning. "I have heard the *mermaids* singing, each to each."

Symbols convey meaning on many levels and frequently on more than one level at one time. A specific and concrete meaning is presented on one level of the discourse, a transcendent and no less important meaning on another level. There is a close connection between the seeing of a material object deeply and intensely and the understanding of transcendent meaning. Depth on the one level of understanding increases comprehension on the other. "Being" is not easily exhausted. It always offers a new aspect to the vision of the sympathetic beholder. Thus, the Spirit of Milton's *Comus* describes, on one level, the effect that music has had upon him.

. . . I was all ear,
And took in strains that might create a soul
Under the ribs of Death.

(560–562)

But the reference to music here has also become a symbol of being, of life. Music and its beauty seem so dominant to the poet-beholder that, as a symbol of life, it is affirmed in the bones of negation. The effectiveness of these lines results from combining the abstract concept of "soul" with the very visual "ribs." An effect of intensity is brought about by the sudden intrusion of the immensely "imagistic" *ribs.*

Symbolism covers multidimensional meanings, combining what is specific, what is individuated, with what is transcendent, what is universal, in expression.

"Symbolism" is a word used in a variety of senses. In the widest and most exalted sense, it can be made to stand for a universal union of values and attitudes. Thus Emerson says that "some stars, lilies, leopards, a crescent, a lion, an eagle, or other figure which came into credit God knows how, an old rag of bunting, blowing in the wind, on a fort at the ends of the earth, shall make the blood tingle under the rudest or most conventional exterior."[36] And Carlyle asserts that

> . . . in the Symbol proper, what we call a Symbol, there is ever, more or less distinctly and directly, some embodiment and revelation of the Infinite; the Infinite is made to blend with the Finite, to stand visible, and as it were attainable there. By Symbols, accordingly, is man guided and commanded, made happy, made wretched. He everywhere finds himself encompassed with Symbols, recognized as such or not recognized: the Universe is but one vast Symbol of God; nay if thou wilt have it, what is man himself but a Symbol of God: is not all that he does symbolical . . . ?[37]

D. H. Lawrence argues that symbols "don't mean something." They stand for units of human feeling, human experience. He argues that it takes centuries to create a really significant symbol, and that no man can invent them. "He can invent an emblem, made up of images: or metaphors: or images: but not symbols. Some images, in the course of many generations of men, become symbols, embedded in the soul and ready to start alive when touched. . . ."[38]

Modern critical practice does not use "symbol" in either such a universal or such a restricted sense, though there is justification for such uses. Originally the word was used by the Greeks to denote the two halves of the tablet they divided between themselves as a pledge of hospitality. It came to be used of every sign, formula, or rite by which those initiated in any mystery made themselves secretly known to one another.

Some distinction has to be made between symbolism operating in a work of art and symbolism functioning directly in human experience (e.g., the national flag, the universe as a revelation of God). Northrop Frye speaks of a poem as a "microcosm of all literature, an individual manifestation of the total order of words." He thinks of all symbols being united "in a single infinite and eternal symbol which is . . . as mythos [myth], the total creative act."[39] Frye observes that it is this conception which Joyce expresses, in terms of subject matter, as *epiphany,* and Hopkins, in terms of form, as *inscape.*[40] Frye thinks of literary symbolism both as a shaping principle (the organizing of the matter) and as the containing principle of meaning holding the work of art together.

Like Emerson and Carlyle, Frye recognizes a genuine mystery and a real place for wonder in art as well as in life. But he finds the wonder of art in a sense more mysterious than the symbols of life extrinsic to it.

> The mystery of the unknown or the unknowable essence is an extrinsic mystery, which involves art only when art is also made illustrative of something else, as religious art is to the person concerned primarily with worship. But the intrinsic mystery is that which remains a mystery in itself no matter how fully known it is, and hence is not a mystery separated from what is known. The mystery in the greatness of *King Lear* or *Macbeth* comes not from concealment but from revelation, not from something unknown or unknowable in the work, but from something unlimited in it.[41]

What has been called the new criticism is particularly concerned with attempting to interpret the elusive, though meaningful and challenging, symbols of literary statement. Its primary concern is the multiple-meaning structure of interlocking images. The new critics warn against any impression that the meaning of the symbolism of a major work of art can be exhausted. Thus John Unterecker states that symbol exists only with its sign value as a fixed meaning.

> Its other meaning or meanings are unassigned. Any analogy we can construct for the symbol, any meaning we assign to it, is legitimate so long as we recognize that that meaning is not its meaning. (Its meaning must always be more elusive than any value we can—with words—fix to it.) All that the meaning we assign to a symbol can ever be is either part of its meaning or one of its possible meanings.[42]

It is quite common today to speak of the *centripetal* use of language, a language pointing to inward meaning. This is distinct from the centrifugal meaning in which we go outward from the individual words to the things they mean. Symbolism is centripetal.

Are important distinctions to be made between symbols, images, and signs? Can their respective meanings and uses be definitely ascertained?

In a sense the word "symbol" is universal, in the most elementary sense of something standing for or pointing to something else. But in literary terminology the meaning has to be narrowed.

We look at the letters *r o s e* on a page. The letters are scientific symbols (merely in the sense of signs) for certain sounds. We arbitrarily say in algebra, let x stand for 5; in language we say, let *rose* stand for a certain flower. As a *sign,* a word simply identifies without other implications. Instantaneously, if we have been trained to read, we mentally recognize the sound of the word "rose" upon seeing the letters of the printed word. We are probably not conscious of mentally hearing the word; almost immediately a fleeting picture (or image) of an actual flower flashes across the mind. If this were the only set of letters on the page, we would wonder "What does this mean? What am I supposed to do next?" Let us suppose the words "Buy a" are added. Now my mind is drawn centrifugally outwards to a meaningful context, *buy a rose,* of which the *sign* "rose" is merely a part. But the rose is itself only a rose, and nothing more. It is only symbolic in the sense that every word is a sign, and it is a symbol only in the restricted sense of a sign.

But isn't the word "rose" an image? An image, yes, but not a *poetic* image. Because the poetic image of rose would point to something beyond its being rose pure and simple. A poetic image goes beyond the stage of mental picture to a new context (centripetal) in which, while the word retains the basic *icon,* or image, of a rose in the mind, it develops new tendrils and new roots in a discourse of other ideas and images. We can see the difference at once if we contrast the rose of "buy a rose" with the rose in Edmund Spenser's line:

Gather the Rose of love, whilest yet is time

The pictorial image remains, but an entirely new contextual focus on *love* has subordinated the purely informative and denotative aspect of the image-picture of rose to something much larger and more arousing: rose of *love.* The centripetal, or inward, meaning of the image-picture of rose, on the other hand, has been enormously increased. It is a more vibrant, emotive rose. But not a rose that one could *buy!*

Is this centripetal image of rose a symbol? The answer depends here largely on how critics use the word. Spenser has pointed not only to sexual love in the complete stanza in which the above line appears, but also to youth, and the destruction of youth by time:

Gather therefore the Rose, whilest yet is prime
For soone comes age, that will her pride deflowre.

(*The Faerie Queene,* II, xii, LXXV–LXXVI)

"Rose" here is indeed a *poetic* image. Is it, in critical language, a symbol? Most critics would say yes, if the image presents a repeated pattern (*motif*), a meaningful theme throughout the work. If it only occurs occasionally in a traditionally conventional way, critics would hesitate to refer to the rose as one of Spenser's symbols.

There is no reluctance, however, to refer to the use of the rose image as a symbol in W. B. Yeats's poetry. Yeats himself noted the meanings symbolized in the image—physical love, Ireland, religion. It is a motif in his work:

Come near; I would, before my time to go,
Sing of old Eire and the ancient ways:
Red Rose, proud Rose, sad Rose of all my days.

("To the Rose upon the Rood of Time," 22–24)

Similarly "The Mystic Rose" in Canto XXXII of Dante's *Paradise* is unequivocally a symbol. As a symbol of the beatific vision, it is used diagrammatically, in the manner of seventeenth-century metaphysical poetry. It falls into the classification of what has recently been called the radical image—that is, an image in which the minor part has no obvious emotive associations. In fact, Dante also employs the image for what might almost be considered scientific classification, arranging the blessed in various categorical tiers of the petals!

Images and symbols must not be thought of as restricted merely to the pictorial. They can be auditory, for example as in Milton's lines:

I hear the far-off Curfew sound,
Over some wide-water'd shore,
Swinging slow with sullen roar.

("Il Penseroso," 74–76)

This is not a symbolic statement but an account of direct experience, standing just for itself. Its effectiveness is in the exactitude with which the auditory aspects of the scene are suggested ("sullen roar"). The almost liturgical movements of the sounds of nature itself symbolize the dramatic tension in Milton's *Comus*—more even than the characters themselves. The characters seem more like a chorus putting into words a drama that has been enacted elsewhere.

Nothing that the characters do is so rich and tense as the following description of a symbolic sound:

At last a soft and solemn breathing sound
Rose like a stream of rich distill'd perfumes,
And stole upon the Air, that even Silence
Was took ere she was ware, and wish't she might
Deny her nature, and be never more,
Still to be so displac't. I was all ear,
And took in strains that might create a soul
Under the ribs of Death.

(*Comus,* 555–562)

Here is an amazing sexual and fertility reference, symbolized through music, so sudden and complete in its germinative power that it creates a soul under the ribs of death! This is a symbolic statement that is even more dramatic than stage action.

Imagery often passes beyond any stage that we can classify as pictorial or auditory. As Northrop Frye has pointed out, we have no technical word to indicate the *moving* body of imagery in a work of art. Or as I. A. Richards has stated, "Too much importance has always been attached to the sensory qualities of images. What gives an image efficacy is less its vividness as an image than its character as a mental event. . . ."[43] The point is that everything in the above lines from Milton unites and mounts to a great climax, *a mental event,* very complex in construction, yet strikingly simple (united) in emotional impact.

ARCHETYPE AND MYTH

In the Greek language, an *archetype* was the original pattern or model after which a thing is made. In Plato's philosophy we speak of the self-subsistent universal ideas as archetypes, which are reflected in the world of sense. The term has a much greater fluidity as applied to literature. Frye says: "I mean by an archetype a symbol which connects one poem with another and thereby helps to unify and integrate our literary experience. And as the archetype is a communicable symbol, archetypal criticism is primarily connected with literature as a social fact and as a mode of communication."[44] Through the impact of the psychology of Carl Jung, who postulates a collective unconscious, the archetype is viewed as a basic human theme going far back into unconscious racial memory and deeply affecting the unconscious mind of the reader. Archetype in this sense signifies a universal theme that touches all mankind. The ancient myths are stressed in contemporary criticism as archetypal.

A reader coming upon the current literary use of the word "myth" might easily be confused by its use and adaptations. The first impression is that myth refers to a large and coordinated system of symbolism.

In "Dragon of the Apocalypse," D. H. Lawrence refers to the myth of Cronos, known as Saturn in Latin. As a story, it seems incomprehensible, though Lawrence says it can be expounded very easily. Cronos was the Titan child of Mother Earth and Father Heaven. He inflicted horrible injuries on his father, who had maltreated him. From the blood of the father sprang the Giants, who were eventually to disappear, and the Furies, who were to remain—with their hair of snakes and eyes that wept blood, walking in darkness, remorselessly avenging crime. Cronos, poetically associated with the golden age of peace and harmony, reigned for ages. But on learning that one of his sons was to dethrone him, he swallowed his children as soon as they were born. His wife managed, however, to save her sixth son, Zeus, through a stratagem: she wrapped a stone in swaddling clothes; Cronos swallowed the stone, and the living Zeus became an exiled infant in Crete. When Zeus became an adult, he forced his father to disgorge the stone and the five previous children. A terrible war ensued between Zeus and his father, in the course of which the universe was nearly wrecked. Tradition says that the dethroned and exiled Cronos fled to Italy, where, as Saturn, he became the symbol of Roman civilization and of the golden age.

Certain themes are indicated here, of course—the passing of time, the conflict of parents and children, the repeated pattern of crime and punishment. Lawrence observes:

> We can explain it, we can even draw the moral conclusion. But we only look a little silly. The myth of Cronos lives on beyond explanation, for it describes a profound experience of the human body and soul, an experience which is never exhausted, for it is being felt and

> suffered now, and it will be felt and suffered while man remains man. You may explain the myths away: but it only means you go on suffering blindly, stupidly, "in the unconscious," instead of healthily and with the imaginative comprehension playing upon the suffering.[45]

Lawrence's words are fairly representative of a good deal of what is said about myth. It is thought to figure forth something of great importance in the psyche and experience of man, but it is hard to state what. In fact, the meaning is supposed to be there, to be felt, to be intuited, but scarcely to be communicated along lines of rational thought. Myth, in the usual sense, refers to a story which is not based on fact or natural explanation. Only gradually in the ancient literature does the tendency emerge to tell a plausible story. Stories of the gods become stories of heroes, and out of the legends of heroes emerge the plots of comedies and tragedies. But the lack of realism, the implausibility of myths, does not seriously weaken the new-found respect that many modern critics have for them. They are respected as systems of symbols, particularly revealing of the unconscious mind of man. This respect parallels the contemporary emphasis on poetry as a system of images that rejects overt statement or assertion.

The contemporary tendency has been to exalt myth, but not every reader can see it in that light. A reader might not object to finding new meaning in the myth of Cronos, but he might be seriously disturbed by considering the book of *Genesis* a myth, or the whole of Christianity a myth. It might seem to him, in this case, that if Cronos has moved up, Christianity has moved down. Obviously the use of the word "myth," even with the best intentions in the world, disturbs the reader who regards the biblical narrative as, at least in some measure, one of historical fact. This tension has been somewhat eased today by a preoccupation with allegorical meaning. *Genesis* is seldom read purely literally today even by theologians. It is read with marked emphasis on language, historical culture, and anthropology, and with increasing amazement at the subtlety of the allegory (the Tree of Knowledge of Good and Evil and the Tree of Life) to be found in so ancient and primitive a document. But even under these conditions, a religious believer would have difficulty in looking at *Genesis* as one of the great repeated symbols. He certainly would not accept the story of Cronos and that of Adam and Eve as being on the same level of myth. And a theologian would have difficulty in applying to *Genesis* Frye's statement that "the allegorization of myth is hampered by the assumption that the explanation 'is' what the myth 'means.' A myth being a centripetal structure of meaning, it can be made to mean an indefinite number of things. . . ."[46] Though the word "myth" is often mechanically applied to indicate the story content of a narrative or dramatic line, in a wider sense, it can mean "any anonymously composed story telling of origins and destinies: the explanations a society offers its young of why the world is and why we do as we do, its pedagogic images of the nature and destiny of man."[47]

Illustration: An Archetypal Poem

T. S. Eliot's *The Waste Land* is an outstanding example of a modern poem that uses symbol and myth, constantly recalling the ancient archetypes of death and life, sterility and fertility. The title is reminiscent of Alfred Lord Tennyson's "The Passing of Arthur" (from *Idylls of the King*):

. . . an agony
Of lamentation, like a wind that shrills
All night in a waste land, where no one comes,
Or hath come, since the making of the world.

(200–203)

The basic symbol in this poem, that of a waste land, is derived from Jessie L. Weston's book, *From Ritual to Romance,* which relates a legend about a land, once flowering, rich, and fruitful, that has been blighted by a curse incurred by the sin against chastity of the lord of the land, the Fisher King. He has been rendered impotent and his land laid waste. The curse can be removed only by the appearance of a knight in search of the Holy Grail who will ask the meanings of the various symbols which are displayed to him in the Castle Perilous. Eliot makes a transition from physical to spiritual sterility, by indirect and complex contrasts and by varied and disjointed symbols which nevertheless have a fine thread of unity and connection.

The major contrast of *The Waste Land* is that of two kinds of life and two kinds of death: life devoid of meaning is death; whereas sacrifice, even sacrificial death, may be life-giving, an awakening to real life. Eliot develops his thesis: "So far as we are human, we must be either evil or good; so far as we do evil or good, we are human; and it is better, in a paradoxical way, to do evil than to do nothing: at least, we exist." The fact that men have lost the knowledge of good and evil keeps them from being alive and is the justification for viewing the modern waste land as a realm in which the inhabitants do not even exist. In a number of life-through-death incidents, those in which a god dies and is resurrected, thereby bringing salvation, the poet seeks to identify as many religions and religious myths as possible with Christianity.

Water, throughout the poem, is the symbol of regeneration. But society is afraid to partake in any rebirth. An analogy is implied between water in *The Waste Land* and the water of baptism. This symbol is akin to the fertility rites in which Osiris died and was resurrected. The rising of the waters of the Nile, a sign of the rebirth of spring, was thought by Egyptians to be due to Isis's weeping for her dead Osiris.

One section of the work employs the Tarot deck of cards, which were originally used by the ancients to determine an event of the highest importance, the rising of the waters. Madame Sosostris employs them in the vulgar act of fortune telling. The card bearing the image of the drowned Phoenician sailor, which represents the fortune of the protagonist, is a type of the fertility god, Adonis. His image was thrown into the sea annually as a symbol of the death of summer and was resurrected the following day as a symbol of the new fertile life which was to come to vegetation. Adonis died in order to find life in the waters of salvation, as modern man must also do. The Hanged Man, which Madame Sosostris is unable to find, represents Christ. Hence she warns: "Fear death by water." The individuals of the waste land are unable to discover their Savior for the simple reason that their search for Him is cloaked in passivity and, therefore, is no real search at all. They cannot know, as a result of their participation in modern civilization's flight from reality, that the way to life is by death in the water of salvation and renewal.

The symbol of regeneration, water, is extensively used here, in striking contrast to rock, the symbol of the waste land and sterility. We are confronted with a journey through the rock and dust. Water is absent and we must go on searching and hoping for it as a means to salvation. The "dry sterile thunder without rain" is a symbol of the superficialities of the waste land which actually bring nothing of value.

LITERATURE AND HUMAN VALUES

Great literature is a major statement touching upon what is universal in human values. It is, as Matthew Arnold once said, the best that has been thought and said in the world. It is a public statement—meant to be communicated to others rather than to oneself; it has, as such, a certain decorum and decency to observe, though this does not preclude great directness and realism.

Literature is related directly to "human values." As early as 1595, the great humanist Sir Philip Sidney observed that literature had certain advantages lacking in history and philosophy. Sidney may have been somewhat opinionated in regard to these other fields, but what he says contains an important element of truth. The philosopher must cast a "largess" of "definitions, divisions, and distinctions." The historian gives man's experience based on facts and records, though some of these are hard to verify and evaluate. The claim of the philosopher is that he gives the precept; that of the historian that he gives the example. For Sidney the creative artist is the "moderator" between them. "The philosopher therefore and the historian are they which would win the goal, the one by precept, the other by example; but not having both, do both halt." Sidney argues that the philosopher stands upon the abstract and the general, and the historian is tied to the particular truth of things and not to the general reason of things. What they both lack the creative artist ("the poet") supplies. What the philosopher and the historian know has to come to light before the "imaginative and judging power"; it has to be illuminated and figured forth.

It is, of course, foolish to set up a table of comparative values between history, philosophy, and literature. They are all of utmost importance to the educated man. But if literature has sometimes been overexalted, it has also at times been foolishly degraded. Thomas Love Peacock, who was disgusted with Romantic poetry, extended his feelings to all literature. "While the historian and the philosopher are advancing in, and accelerating, the progress of knowledge, the poet is wallowing in the rubbish of departed ignorance, and raking up the ashes of dead savages and rattles for the grown babics of thc agc." This sort of prejudice has never been quite dead.[48]

But the fact remains that literature is not merely a craft or technique. It is a focal point where the leading concepts of the other subjects—history, philosophy, and also science—are expressed in terms of concrete human experience, where these matters deeply touch what is human. It is one thing to be a thermonuclear physicist, spending years of research under the guidance of a powerful intelligence; it is another thing to consider the end result of such research as it may touch human beings, as in the popular novel, *Fail-Safe*.

It is not just a verbal accident that the term "humanist" was first applied to the type of classical scholar who read the classics less as history and philosophy than as literature. The term "humanities" came from the renaissance emphasis on *literae humaniores* ("the more humane letters"). The first humanists, interested in literature for form as well as content, were also frequently moral philosophers, especially expounding the texts of Plato. Like Matthew Arnold of a later date, they thought of literature in terms of "the need of relating what we have learnt and known to the sense which we have in us for conduct, to the sense which we have in us for beauty."[49] It is only in the nineteenth century that the idea of "art for art's sake" is projected. Walter Pater's view is the other extreme to that of the renaissance humanist: "Art comes to you proposing frankly to give nothing but the highest quality to your moments as they pass, and simply for these moments' sake."[50] The renaissance humanist, in contrast, was fond of relating literature to those large universal values that he considered lasting and permanent.

Literature's Role of Integration

Walter Pater demarcated literature too narrowly, though he was right in viewing it primarily as an art. Another exaggeration along similar lines is to make art, including literature, a substitute for religious truth, to give a narrow interpretation, for example, to the "inspiration" of literature. The role of ideas and values in literature as extremely important, as long as such ideas and values are truly assimilated in the work of art and do not stand out of the context like separate discourses. The works of literature themselves prove this.

Besides being an expression of beauty, literature is, as we have mentioned, a medium for communicating ideas of social significance. To literature we may rightly go for that criticism of ideas which is based on experience. Zamiatin's *We,* for example (see p. 132), does not argue about totalitarianism; on the surface, it endorses it. But it shows how such a state of affairs is obnoxious to human experience. The work is, in short, a satire on the totalitarian structure.

Because literature criticizes and tests experience, it is closely related to the general field of ideas and it gains, therefore, by being closely correlated with other avenues of knowledge.

Literature illuminates intellectual and cultural history. It reflects the thoughts of the past, giving them a concrete and permanent form. A play like *Antigone,* for example, tells us a great deal about different levels of Greek thinking and makes them all come alive for us again. Some literary works, as a collateral result, actually help to make intellectual history as, for example, Rousseau's *Émile.* And a major artist like Shakespeare is deeply interwoven with the culture and even the language of the English-speaking people.

If we were to compare the roles of the historian, the philosopher, and the literary artist in intellectual history, we might say that history studies the vicissitudes through which an idea has passed and traces the powerful effects of an idea upon people and political events; that philosophy actually defines, gives the specific meaning of the idea; that literature tells us what this idea meant to people in terms of flesh and blood.

Herein lies the integrating role of literature. We sometimes speak of Dante's work as a "compendium" of medieval thought. *The Divine Comedy* evaluates history and philosophy while at the same time showing us real people—not merely *telling* us about people, but *showing* them. The integrating principle is that literature, however loaded with philosophical and historical concepts, always brings us back to the human condition. Tolstoi's *War and Peace* is actually a penetrating study of history, but what it is always telling us is how this juggernaut of complex events and motives affects specific individuals, their way of life, their marriages, their dreams.

All that is deeply and essentially human concerns everyone. This is the concern of great literature. We are fond of saying in recent times that a person has no alternative but to be a specialist, that no one in our period could possibly learn everything in a lifetime. This, of course, is true in the main. But one can, through a study of great literature, get a line on what is deeply and essentially human in sufficient time to apply this knowledge for the conduct and understanding of life. Certainly literature cannot be expected to integrate all fields of knowledge dealing with man. But it can help one develop a response to the leading human values whenever they are met.

"This is all very well," one may say, "but what happens when you meet a work of art that has an ideological premise with which you deeply disagree? What then?"

It is obvious that an educated man is concerned with the justness and rightness of universal ideas. As Lecomte Du Noüy once observed, "What characterizes man, as *Man,* is precisely the presence in him of abstract ideas, of moral ideas, of spiritual ideas, and it is only of these that he can be proud. They are as real as his body, and confer to this body a value and importance which it would be far from possessing without them."[51] But the person who meets in literature ideas opposed to his own does not necessarily lose his hold on his own ideas. In fact, it may help him to realize his ideas in *depth* by knowing other ideas objectively and critically. The basic urge in any tradition of humanism is to assimilate and embrace the good wherever it may be found.

Actually we are equipped better to deal with ideas opposing our own through examining and studying them, especially in the kind of human context that literature provides. In our studies, it is well not only to realize that misleading ideas have deeply influenced society at times but also to understand their causalities and effects. While we may not accept the interpretation of life that such literature offers (we may, for example, reject the nostalgic fatalism of Omar Khayyám which appealed to some Victorians), it is also true that we can learn by literary study the historical and social influence of such ideas on individuals. We come to understand some of the causes which led an artist to present life in a specific way, even if we do not endorse that way. This knowledge is very helpful to us in obtaining perspective in regard to our own cultural problems and in regard to the universal problems of human experience. We learn to estimate the sincerity, the poignancy, the quality of man's thought even when it is in error or leads to erroneous results.

A great pagan artist like Homer may assume values that might not square with later religious principles. But this depicting of humanity may still be universally true. Take the great scene in

Homer's *Iliad* between Priam and Achilles. Achilles has killed Hector, the most loved of Priam's sons, because Hector killed Patroclos, Achilles' closest friend. Three times the enraged Achilles has dragged the body of Hector, tied to the chariot wheels, around the walls of Troy. Yet Priam has the courage now to go to the tent of his enemy to beg back the body of his son. Uncertain of Achilles' temper and impulsiveness, Priam faces a humiliating and dangerous mission that only a great love could undertake. Priam pleads in terms of a common humanity:

> Remember your own father, most noble prince Achilles, an old man like me near the end of his days. It may be that *he* is distressed by those who live round about him, and there is no one to defend him from peril and death. But he indeed, so long as he hears that you still live, is glad at heart and hopes every day that he will see his well-loved son return from Troy.[52]

Homer tells us that

> . . . the heart of Achilles ached with anguish at the thought of his own father. He took the old man's hand, and pushed him gently away. So the two thought of their dead and wept, one for his Hector while he crouched before the feet of Achilles, and Achilles for his own father and then for Patroclos. When his agony had passed, and he could move again, he got up from his seat and raised the old man by the hand, pitying his white hairs and white beard, and spoke simply from heart to heart: "Ah, poor man, indeed your heart has borne many sorrows! How could you come to the Achaian camp alone? How could you bear to look on the man who killed all your noble sons, as I have done? Your heart must be made of steel. Come now, sit down upon a seat. We will let our sorrows lie deep in our hearts awhile, for there is no profit in freezing lamentation. This is the way the gods have spun their threads for poor mortals! Our life is all sorrow, but they are untroubled themselves."

Homer gives us a great human scene, utterly believable, showing how two quite opposed men have their great moment of trust and understanding approaching what medieval people meant by *Saint Charity*. Both schooled by sorrow, Priam and Achilles share a companionship in observing the common plight of man.

In terms of their pagan culture, we can, of course, understand their bleak attitude to the gods, who seem to have little understanding of men. Zeus is shown as completely willful, arbitrary, and lacking in compassion. From the religious viewpoint of the Judaic-

Christian tradition, this attitude would open serious error. Such pessimism would be at least as opposed to the Christian idea of Providence as "totalitarianism" is to "freedom."

But why does it not seem to matter very much in Homer's narrative? The answer lies in the fact that the essential thing offered by Homer is a great human picture. This is the truly universal thing that moves our emotions. The overtly universal pronouncements about men and the gods are not important as theological statements—only as indications of understandable frustrations and feelings. The *human experience* is the important thing that Homer offers—sincere, poignant, inspiring—and not his facile theology, which is unacceptable. Homer graphically conveys to us how helpless we feel in the face of human disaster. He does this as an *artist.* As a theologian and philosopher, he provides no coherent account of Zeus. "Zeus has two jars of the gifts he gives, standing on the floor beside him, one of good things and one of evil things. When the thunderer mixes and gives, a man meets with good sometimes and bad other times: when he gives all bad, he makes the man despised and rejected; grinding misery drives him over the face of the earth, and he walks without honor from gods or from men." We might quite justifiably regard such a view of the universe as capricious and irrational, even "unclassical." But, in studying Homer, we understand why he presented the universe in this way. And, in doing so, do we not sharpen our own perspectives and our own values? Having learned about life from Homer, we realize how important it is for us *really* to know "what we think we know." Some of our own values, which we may accept casually as a matter of routine, suddenly seem worth examining in depth. If we have a wisdom that is in certain areas superior to that of Homer, because it offers a more adequate answer to the experience Homer has transferred to us, does not the great artist give us an urgency to substantiate and realize such wisdom?

A great artist like Homer, Dante, Shakespeare, Milton, or Tolstoi transcends the values and "errors" of his time because, as a penetrating observer of experience, he sees what is universal and generic, what is emphasized through the generations of mankind. The human values that the great artist offers us are universal and cosmic and are, in that sense, always new, always modern. Some of these writers are "antique" but you could never call them "old hat."

In many great works of literature, such as *Paradise Lost, Anna*

Karenina, and *Antigone,* we see man caught in the irony of his initial decisions. We learn from such works what to *be human* means. In a deep sense, we are looking in literature for ourselves. Not even kings, not even the most farsighted and gifted men, have any way, merely as men, to avoid the common plight of all. All men are under sentence of death, but some, through the quality of their vision, create happiness; others, unhappiness.

What we look for in a great artist are values—not primarily words (though these are remarkable enough and are themselves the vehicles of values). But we must avoid that kind of left-handed compliment which says, in effect, that it doesn't really matter what the artist has to say—he has such a beautiful way of saying it! A great artist does not necessarily intellectually explain, put into mental definitions, the mysteries of experience appreciably better than anyone else. Every artist, since he is also a human being limited by space and time, will share in some of the current opinions and values of his epoch which may have only localized meaning. But the great artist can often see in one view more angles, more levels; he can get a more comprehensive picture than most of us. And the more comprehensive the picture, somehow the more basically encouraging it is. A great artist is organic in his view—that is, his various perceptions grow together and strengthen one another and, if they admit of apparent contradiction, it is the kind of contradiction found in experience itself, even like the paradoxes of religion, which are not negative or sterile but await resolution and fulfillment. A great artist brings about synthesis, the fusion of the different legitimate approaches to truth. And if a Shakespeare is at loose ends, inconclusive, undefined, it simply means that though one may be extremely perceptive about all the elements that enter the structure of life it is not in the power of any man to fit them together completely. Too many forces enter into the Creator's many-dimensional plan to be reduced, even in an age of extreme rationalism, to a neat human plan. The poet Henry Vaughan may triumph over death but he cannot solve its mystery; he can experience love but he cannot chart it. Yet a great artist responds to the universe with great creative emotion. If he cannot explain everything, he can tell us how we should feel—and feeling is no less essential a part of life than intellection. And for thought to be really alive, it must not be merely speculative. There must also be the testimony of living experience. And that is what the artist gives us.

Discussion Questions

1. Why is literature primarily concerned with human experience?
2. Besides telling us about experience, what other benefits can literature give us?
3. How can literature be specifically distinguished from the other arts?
4. How can literature be said to aid in the development of a human culture?
5. In what way is literature responsible to truth?
6. What distinction does Aristotle make between the poet and the historian?
7. What meanings are suggested by "holding the mirror up to nature"?
8. What is the relationship of literature to contemplation?
9. Why is the perception of the *individuated* important for a sense of the beautiful?
10. How would you distinguish *function* and *being*?
11. What are three traditional characteristics of the beautiful?
12. What is meant by *integrity* in relation to a work of art?
13. How would you distinguish *organic* from *mechanical* form?
14. What is meant by the principle of tension in regard to a work of art?
15. What misunderstanding lies behind St. Augustine's objection to art?
16. What moral problems may arise in *art of conflict*?
17. How would you explain *aesthetic distance*?
18. What might be a good test to determine the morality of a work of art?
19. How would you explain *symbol*?
20. What merit is possessed by Plato's view that the furniture before him is *a* table but not *the* table?
21. Give some examples of *overtones* of meaning.
22. Can you show why there may be several levels of meaning in a literary statement?
23. What is meant by an archetype?
24. What is signified by myth?
25. Why might an image be considered a mental event?
26. What position relative to that of the philosopher and that of the historian might be assigned to the creative artist?
27. Why may literature be considered a focal point of other disciplines?
28. What characterized the approach of the renaissance humanist to literature?

29. In what sense may we say that literature illuminates intellectual and cultural history?
30. Illustrate the *integrating* role of literature from a work of your own selection.
31. Why is Homer's ideology comparatively unimportant in his work?
32. What might be considered the specific contribution of the great artist?

PART TWO

Response to Poetry

No word, but as it beats upon the mind's ear,
carries, not merely in meaning, but in the mere
sound of it, infinite varieties of association.
It comes, not merely with the sound of itself,
but with waifs, with errant glories, from all the
sound contexts with which ever in speech
or in song it has been associated.

H. W. GARROD

ART ASKS FOR RESPONSE

It is important to try to understand as closely as possible what the literary artist is saying and making. But simultaneously, too, we should be aware of our own reactions, study them, and perfect them in awareness and sensitivity.

A work of art is designed to elicit certain emotional responses. The communication of literature misses its purpose if we respond to it only with one corner of our mind—if we, for example, master the necessary factual information about a work but fail to read it with genuine empathy, with a capacity to enter fully and imaginatively into its emotional life. It is possible to know everything about a book and still miss the experience the artist worked so hard to convey. There is always this danger about a work of art—of "knowing" all about it without really understanding it, just as in everyday life a person may have all sorts of contacts with someone without in the least understanding him.

Just as the normal process of progressing from the egocentricity of childhood toward a certain social awareness and a capacity to put ourselves sympathetically in our neighbor's shoes, see his troubles, his point of view, takes time and experience, so sympathy and emotional maturity in responding to a work of art do not come all at once. They come only as one travels the slow path to maturity past mistakes and shallow judgments, until one reaches a true capacity for both intellectually seeing and emotionally feeling the work of art. Actually, as information ceases to be mere information and becomes part of our real intellectual processes, our emotional growth tends to correlate with it.

Some idea of the various responses called for by the different forms of literary art can be very helpful. And we shall consider some aspects of the responses to poetry, creative prose, and drama. Emotional responses of this sort are of the highest importance in the development of the individual. The arts were not created for the purpose of setting up courses in them, or for making people pass examinations in them. They were primarily meant to excite and move people in some way or other. The fact that such responses cannot easily be examined or graded in a school system should not blind us to their primary importance.

RESPONSE TO POETRY

We may say initially that in poetry words are not simply symbols of ideas. Prose speaks *about* something through words, poetry *makes* something *through* words. A prose creation depends upon elements of construction—of plot and the building of situation as in a narrative, of definition, of exposition and argumentation as in other prose forms—for which words are tools rather than essences in themselves.

Let's try an illustration. Let us take one of the great ideas of the Greeks. They were particularly concerned, as in the case of Plato, with the art of measurement. The universe was a harmonious place in which everything had its due limits in relation to everything else. The great virtue was moderation, the observance of the due boundaries of decorum, "of what is *fitting*." To jump over the proper measurements, the proper ratios, the proper balances, was to commit the great sin of *hubris* (overweening self-confidence or pride). In a state of *hubris,* a man becomes unable to make sound judgments, to listen to good advice. He begins to make serious blunders in his affairs, in his relationships with other people. He moves in the direction of *ate* (mental derangement, insanity). Listening only to his own ego, he becomes increasingly foolish. A standard Greek platitude is "those whom the Gods would destroy they first make mad." The Gods do not have to destroy the individual who has attacked the cosmic harmony. He will inevitably destroy himself. This is a basic subject matter of Greek tragedy.

The positive side of this principle is a vision of the universe as a great cosmic harmony, in which all the spheres join their tunes to the universal pattern. This is the macrocosm (the greater world) which man can choose to reflect in his own person, his own microcosm (the lesser world). The body itself is great harmony; the spirit constitutes even a more remarkable harmony. The secret of the good life consists in "knowing oneself," one's due place and function, and responding to the universal harmony. The Greek emphasis on mathematics, music, gymnastics (all concerned with measure) as the basis of their educational system helped to reinforce this pivotal idea.

So far now we have been *telling* about something through words. We have been making an explanation, an *exposition.* The only response expected of the reader is one of intellectual curiosity and satisfaction.

Now let us see what Shakespeare does with this kind of idea in a poetic context:

How sweet the moonlight sleeps upon this bank!
Here we will sit and let the sounds of music
Creep in our ears: soft stillness and the night
Become the touches of sweet harmony.
Sit, Jessica. Look how the floor of heaven
Is thick inlaid with patines of bright gold.
There's not the smallest orb which thou behold'st
But in his motion like an angel sings,
Still quiring to the young-eyed cherubins.
Such harmony is in immortal souls. . . .

(*Merchant of Venice*, V, i, 54–63)

Here you see harmony visualized, made vivid. Here you have an *imagistic* experience of harmony. The Greek *idea* has become indissolubly welded with a vivid picture. You do not get as much information as in the prose discourse above; you may not understand the background of the idea so well. On the other hand, you get a vivid picture, extremely beautiful, that moves you deeply. The idea of harmony has ceased to be merely an idea; it has become part of one psychologically and emotionally as well as intellectually. It has been argued that the intrinsic law by which poetry is ruled is that of beauty—beauty understood in its widest, most generous sense. Edgar Allan Poe argues that when people speak of beauty in poetry, "they are not speaking of a quality as supposed, but an *effect;* they refer, in short, to an intense and pure *elevation of soul* rather than of intellect or of heart."[1] Beauty is for Poe the legitimate province of the poem. "Now the object Truth, or the satisfaction of the intellect, and the object Passion, or the excitement of the heart are, although attainable to a certain extent in poetry, far more readily obtainable in prose."[2]

You might well quarrel with Poe's semantics but he is obviously getting at something that characterizes poetry and the emotional response it requires. Somehow, a generalization becomes particularized when it becomes part of the poetic process. A generalization scarcely exists in the highest poetry; it has become concrete, it has become *incarnated.*

There is something unusual and distinct about poetry, something hard to define but somehow of the highest importance. As one critic has said, "The expectation with which we approach poetry is utterly different from the expectation with which we approach prose."[3] What is not explicitly said, what is only suggested, is no less important than the overt statement. In the words of John Stuart Mill, "Eloquence is heard; poetry is overheard."[4] Or, as another critic has put it, "It is the successful blending of the undefined and definite in words that constitute the triumph of the poet's art."[5]

The undefined, what is "overheard," so important in poetry, will not seem quite as mysterious to us if we realize what is meant by the creative imagination, by the laws of mental association, and if we acknowledge the importance of the unconscious as well as of the conscious mind.

But first we may ask what are the general characteristics of poetry in an *essential* sense, not merely in terms of surface techniques and appearances.

CHARACTERISTICS OF POETRY

One of the most productive approaches to forming an idea of the nature of poetry is to make a distinction between its characteristics and those of prose, particularly in reference to *organic* form rather than *surface* form.

According to the English critic Herbert Read, poetry is "predominantly intuitive, imaginative and synthetic."[6] Read deliberately chooses the word "predominantly" because those qualities which are present in prose are present as well in poetry, but in a subordinate capacity. Prose, on the other hand, is "predominantly logical, constructive, and analytical." Poetry attains its end by synthesis, prose by analysis.

Some of the terms in the distinction need clarification. Some are self-explanatory and can be briefly dismissed. "Logic," "construction," "analysis" carry fairly clear meaning. In prose the idea is important, the *intellectual* communication. The particular *mode* of expression is not so pivotally important as long as the prose writer makes his ideas and the connections between them clear. Of course, a work of prose may contain within itself moments of poetry, but these are subordinated to the overriding design of the prose, which is that of intellectual clarity and demonstration. It is also true that poetry, especially in the longer and more architectonic forms, embraces a good deal of the prose elements of logic, construction, and analysis. A poem like *Paradise Lost,* for example, has to incorporate a considerable amount of definition, argumentation, and exposition. Poe once stated there was no such thing as a long poem. A long poem for him was merely a series of short poems strung together. Such a statement actually has justification in so far as prose elements are bound to enter (and quite rightly) into longer poems.

Intuition, imagination, synthesis are terms that cause greater difficulty, and we shall consider these separately.

Intuition

Without going into all the possible philosophical difficulties that surround the word "intuition," we can recognize it in its general connotation as characteristic of poetic discourse. Poetry is a comparatively excited statement, and it arises from the poet's seeing something with great directness and enthusiasm. The etymological background of the word signifies a direct "looking at." The poet constantly "asserts" what he sees rather than argues about it. Intuition means a capacity to see into truth directly without the necessity of going through a painstaking logical process.

How does such intuition arise? Intuition often results from previously accumulated exercises of reason, so that something can be seen in a compressed way by a kind of sixth sense. A line in Dante, for example, exhibits this kind of compressed insight, in his case in a religious context: "In God's will is our peace" *(In la sua volontade e nostra pace).*[7] This line might almost be said to compress the basic outlook of Christian faith.

There is another aspect of poetry, too, which accounts for our frequent connection of intuition with it. This point will become clearer as we discuss the function of the image and of mental association in poetry. Intuition in poetry is seldom *merely* an intellectual perception. It is an intuition expressed in image-bearing words. An image may carry with it many overtones, many mental associations. The poetic intuition is an imaginative one rooted in the image rather than in the concept. Because the image is not confined to denotation (the specific universally recognized meaning of a word) but suggests many other possibilities, great poetry is distinguished by a multidimensional seizure of reality. This is the fact realized by what is called *levels of meaning* in modern criticism.

When we speak of intuition in poetry we also speak of those flashes of truth which win universal acceptance. It is because of the presence of intuition in this sense that we may say that a great poet does not have to seek after the unusual but only to make us *see* what we already *know*. This also explains why many people are attracted to poetry because they find in it a concise and simple (at least, *apparently* simple) way of saying great things. As Keats once observed, "Poetry should strike the reader as a wording of his own highest thoughts, and appear almost as a remembrance."[8]

Take a statement like this from Henry Vaughan:

I saw eternity the other night
Like a great ring of pure and endless light,
All calm as it was bright.[9]

It reads very casually, like an absent-minded jotting in a diary. This is concise and simple—yet not so simple. Many assertions are made through the image of *ring*. A ring signifies unity, as in a wedding ring. It means interdependence and harmonious dynamicism, for, being circular, the ring signifies movement within and back to itself. It therefore symbolizes permanence and friendship among all men, who, in the religious sense, compose eternity. As a ring of *light*, it symbolizes glory, and, as a circle isolated from what lies outside, it indicates self-possession. The light is *endless* but how is it endless? It is endless *within* the ring, not radiating outwards from the circle (in which case we would not *see* the circle). The light, in other words, is endless but in terms of a *depth within* the circle. The ring binds and bounds all within it, not diminishing the endless depth. Outside the ring there can be nothing. Here, then, is Vaughan's intuition, multidimensional and perhaps not thought out consciously in every detail. While Vaughan's style is apparently casual, he intuits the unity, dynamicism, interrelationship, permanence, glory, self-possession, and the endless depth of light in *eternity*.

In dramatic poetry, particularly in the work of Shakespeare, a powerful intuition comes as a result of intensive amplification and the building up of climax. Under the indomitable guidance of his wife, Macbeth has steeled himself to murder the king. She remains cool, collected, practical. He has not been able to say "Amen" in response to one of the guards talking in his sleep; he realizes that his nerves are giving away. He is further shaken by the sudden knocking at the door, "How is't with me when every noise appals me?" But suddenly he is hit with something much harder, something he had not bargained for at all, a terrifying intuition about moral guilt, a transcendent guilt that swallows up everything else:

What hands are here? Ha! they pluck out mine eyes!
Will all great Neptune's ocean wash this blood
Clean from my hand? No, this my hand will rather
The multitudinous seas incarnadine,
Making the green one red.

(*Macbeth*, II, ii, 59–63)

The imagistic intuition here used by Shakespeare signifies the transcendent nature of moral guilt. Lady Macbeth had previously told him to get some water and wash the blood off his hands. But water will not wash off blood; blood, as a moral symbol, covers everything. It "incarnadines" (turns to crimson, to blood color) the multitudinous seas, making the green ocean one red color. A whole medieval philosophy and theology is compressed into the image of incarnadining the multitudinous seas. It is not a wild exaggeration but a vivid perception. The enormity of Macbeth's sin has shattered his whole relationship to life and to the natural universe.

Imagination

As far as the second word of the distinction is concerned, "imagination," we have in mind the predominance of the imagistic method in poetry. Our minds are like extrasensitive, high-speed cameras. We form mental images and retain them in our memories. It is this human ability that enables us to identify our surroundings and get a great deal of our business done. But when we speak of imagination in the arts, we have something more complex in mind. We mean the use of the image in a *symbolic* sense. A symbol is a sign of something that goes beyond, that transcends, the identification of the particular object before us. The image "bread" denotes a flour product with certain ingredients, though, by mental association, one man may think of rye bread, another of French rolls, a third of pumpernickel. But when we use a phrase like "bread of life" we have gone beyond considering pumpernickel or French rolls; we have combined and synthesized in our minds certain essential characteristics of bread with certain characteristics of life. We are talking about something transcendental, life, through the *symbolic* image of bread.

Herbert Read goes so far as to identify imagination, in this sense, with the creative faculty of the mind. The imagination is creative, he says, "if we keep to the etymological significance of the word, in that it bodies forth images! In this sense I maintain that it is a poetical faculty. The 'maker' of imagery is the poet. This is the plain significance of the words and their historical origin."[10]

Eric Gill argued in "The Value of the Creative Faculty in Man" that when we say a man has imagination "we mean not merely that he registers his sense-impressions but that he *creates* images; and when a child draws or a poet 'makes,' likeness to sensory appearance is the least important as well as the least obvious character of their productions. Now, this creative 'image' is not purely sensory; on the other hand, it is . . . not a purely intellectual form either, it concerns 'not only the intellect . . . but the imagination and the sensibility of the artist . . . and for this reason cannot be expressed in concepts.' "[11]

Synthesis

Synthesis, our third differentiating word, means a uniting, a bringing together, in contrast to *analysis,* which means taking something apart to see the elements that compose it. Poetry, we have said, is a *welding* process in contrast to the step-by-step construction of a prose work; it *fuses* elements, whereas prose defines and particularizes the elements entering into its total construction. An interesting example, because it was so adversely criticized by Dr. Samuel Johnson as a mixed metaphor (which it is, but who cares), is Milton's "blind mouths" in "Lycidas":

Blind mouths! that scarce themselves know how to hold
A sheep-hook, or have learnt aught else the least
That to the faithful herdsman's art belongs!

("Lycidas," 119–121)

"Blind mouths" are clergymen who are intellectually and spiritually without vision but look after their own selves, particularly their physical selves, extremely well. You could explain this indefinitely in terms of analysis but the compressed synthesis, *blind mouths,* has hit the situation with a force that no amount of analysis could drive home. For another synthesis, on a highly colored and climactic emotional level, think of the "multitudinous seas incarnadine" that we discussed before.

A characteristic of the poetic synthesis is that the statement is unique; it does not permit any verbal substitutions. A synthesis cannot be adequately expressed otherwise. "Turning many seas to crimson," while expressing the surface meaning of "multitudinous seas incarnadine," is obviously unsatisfactory.

Because of these characteristics of intuition, imagination, and synthesis, poetry does not arise primarily from planning and abstract intellectual thinking; it arises from, and is based on, the image brought about by mental association and then indissolubly wedded to an underlying intellectual idea. Once the union, the *concretization,* has taken place, there stands the total poetic meaning. For the poet, there is no prior *conceptual* meaning which is then illustrated or *demonstrated,* and there can be no other meaning, or translation of meaning, than the poetic phrase itself contains. In this sense, to paraphrase Cleanth Brooks, "a poem says what it says."[12] That is why the paraphrasing of a poem, or its translation into another language, is so unsatisfactory. We give a watered version of the poetic statement—merely its conceptual significance.

Matthew Arnold in his essay "Literature and Science" gives an amusing illustration of the frustrations frequently met with in the teaching of poetry because of this mysterious fact about it:

> I once mentioned in a school-report, how a young man in one of our English training colleges having to paraphrase the passage in *Macbeth* beginning
>
> Can't thou not minister to a mind diseased?
>
> turned this line into, "Can you not wait upon the lunatic?" And I remarked what a curious state of things it would be, if every pupil of our national schools knew, let us say, that the moon is two thousand one hundred and sixty miles in diameter, and thought at the same time that a good paraphrase for
>
> Can'st thou not minister to a mind diseased?
>
> was, "Can you not wait upon the lunatic?"[13]

But the trouble is that the young man had an almost impossible assignment. Can anyone think of a paraphrase that would be much better?

The fact is that the imagistic significance of poetry remains in the original statement. It is not transferable. So we must always fail, in some degree, in "explaining" what a poem means. At the best, we can through interpretative criticism throw light on the background of the poetic statement so that it can get to be recognized more easily. Such criticism is like giving *A* a letter of introduction to *B*. It is still up to *A* to know *B*.

MENTAL ASSOCIATION

It is most helpful to understand the relationship between poetry and mental association. Because of a certain kind of conditioning in our educational system, we are likely to underrate the stream of images that passes through our minds during our working hours. We feel that we should be thinking logically, constantly seeing useful and productive relationships. Actually only a minor portion of our mental time is spent in this logical way.

In the midst of mechanical work and even of creative intellectual work, images pass through the mind of what we are going to have for lunch, of the corner in the lake where we caught the large trout last summer, of the wife or sweetheart we are going to meet at six o'clock. Or someone might casually or accidentally say something that brings a stream of memories to us—the house we knew in childhood, or our first baseball game, or some elementary school teacher whom we liked or who frightened us.

Obviously the more we are developed in self-awareness, in consciousness of ourselves, the richer and more varied are our mental associations. The greater the power of our mental associations, the greater our response to poetry. Every word *denotes* something specific. Everyone is agreed, for example, that "ocean" means a large body of salt water. But "ocean" *connotes* many different things and many different ideas to various people. Mental associations are the ideas, images, formulated feelings that we connect with the real object suggested by the word. "Ocean—I don't like it—seasickness, you know," might be one man's response in terms of mental association. Another might say to himself, "Ocean—sailboat, blue skies, fresh breeze, freedom." While many mental associations are purely conventional and simply reflect an unawakened conformity on the part of the subject ("ocean" is "blue," though in fact it is often characterized by different colors), others are uniquely personal and are based upon real experience emotionally and imaginatively perceived. Some of these associations are *images* in a very specific sense, for they indicate real objects associated with the word—for example, such objects as lobster, shipwreck, or black timber might be connected with "ocean." Some are intellectual ideas, symbols of thoughts that were engendered by experience—for example, in reference to "ocean" such words as "unknown," "secret," "immensity," "wisdom," "ebb and return," "tranquility."

The uniqueness of the poetic statement is directly related to the uniqueness and intensity of the individual experience, at least as far as the creation of the original mental association is concerned. That is why unconscious factors, or factors that have been dead or dormant in the memory, are so frequently resuscitated in poetry with great vehemence.

The poet has learned the art of navigating the high seas of mental association, with their subtle and even concealed relationships, while most of us have been content to operate safely in the narrow and well-marked harbors of expository and logical discourse.

By employing the possibilities of mental association, the poet often says more than he consciously plans. He arouses unforeseen mental associations in the mind of a sensitive listener. The poet deals with a force that has a life of its own; he is never confined to the basic meaning of his statement. Take a factual statement such as, "It's snowing heavily now." After you have learned the fact, what more can you do with the expression? But take an imagistic statement such as, "The spinning, spiraling gift of snow like the eloquence of unloosed bells." This statement lacks the narrow accuracy of the first. It might be hard to *explain* just what has been said. But obviously it is saying much; it challenges you to brood over it, to build an emotional experience of your own derived from it. It is the kind of phrase you might treasure; it has a kind of undefined vitality about it that cannot be easily exhausted. In fact, you might feel inclined to return to it often for its sheer beauty. The first statement was purely functional but this statement has *being*.

It is the poet's capacity to harness the forces of mental association to his purpose, and to invite us to bring our own associations into union with his, that is the technical basis of what has been called *verbal magic* and *poetic vision.*

Because of mental association, the poet's imagery tells us many things besides what is overtly presented. The overt presentation may be the least important aspect of what he has to say.

John Ruskin says that these lines from Oliver Wendell Holmes's "Spring"

The spendthrift crocus, bursting through the mold
Naked and shivering, with his cup of gold

are very beautiful and "yet very untrue." "The crocus is not a spendthrift, but a hardy plant; its yellow is not gold but saffron. How is it that we enjoy so much having it put into our heads that it is anything else but a plain crocus?"[14]

The answer to this question is, in part at least, that the overt statement about the crocus is not of major importance. What the poet is describing through his image is the power and beauty of the germinating spring *courageously* bursting through what opposes it—the mold and the frigidity. And implied here is an attitude toward life itself which we might like to share and fulfill, a sort of splendid courage so rich in what it has to offer that suffering is only noteworthy as a contrast.

Keats once said that "poetry should surprise by a fine excess."[15] The greatest poetry gives the impression of a treasured value expressed with a driving passion. Milton in his tractate *On Education* described poetry as "simple, sensuous and passionate."[16] If by "simple" we mean an interior organic unity following the laws of imagination, "sensuous" in the sense of the close bond between images and sense impressions, the additional word "passionate" adequately completes a description of the greatest poetry.

Poetic statement is almost always an *exaggerated* statement if we were to take some other norm than poetry itself; say, truth to fact or scientific accuracy. We must remember that poetry touches the emotions deeply. The poet himself is emotional. He is not giving us just a transcript of a world external to himself. He is seeing the external world, it is true. But he is also seeing *himself seeing* and *feeling* it. His reaction is communicated to us and we share it. Emotional language is emphatic language; its alleged excess corresponds to the reality of the emotion communicated. As one critic says:

The intensity of the feeling makes up for the disproportion of the objects. Things are equal to the imagination which have the power of affecting the mind with an equal degree of terror, admiration, delight, or love. When Lear calls upon the heavens to avenge his cause, "for they are old like him," there is nothing extravagant or impious in this sublime identification of his age with theirs; for there is no other image which could do justice to the agonizing sense of his wrongs and his despair.[17]

Examples of this "fine excess" are innumerable. As good a one as any is this powerful exaggeration from *Isaiah* 55:12 that entirely suits its subject, the operative presence of God, emphasizing his dynamism and creative power: "The mountains and the hills shall break forth before you into singing, and all the trees of the field shall clap their hands."

THE INSPIRING POWER OF POETRY

The peculiar power of some poetry in its "fine excess" is so great that it has often been called *inspired* utterance. This adjective attests to the unusual power of poetry at its highest, though it would seem an exaggeration to use "inspired" in a theological sense, even if poetry truly inspires the audience.

Poetry, closely allied to mental association, is also a carefully wrought art, allowing for a great deal of technical and intellectual elaboration. In the case of surviving work sheets of poets, including their erasures and changes, we can see the working, even plodding, side of poetry. To some this sort of knowledge comes as a shock. Thus Charles Lamb, describing the Milton manuscripts at Trinity, finds "taking a peek behind the scenes" particularly horrifying:

I had thought of Lycidas as of a full grown beauty–as springing up with all its parts absolute–till, in an evil hour, I was shown the original copy of it, together with the other minor poems of its author, in the library at Trinity, kept like some treasure to be proud of. I wish they had thrown them into the Cam, or sent them after the latter cantos of Spenser into the Irish Channel. How it staggered me to see the fine things in their ore, interlined, corrected, as if their words were mortal, alterable, displaceable at pleasure! As if inspiration were made up of parts, and these fluctuating, successive, indifferent. I will never go into the workshop of any great artist again.[18]

Other examples could be cited, such as, for instance, Roy Ridley's uneasiness in looking into the artist's work in *Keats's Craftsmanship,* where he discusses Keats's holograph.[19]

One thing abundantly proved by the manuscripts of Milton and Keats is that they did not write from any full-blown inspiration in the first place but through persistent struggle with recalcitrant material. W. P. Ker in *Form and Style in Poetry* indicates that scene of struggle which is ultimately transcended in the final product, but still carries the odor of the workshop. In speaking of these lines in "Lycidas,"

Sleep'st by the fable of Bellerus old,
Where the great vision of the guarded Mount
Looks toward Namancos and Bayona's hold. . . .

(160–162)

Ker says:

> "The fable of Bellerus old" is pedantic mythology. It means Cornwall, Land's End. Milton, writing in the fashion of the solemn ode, thinks himself bound to use mythological ornament. First he puts "Corineus" because "Corineus" comes first in British mythology; but this did not sound well enough. Just as he changed "humming tide" to "whelming tide" for fuller sound, so he substituted here "Bellerus," Bellerion being an old name for Cornwall. Milton takes a sham mythological figure, whom he knows nothing of and about whom he does not want his readers to inquire. . . . What one gets from it, if one tries to express the meaning of it in prose, is the mood of sorrow, of regret, expressed through thoughts of the spaces of the sea. And though Bellerus is nothing, "the great vision of the guarded Mount" is one of the most glorious images in the whole of Christendom, the appearing of St. Michael on his own mountain, looking out over the Atlantic.[20]

The testimony of poets themselves clashes about the reality of *inspiration* and about its nature. William Blake claimed he was an inspired, even an automatic writer. "I write," he once said, "when commanded by the spirits, and the moment I have written I see the words fly about the room in all directions."[21] He claimed that he wrote his *Milton* "from immediate dictation, twelve or sometimes twenty or thirty lines at a time, without premeditation, and even against my will."[22] Goethe once said in regard to inspiration that "the good ideas stand suddenly before us like free children of God and cry out, 'Here we are.' Things that so come we must regard as unlooked-for gifts from above, as veritable children of God, to be received with reverence and with joyful gratitude. They are akin to the daemonic. . . ."[23]

But here is Edgar Allan Poe insisting that poetry is basically a technique:

> Most writers—poets especial—prefer having it understood that they compose by a species of fine frenzy and ecstatic intuition—and would positively shudder at letting the public take a peek behind the scenes, at the elaborate and vacillating crudities of thought—at the true purposes seized only at the last moment—at the innumerable glimpses of the idea that arrived not at the maturity of full view—at the fully matured fancies discarded in despair as unmanageable—at the cautious selections and rejections—at the painful erasures and interpolations—in a word, at the wheels and pinions—the tackle for scene lifting—the step-ladders, and demon-traps, the red paint and the black patches. . . .[24]

Romantic tradition in the nineteenth century powerfully emphasized the notion of inspiration. It is said that Browning, on being asked to interpret a line of his own verse, replied that when the poem was first written God and Robert Browning knew what the line meant, but now only God knew.[25] Shelley in his *Defence of Poetry* (1831) says that "poets are the hierophants [sacred interpreters] of an unapprehended inspiration; the mirrors of the gigantic shadows which futurity casts upon the present; the words which express what they understand not. . . ." For Shelley poetry is the visitation of the Divine to man: "Poetry is indeed something divine. It is at once the centre and circumference of knowledge; it is that which comprehends all science, and that to which all science must be referred." Wordsworth, in the preface to the second edition of *Lyrical Ballads* (1800), says: "Poetry is the breath and finer spirit of all knowledge; it is the impassioned expression which is the countenance of all science." And again, "Poetry is the first and last of all knowledge—it is as immortal as the heart of man." The Romantics went so far as to view the poet as a prophet and priest. Poetry for Wordsworth is the voice of religion:

> *. . . to the open fields I told*
> *A prophecy: poetic numbers came*

Spontaneously, and cloth'd in priestly robe
My spirit, thus singled out, as it might seem,
For holy services. . . .

(*Prelude,* 1805 text, I, 50–54)

In *Sleep and Poetry* (1817) Keats similarly views poetry as a religious vocation:

No one who once the glorious sun has seen
And all the clouds, and felt his bosom clean
For his great Maker's presence, but must know
What 'tis I mean, and feel his being glow.

The concept of poetic inspiration in this sense owes something to Platonic tradition. In the *Apology* Plato says: "Then I knew that not by wisdom do poets write poetry, but by a sort of genius and inspiration; they are like diviners or soothsayers who also say many fine things, but do not understand the meaning of them."[26] Even Francis Thompson, who rejects the Romantic concept of nature, yields to this particular idea:

We speak a lesson taught we know not how,
And what it is that from us flows,
The hearer better than the utterer knows.[27]

The Romantics, often departing from religious orthodoxy, were religiously minded and often constructed new religious values from scattered and antagonistic sources. They were the priests of their own religion, and their poetry was their theology. They identified art and religion, with the result that art lost responsibility to religion as a higher source of truth than that of art. As the nineteenth century drew on, however, poetry for many became more and more divorced from any connection with traditional theology. Artists were often agnostics, and occasionally atheists. Nevertheless the concept of art as its own religion continued. From Romantic tradition stemmed a nonreligious version of the older belief that inspiration of the poet is a direct revelation of spiritual power. From it derived the nineteenth-century principle of "art for art's sake."

LEVELS OF MEANING

Today it is rather uncommon to talk about inspiration in literature, even if the word points to a certain truth, though not absolutely definable, and even confused, about the art of poetry. In line with what is called the new criticism, we are today particularly concerned with what are termed levels of meaning.

Today you come across certain phrases that by now are almost clichés. The contemporary critic, especially in regard to poetry rather than to prose, speaks not only of levels of meaning, but of ambiguities, ambivalences, tensions, polarities, and so on.

What this indicates is a growing preoccupation with the suggestive powers of imagery and the desire to prod this suggestiveness as deeply as possible. One effect of this concern is a more concentrated reading of a lesser number of texts. It indicates entering into a work of art for a thorough intellectual and emotional experience, with a consequent lesser interest on literary trends, history, and classification.

Concentration rather than dispersion is the keynote of the new criticism.

What is meant by some of these new terms? Basically they stem from the problems suggested by the older term "irony." This means more, in the new criticism, than the traditional rhetorical device in which the surface statement is the opposite of the intended inner meaning (allied to *humor* discussed in Part 3, "Response to Prose"). Irony, in the largest sense, is allied to what may be called the plight of man. Man has a capacity for great intelligence, imagination, generosity, a zest for life, but he is constantly faced with frustration, the problem of evil, and death itself. The essence of irony is contrast, either explicit or implicit, especially between the world we actually experience and the world of harmony, love, and sympathy that we eternally desire—the contrast also between the tensions of our internal life and the frequent indifference of the outside world to the private individual self. Fresh areas of irony have appeared in modern literature because of the increasing subtlety of psychological studies. What we think and do consciously may not be a true index of how we really feel and want to do. There is the new contrast, springing from psychoanalytical studies, between the real self, which may be hidden to us, and the image of the self that we have projected and deliberately try to adhere to. While literature has constantly recognized the common fact of self-deception, its inner causes have never been so explored as in the contemporary preoccupation with the conscious and the unconscious, stemming from the studies of Jung and Freud.

It is the world of contrasts that irony explores in writing. A complex response enters into the perception of irony. To some extent, there is an element of surprise, of shock. In Synge's *Riders to the Sea,* a semipoetic drama, Maurya, the aged mother, has lost the last of her seven sons to the sea. Eamon, a neighbor Aran Islander, has been asked by her daughter to make a coffin for the last son. "But where are the nails?" he asks. "It's a great wonder she wouldn't think of the nails, and all the coffins she's seen already." Or think of Cleopatra in Shakespeare's play. She is to die in tragic despair ("Immortal longings are upon me"), but even to die is partly a technical operation. She buys a serpent from a merchant specialist, who, as a matter of course, extols his wares. "I wish you all the joy of the worm," he says politely. This is the sort of thing that people have called, with *unconscious* irony, *comic* relief!

Irony in these examples has a poignant emotional impact. To the element of surprise and shock must be added a sense of justice—or, at the very least, a sense of the reality of man's condition. An Eamon or the serpent merchant has his own right and validity; each says what he has the right to say even if, by contrast, it underscores emotional and tragic depths of which he is unaware.

Irony of this kind often arises from the context itself. In *Hamlet,* for example, the King tells Laertes

There's such divinity doth hedge a king
That treason can but peep to what it would,
Acts little of his will.

(IV, v, 123–125)

No one can reproach Claudius, now the *actual* king, on the grounds of intelligence; we have no certain grounds of knowing whether he is meant to be sincere in this statement. But the statement is made in a context where Claudius had already committed successful treason against the older Hamlet and where shortly he is to be liquidated himself. And here is where *ambiguity* arises—is Claudius a fool, or a Machiavellian saying anything that suits his purpose at the moment? Are we to go along, independently of Claudius, with the principle that divinity *doth hedge* a king?

Just as *tension* arises in ordinary life because of uncertainty about meaning and mutual attitudes, about the unpredictabilities that may follow from already tentative or uncertain situations, so in poetry or literature itself. *Ambiguity* originally meant a doubtfulness or uncertainty of meaning—the idea being that two alternative interpretations were open to one from a given statement. Actually, the new criticism, which seeks some certitude in pinning down a variety of suggested meanings, has frequently discovered that an artist is not actually giving us an *answer* to a question, which a superficial interpretative reading might indicate, but rather is asking *us* a question and, in a sense, dropping a problem in *our* laps. Shakespeare might, in effect, be asking in reference to Claudius, "And what do *you* think about this proposition of the King's divinity?" *Ambivalence* relates to basic tension in that it implies the coexistence of opposite and conflicting feelings about the same person or object. The new criticism frequently extends ambivalence to include the existence of *conflicting intellectual values* in a piece of literature. A work like *Hamlet,* under this terminology, is full of ambiguities and ambivalences, particularly because it is open-ended, and for Shakespeare, while he may be giving us some values, he is also *searching* for values.

The new criticism has not extended its terminology so successfully to the interpretation of prose, partly because prose operates on a more denotative, unilateral level than poetry.

Let us see how such terms could be applied to the following seventeenth-century poem, "They Are All Gone into the World of Light!" by Henry Vaughan.

They are all gone into the world of light!
And I alone sit lingering here;
Their very memory is fair and bright
And my sad thoughts doth clear.

It glows and glitters in my cloudy breast
Like stars upon some gloomy grove,
Or those faint beams in which this hill is drest
After the sun's remove.

I see them walking in an air of glory,
Whose light doth trample on my days;
My days, which are at best but dull and hoary,
Mere glimmering and decays.

O holy Hope! and high Humility,
High as the heavens above!
These are your walks, and you have show'd them me,
To kindle my cold love.

Dear, beauteous Death! the jewel of the Just,
Shining nowhere but in the dark;
What mysteries do lie beyond thy dust,
Could man outlook that mark!

He that hath found some fledged bird's nest, may know
At first sight if the bird be flown;
But what fair well or grove he sings in now,
That is to him unknown.

And yet, as Angels in some brighter dreams
Call to the soul, when man doth sleep,
So some strange thoughts transcend our wonted themes,
And into glory peep.

If a star were confined into a tomb,
Her captive flames must needs burn there;
But when the hand that locked her up gives room,
She'll shine through all the sphere.

O Father of eternal life, and all
Created glories under Thee!
Resume thy spirit from this world of thrall
Into true liberty.

Either disperse these mists, which blot and fill
My perspective still as they pass;
Or else remove me hence unto that hill
Where I shall need no glass.

Without trying to enumerate all the possible ambiguities and ambivalences in Vaughan's creation, we might mention the most obvious. His dead friends are gone into the world of light and are walking in an air of glory. Apparently this fact depresses the poet ("Whose light doth trample on my days"), but on another level their memory is fair and bright ("And my sad thoughts doth clear"). We presently come to a brilliant ambiguity, though we could quarrel with the question of whether the poet himself does not resolve it. But, anyhow, it is ambiguous as a statement:

O holy Hope! and high Humility,
High as the heavens above!
These are your walks, and you have show'd them me,
To kindle my cold love.

On reflection, since humility is a virtue, it can be seen as a *high,* a glorious thing. In fact, this concept seems much more justified than the common association with humility of self-depreciation, feelings of inferiority. Here we have ambivalence—the various values that can be given the concept of humility. We also have an ambivalence within an ambivalence, because Vaughan's departed friends in "trampling" on his days have mysteriously "kindled" his cold love. "Trampling," far from being obnoxious, is actually constructive of a valuable spiritual experience. An ambivalent mental association arises almost immediately with the idea of death, for death has been the instrumentality of this new relationship that Vaughan is experiencing—it is a beautiful thing!

Dear, beauteous Death! the jewel of the Just,
Shining nowhere but in the dark;
What mysteries do lie beyond thy dust,
Could man outlook that mark!

Another important ambiguity arises from Vaughan's evaluation of his own complex feelings. A potential envy has become a vision of glory, not only his own, but that of all mankind:

If a star were confined into a tomb,
Her captive flames must needs burn there;
But when the hand that locked her up gives room,
She'll shine through all the sphere.

It is a valuable experience to examine levels of meaning in respect to the presentation of major characters in the great epics and the great novels. Below we show such an analysis carried out with respect to Satan in Milton's *Paradise Lost.*

Illustration: Levels of Meaning in *Paradise Lost*

A great artist can generally see on many levels at once, and he can convey what he sees, though not always in an *overt* way (for the simple reason that the particular conventions of the art in which he is working do not always make this possible).

An interesting example of the synthesis of a number of levels of meaning is to be found in Milton's presentation of the great figure of Satan in *Paradise Lost.*

As we have said, a great poet says more than he consciously plans because of the way in which mental association works, and one of the functions of a critic is to bring to light all the insights that are implicit in the poetic statement. It is also true that a great artist consciously plans a great many levels of meaning to which he expects a sensitive audience to respond, as Shakespeare does in *Hamlet,* or Milton in *Paradise Lost.*

Even major critics catch only one side of Milton's presentation. William Blake initiated a whole trend in the criticism of the Romantics when he stated in *The Marriage of Heaven and Hell* that Milton was of the devil's own party without knowing it. In other words, Blake was saying, the real hero of *Paradise Lost* is Satan. One modern critic puts forward this point of view with some wit. "Here indeed is the basic flaw of our great Epic: to set Omniscience arguing is as superfluous as challenging Omnipotence to fight. Satan in the story has no call to explain himself. His cause is prejudged, his defeat determined. But he faces up to it with our sympathy. In short Milton's God, creating man in His image, forgot to anticipate his development into a sportsman."[28]

Milton, who was attempting to "justify the ways of God to men," may not have been so nearsighted, such a fool as that. Maybe this viewpoint has missed some of Milton's levels, particularly his keen sense of irony.

Satan reflects some of renaissance man's preoccupation with the sense of *glory.* This is an idea that has weakened or disappeared in contemporary society, where our main concern might be said to be *security* and good *public relations.* Anyone ambitious to achieve glory in the renaissance sense might be viewed now as an awkward figure in need of psychotherapy. But this idea in Milton's time was the basis of much driving ambition. Edmund Spenser died with his ambition to bring the glory of a great national epic to England only partly fulfilled. Milton himself, perhaps the last great man of the renaissance, realizes the compulsion of this idea in "Lycidas," where under the word "fame" he refers to it as "That last infirmity of Noble mind." "To the Greater Glory of God" was a typical renaissance phrase, whereas today we might more honestly say "To the Greater Security of the Public Welfare."

Satan is infatuated with the sense of glory. Why did he start his particular conspiracy? Milton's answer in the opening lines is that he aspired "To set himself in Glory above his Peers." Satan is willing to gamble everything in his warfare with Deity, but there is one thing he can never face losing—*glory:*

That glory never shall his wrath or might
Extort from me.

(I, 110–111)

A great deal of Satan's mental process consists of creating psychological supports for his sense of glory. In the first book of *Paradise Lost* he thinks of the will as "unconquerable," of himself as "One who brings/A mind not to be chang'd by place or time." He has argued that the mind and spirit remains invincible (I, 140–141).

It is this strong sense of his glory that causes Satan to make a series of misjudgments that a lesser person would have avoided. An outside observer, not under Satan's hypnotic persuasion, would clearly see that he had been decisively beaten in the warfare with God. Satan frequently talks about his defeat, but somehow he never quite manages to believe it, and it never occurs to him that it is decisive.

God's apparent victory, according to Satan, must have been due to some technical innovation, fraud, or sheer vulgar power. It was unfair, it was *inglorious,* in the sense that God derived no glory from it. It was due to thunder (I, 93); to force, not to reason—"Whom reason hath equall'd, force hath made supreme/Above his equals" (I, 248–249). He even goes so far as to accuse God of Machiavellian devices. God concealed his real power, caused the angelic revolution to be touched off before the full preparations had been made:

. . . but still his strength conceal'd,
Which tempted our attempt, and wrought our fall.

(I, 641–642)

Nor can he view God's power as an insurmountable fact—God is merely upheld "by old repute, consent, or custom" (I, 639–640). Satan's inability to come to terms with a state of facts is expressed with unconscious irony. Like a prize fighter who underhandedly compliments himself by saying "only a real champion could have defeated me," Satan says of his opponent:

. . . whom I now
Of force believe almighty, since no less
Than such could have o'erpowered such force as ours. . . .

(I, 143–145)

Milton can combine several levels of meaning about the concept of glory. Satan's sense of glory has, in modern parlance, made him neurotic. In his drive to glory (as in a drive to power) he is trying to reduce God to nothingness; he is trying to make an inescapable state of facts evaporate. As *Paradise Lost* progresses, Satan loses more and more contact with reality. But Milton reminds us of a real complexity, a real ambiguity: Satan's judgment is rapidly deteriorating and he has insight into his own neuroticism—his unreversible compulsion that must bring only misery:

With diadem and Sceptre high advanc'd
The lower still I fall, only Supreme
In misery; such joy ambition finds.

(IV, 90–92)

On the other hand, he himself *has* glory—a glory he is destroying in *seeking* glory:

. . . his form had yet not lost
All her original brightness, nor appear'd
Less than Arch Angel ruin'd, and th' excess
Of Glory obscured. . . .

(I, 591–594)

Now we begin to glimpse the complex depths of Milton's irony. Satan's own glory has been the free gift of God. In a sense, it is the reflection of God's grandeur. As he continues to lose his *true* glory, his participation in the grandeur of God, his counterfeit glory becomes more resplendent. The key words, "pride" and "glory," subtly develop opposite meanings:

. . . And now his heart
Distends with pride, and hard'ning in his strength
Glories. . . .

(I, 571–573)

His *strength* is now really weakness, and his glory really *shame.*

Milton is a master artist in the many ways he reveals Satan's inner confusions, although Milton might not have appreciated the irony of the Romantic critics in viewing concepts which Milton is exposing as shallow as the true expressions of Milton's inner self.

Take the concept of freedom, for example. Milton's own view of freedom is strenuous and austere. In *Comus* he has said that *"virtue* she alone is free."[29] Virtue must be tested; "that immortal garland is to be run for, not without dust and heat."[30] What a noble person strives for is the right to do what he should. The idea of freedom in the sense of the absence of responsibility, of doing just what one pleases, never occurred to Milton. He insists on the freedom *to* assent to what is right, to do what is right. I should do what is right for myself; no one else should do it for me. Nor should man-made laws or institutions hamper my *right* to do what is right. Book V of *Paradise Lost* is itself a conclusive debate between Satan and Abdiel about the meaning of freedom. Freedom, to Milton, consists in obeying positively and loving what is the truly legitimate authority. Mammon's view of freedom is the opposite to that of Milton himself:

Free, and to none accountable, preferring
Hard liberty before the easy yoke
Of servile pomp.

(II, 255–257)

Mammon had just stated that we should "Rather seek our own good from ourselves, and from our own live to ourselves. . . ."

And here we come to what is probably the biggest irony of all in *Paradise Lost,* as frequently stated by Satan and his lieutenants. They constantly are thinking of attacking heaven's "battlements." Though Satan has said that "The mind is its own place, and in itself/Can make a Heav'n of Hell, a Hell of Heav'n," he also suggests to his cohorts that they can "re-ascend,/Self-rais'd, and repossess their native seat." Although the confused Satan at one time makes the concept of heaven purely mental and subjective, at other times it is a definite place, a material object. The whole point of *Paradise Lost* is that heaven is a relationship, a relationship between God and his creatures. In destroying this relationship, Satan has destroyed the essence of heaven. He is seeking a house rather than a home, a symbol rather than a reality. No theologian, however limited in vision, ever thought of heaven as a mere piece of real estate.

Satan's power to think clearly has been seriously disturbed in many directions. He has become clever rather than wise. And he constantly traps himself. At the great Council of Devils at the beginning of Book II he has arranged a loaded convention, with Beelzebub more or less acting as his stage manager. He has sophistically argued, amazingly enough, by reference to "the fixt Laws of Heaven" (the heaven he has rejected) that he was created "your leader." No one should envy him his preeminence, he says, because as the leader of the insurrection he is most exposed to punishment. It is doubtful whether Satan really believes this when he is saying it; he wants to secure leadership much more than he fears potential punishment—it is a matter of political strategy. But ironically what he doesn't believe in, and is falsely presenting as true, is, in *actual* fact, true. Here is a real ironic boomerang. Although he himself is a rebel against hierarchy and authority, he constantly appeals to feudal law in addressing the devils:

. . . Wherefore do I assume
These royaltie's, and not refuse to Reign,
Refusing to accept as great a share
Of hazard as of honor, due alike
To him who Reigns, and so much to him due
Of hazard more, as he above the rest
High honor'd sits?

(II, 450–456)

Does Milton use a certain amount of ambiguity and ambivalence in the presentation of Satan, in a certain sense did he contribute to the misunderstanding that he was consciously or unconsciously sympathetic to the figure of Satan as the hero of *Paradise Lost?*

Well, in one sense, Milton presents what Aristotle termed a "fatal flaw" (see the section on "Response to Drama") in the characterization of Satan—his misunderstanding of the true nature of glory and his seeking after a false glory. Satan is far from being entirely egocentric; he seems to have real feelings for his associates:

Thrice he assayed, and thrice in spite of scorn,
Tears, such as Angels weep, burst forth. . . .

(I, 619–620)

His attitude toward Adam and Eve is not one of pure malice, though he never deviates from his politic purpose of injuring the Deity:

. . . yet no purpos'd foe
To you whom I could pity thus forlorn
Though I unpitied. . . .

(IV, 373–375)

He has not lost all his virtue—he is "th' excess of Glory obscur'd."

Nor fail'd they to express how much they prais'd,
That for the general safety he despis'd
His own: for neither do the Spirits damn'd
Lose all their virtue. . . .

(II, 480–483)

Actually Milton incorporates a long tradition of medieval irony. The sinner can enter an endless vicious circle—the commission of sin warps his judgment, and the warping of judgment leads more deeply into sin. Sin is accompanied by a growing stupidity—the stupidity being marked by an increasing self-assurance. Thus Dr. Faustus in Marlowe's play, having actually signed a contract with Mephistopheles in his own blood, begins to argue with the devil himself that "Hell's a fable." He has previously told Mephistopheles, "Learn thou of Faustus manly fortitude"! Mephistopheles, who really knows what's what, is actually shocked by Faustus's frivolity:

O Faustus, leave these frivolous demands
Which strike a terror to my fainting soul!

(*The Tragical History of Doctor Faustus*, I, iii, 85–86)

As Roger Ascham, tutor of Queen Elizabeth I, said in *The Schoolmaster:* "Where will inclineth to goodness, the mind is bent to truth. Where will is carried from goodness to vanity, the mind is soon drawn from truth to false opinion."[31]

The underlying irony in Milton's presentation of Satan is that his apparent heroism, his long isolated flight (symbol of his pride) to the strange new world, his audacity, his arrogance are the overt signs of an inward degeneration of mind. He has chosen to attempt to defeat an unbeatable ambiguity—to take positive action in terms of negatives, to reject the relationship that makes things fruitful:

To do aught good never will be our task,
But ever to do ill our sole delight,
As being the contrary to his high will
Whom we resist.

(*Paradise Lost*, I, 159–162)

POETIC MOOD

Levels of meaning are seldom, if ever, overtly explained in poetry. A novelist, as long as he remains interesting, can take plenty of time to show everything that he can possibly mean. But a poet *presents* by symbolic imagery; he has to leave a good deal to the audience's associative powers, and to their powers of inference.

A poet creates his peculiar effects not by a rationalistic ordering but by a climax of mood. The climax of one of his statements generally lies not in the intellectual statement but in the image that evokes the culminating emotional response. In the following passage from Milton, the last line, "*Gorgons* and *Hydras* and *Chimeras* dire," is intellectually purely an addendum that does not increase the basic intellectual meaning of the passage. But, on the other hand, does it not extend enormously the emotional meaning of the passage by evoking mythical and historical memories of ancient terrors?

. . . Thus roving on
In confus'd march forlorn, th' adventurous Bands
With shudd'ring horror pale, and eyes aghast
View'd first their lamentable lot, and found
No rest; through many a dark and dreary Vale
They pass'd, and many a region dolorous,
O'er many a Frozen, many a Fiery Alp,
Rocks, Caves, Lakes, Fens, Bogs, Dens, and shades of death
A Universe of death, which God by curse
Created evil, for evil only good,
Where all life dies, death lives, and Nature breeds,
Perverse, all monstrous, all prodigious things,
Abominable, inutterable, and worse
Than Fables yet have feign'd, or fear conceiv'd,
Gorgons *and* Hydras *and* Chimeras *dire.*

(*Paradise Lost*, II, 614–628)

Repetition, which is normally avoided in prose because it interrupts the continuing direction of analytical thought, is frequent in poetry as a means of arousing certain kinds of emotion. Great passages in the Bible, for example, make full use of parallelism and the repetition of the underlying thought in different image sequences.

But where shall wisdom be found? and where is the place of understanding? The depth saith, It is not in me: and the sea saith, It is not with me. It cannot be gotten for gold, neither shall silver be weighed for the price thereof. It cannot be valued with the gold of Ophir, with the precious onyx, or the sapphire. The gold and the crystal cannot equal it: and the exchange of it shall not be for jewels of fine gold. No mention shall be made of coral, or of pearls: for the price of wisdom is above rubies. The topaz of Ethiopia shall not equal it, neither shall it be valued with pure gold. Whence then cometh wisdom? and where is the place of understanding?—Behold, the fear of the Lord, that is wisdom; and to depart from evil is understanding.

(Job 28:12–28)

Milton provides a rather extraordinary example of a repetition in exactly the *same* words, without even a break! What might seem at the outset a tired secretary's mistake, however, becomes a passage of great pathos and tenderness. Adam is speaking of his love to Eve:

Sweet is the breath of morn, her rising sweet,
With charm of earliest birds; pleasant the Sun
When first on this delightful land he spreads
His orient Beams, on herb, tree, fruit, and flow'r,
Glist'ring with dew; fragrant the fertile earth
After soft showers; and sweet the coming on
Of grateful Ev'ning mild, then silent Night
With this her solemn Bird and this fair Moon,
And these the Gems of Heav'n, her starry train:
But neither breath of Morn when she ascends
With charm of earliest birds, nor rising Sun
On this delightful land, nor herb, fruit, flow'r,
Glist'ring with dew, nor fragrance after showers,
Nor grateful Ev'ning mild, nor silent Night
With this her solemn Bird, nor walk by Moon,
Or glittering Star-light without thee is sweet.

(*Paradise Lost*, IV, 641–656)

Numerous technical devices exist in the poetic art to help create mood. One of the most obvious is that of *onomatopoeia,* whereby the sound *echoes* the sense. This, if not overdone, vividly touches our senses and makes us quick to participate in the imaginary world of the artist. The following lines from Tennyson are very effective:

So saying, from the ruined shrine he stept,
And, in the moon, athwart the place of tombs,
Where lay the mighty bones of ancient men,
Old knights, and over them the sea wind sang
Shrill, chill, with flakes of foam. He, stepping down
By zigzag paths and juts of pointed rock,
Came on the shining levels of the lake.

("Passing of Arthur," 96–102)

The first few lines are characterized by long sonorous vowels, which are then broken by "shrill, chill"; these parallel and echoing "l's" suggest the sudden energy of the sea, beating against the shore. The harsh consonants of "zigzag" and "juts" suggest the terrific roughness of the landscape in contrast to the sudden calm, abruptly come upon, of "the shining levels of the lake."

But outside the exactitude and originality of his imagistic language—which are the essential thing—the most important aid to the creation of poetic mood is the poet's choice of word order. The emotional impact of poetry often depends on an orchestration that leads up to the climactic use of the particular word. Take, for example, the line "Blooms again the broad blue flower of day." The effect of movement, of surprise, of broadening grandeur, depends on the position of "blooms" as first in the line. Placed in another position, the word will fail to win the emotional impact it has here. Note how flat the reverse order would be: "The broad blue flower of day blooms again." The line now suggests boredom rather than dramatic impact.

The following lines afford a relevant illustration of the impact of word order in poetry:

Over the breast of the spring, the land, amid cities,
Amid lanes and through old woods, where lately the violets peeped from the ground, spotting the gray debris,
Amid the grass in the fields each side of the lanes, passing the endless grass,
Passing the yellow-speared wheat, every grain from its shroud in the dark-brown fields uprisen,
Passing the apple-tree blows of white and pink in the orchards,
Carrying a corpse to where it shall rest in the grave,
Night and day journeys a coffin.

(Walt Whitman, "When Lilacs Last in the Dooryard Bloom'd," 26–32)

This passage is directed toward the emotional climax suggested by the word "coffin." The whole of the setting, skillfully vivid, is closely identified ("every grain from its shroud in the dark-brown fields uprisen") with death by the method of suggestion and of symbolism. The whole of nature seems to bear the weight and momentousness of the coffin. The writer isolates by his symbols the essential fact, the death of the man for whom all mourn as one. To speak profanely, we are made to feel that there is only one coffin in the world of any importance.

Whitman is not primarily appealing to our reason. His intention is to make us feel the emotional weight of the occasion. He is making a direct appeal to our emotions through imagery, especially through the symbolism of the word "coffin."

The word "coffin" is a unique poetic expression in Whitman's poem by reason of its *placement*. It only accidentally means what is usually meant by a coffin. Rather, here it is a symbol of the abrupt tragedy that is passing over the surface of the earth. But the word would not contain this suggestive power if it were not for the preceding elements fused with it.

To illustrate this point, it is interesting to see what happens when "coffin" is transferred to the first line:

Night and day journeys a coffin
Carrying a corpse to where it shall rest in the grave,
Over the breast of the spring, the land, amid cities,
Amid lanes and through old woods. . . .

The subsequent expressions here simply give the itinerary of the coffin, and it seems to be somewhat like a commercial bus taking a detour.

POETRY, RHYTHM, METER

In making distinctions between poetry and creative prose, we should not consider poetry essentially dependent upon meter or "fixed rhythm." All language, in fact, has rhythm. But metrical form consists in a special pattern of repeated rhythms.

For example, in what light are we to consider the great psalms of David? They are obviously poetry, but they do not possess a metrical pattern in the usual sense of the word.

By the rivers of Babylon,
There we sat down, yea, we wept,
When we remembered Zion.
Upon the willows in the midst thereof
We hanged our harps.
For there they that led us captive required of us songs,
And they that wasted us required of us mirth, saying,
Sing us one of the songs of Zion.
How shall we sing Jehovah's song

In a foreign land?
If I forget thee, O Jerusalem,
Let my right hand forget her skill.
Let my tongue cleave to the roof of my mouth,
If I remember thee not;
If I prefer not Jerusalem
Above my chief joy.

(*Psalms* 137)

For a more modern example, we may take Whitman. Consider these few lines, and ask whether it is not possible for the highest lyricism—and by that we mean the highest lyricism from the point of view of *music*—to be obtained without any regular metrical pattern at all.

Soothe! Soothe! Soothe!
Close on its wave soothes the wave behind,
And again another behind embracing and lapping, every one close,
But my love soothes not me, not me.

Low hangs the moon, it rose late,
It is lagging—O I think it is heavy with love, with love,

O madly the sea pushes upon the land,
With love, with love.

O night! do I not see my love fluttering out among the breakers?
What is that little black thing I see there in the white?

Loud! Loud! Loud!
Loud I call to you, my love!
High and clear I shout my voice over the waves,
Surely you must know who I am, my love.

Low-hanging moon!
What is that dusky spot in your brown yellow?

("Out of the Cradle Endlessly Rocking," 71–86)

It is difficult to appreciate the beauty of Whitman's rhythm in a short extract, because his structure, like that of the Psalms, is symphonic. Free rhythms are very suitable for what we might call architectonic poetry. Even a classical writer such as Milton loved the freer forms. Yet Milton felt that he had to make some defense of his use of blank verse, and his disregard of rhyme; he himself says in regard to *Paradise Lost:*

> The measure is English heroic verse without rime, as that of Homer in Greek, and of Virgil in Latin—rime being no necessary adjunct or true ornament of poem or good verse, in longer works especially, but the invention of a barbarous age, to set off wretched matter and lame metre; graced indeed since by the use of famous modern poets, carried away by custom, but much to their own vexation, hindrance, and constraint to express many things otherwise, and for the most part worse, than else they would have expressed them.[32]

He went even further in practice and was on the point of approaching the *free verse* of today in his *Samson Agonistes,* although he still adheres to an *iambic* undercurrent in the rhythm. The following extract indicates the direction that Milton was taking in his latest work.

The Sun to me is dark
And silent as the Moon,
When she deserts the night,
Hid in her vacant interlunar cave.
Since light so necessary is to life,
And almost life itself, if it be true
That light is in the Soul.
She all in every part, why was the sight
To such a tender ball as the eye confined,
So obvious and so easy to be quenched,
And not, as feeling, through all parts diffused,
That she might look at will through every pore?
Then had I not been thus exiled from light,
As in the land of darkness, yet in light.
To live a life half dead, a living death,
And buried; but, O yet more miserable!
Myself my Sepulchre, a moving Grave;
Buried, yet not exempt,
By privilege of death and burial,
From worst of other evils, pains, and wrongs;

But made hereby obnoxious more
To all the miseries of life,
Life in captivity
Among inhuman foes.

(86–109)

In more recent times, when so much of our finest poetry has been written in free verse, we are forced to depart from the traditional assumption that meter, in the sense of a *regular* metrical pattern, is an essential of poetry. In fact, we realize that free verse is in itself a very adequate form of poetic expression. The following lines from William Ernest Henley's "Margaritae Sorori," leading economically to its quiet climax, gain their power from the fact that each part of the structure carries the necessary weight of meaning without being in any way forced by adherence to meter.

A late lark twitters from the quiet skies;
And from the West,
Where the sun, his day's work ended,
Lingers as in content,
There falls on the old, gray city
An influence luminous and serene,
A shining peace.

The smoke ascends
In a rosy-and-golden haze. The spires
Shine and are changed. In the valley
Shadows rise. The lark sings on. The sun,
Closing his benediction,
Sinks, and the darkening air
Thrills with a sense of the triumphant night—
Night with her train of stars
And her great gift of sleep.

So be my passing!
My task accomplished and the long day done,
My wages taken, and in my heart
Some late lark singing,
Let me be gathered to the quiet West,
The sundown splendid and serene,
Death.

Free verse, merely because it is *free,* demands particular restraint and judgment to obtain its greatest effects. In other words, the sense of form, of control, does not depend upon any external and fixed pattern. Many of the great passages of the Bible, particularly the Psalms, offer important free verse structures, as in the extract quoted earlier. Ideological contrasts, irony, dramatic tension are particularly well conveyed through the medium of free verse. In free verse the artist has to devise his own sense of emphasis. The emphasis can be at the end of lines, or lines can be run on, with the emphasis coming in the next line or in a single isolated word.

The rhythms of free verse are very close to the rhythms of good natural speech. Each line corresponds to a unit of vocal delivery. Thus in "Margaritae Sorori," Henley, in his special sense of emphasis, makes the climactic word "death" one line, just as he makes the much longer statement "thrills with a sense of the triumphant night" one line.

Free verse demands modulation, cadence, economy, and climax. Looking at Henley's lines, one sees:

1. *Modulation:* "a transition from one key to another." Note the abrupt and broken effect of the following lines; note how the transitions, through constant interruption, suggest impetuous movement:

The smoke ascends
In a rosy-and-golden haze. The spires
Shine and are changed. In the valley
Shadows rise. The lark sings on. The sun. . . .

2. *Cadence:* "the fall of the voice as in speaking." Note the change in tempo after "content":

. . . the sun, his day's work ended,
Lingers as in content,
There falls on the old, gray city
An influence luminous and serene,
A shining peace.

3. *Economy:* in the sense of nothing wasted or extraneous, as in the climactic word "death" at the end of the poem:

The sundown splendid and serene,
Death.

4. *Climax:* the phrase of culminative importance, even if it is as brief as one word, has a line to itself:

There falls on the old, gray city
An influence luminous and serene,
A shining peace.

In rejecting the narrowness of formalized approaches to creativity, we do not wish to overlook the possibility that for a particular writer a traditional form may well be such a matter of second nature to him that it actually helps him toward the conceiving and executing of a work.

In meeting the demands of a rigid form, an artist is often compelled to take extra pains so that his work has the extra tension, the tautness of *difficulty overcome.* It is, of course, possible to meet the requirements of a rigid form by dilution—the addition of extra wordage, illustration to fill out meter and rhyme requirements. The first approach indicates the right use of traditional form; the second, the wrong use. Keats, in "The Eve of St. Agnes," first wrote these lines: [33]

Sudden a thought more rosy than the rose
Flush'd his young cheek and in his painfle heart
. . . riot fierce. . . .

Keats's second version, an improvement, ran as follows:

Sudden a rosy thought
Heated his brow and in his painfle heart
Made purple riot. . . .

Constantly struggling with the form, Keats eventually evolved these great, tense lines:

Sudden a thought came like a full-blown rose,
Flushing his brow, and in his pained heart
Made purple riot. . . .

(136–138)

The "full-blown rose" as an image expressing *action* ("came") is a magnificent image, suggesting color in violent and fluid movement, passionate and beautiful. It was not exactly spontaneous, however; it arose from difficulty overcome.

Difficulty overcome must not destroy spontaneity; it must merely canalize spontaneity. We are told in Dorothy Wordsworth's *Journal* that "William tired himself seeking an epithet for the cuckoo."[34] It is well to seek, but creativity seldom issues from tiredness, from forcing oneself to meet the required form. On the other hand, it is undoubtedly true that some of the great statements to be found in the realm of poetry have been the result of "the happy guidance of a rhyme."

We must not think of traditional forms as static. Great traditional work has variety and tension within a settled order. We have said that a fixed metrical pattern is not essential to poetry, but it may be *essential* to a *specific* poem. The poem is a thing that is made—it is what it is. The finished product is a whole and all that enters into its unity is essential to it. But metrical pattern is not essential in the sense that it must be characteristic of *all* poetry. In this sense, Edgar Allan Poe exaggerated when he said that poetry was "musical thought."

Aldous Huxley illustrates the danger of making poetry too *poetical* in the common sense of that term.[35]

> It is when Poe tries to make it too poetical that his poetry takes on its peculiar tinge of badness. Protesting too much that he is a gentleman, and opulent into the bargain, he falls into vulgarity. Diamond rings on every finger proclaim the parvenu.
>
> Consider, for example, the first two stanzas of "Ulalume."
>
> *The skies they were ashen and sober;*
> *The leaves they were crisped and sere—*
> *The leaves they were withering and sere;*
> *It was night in the lonesome October*
> *Of my most immemorial year;*
> *It was hard by the dim lake of Auber,*
> *In the misty mid region of Weir—*
> *It was down by the dank tarn of Auber*
> *In the ghoul-haunted woodland of Weir.*

Here once, through an alley Titanic,
Of cypress, I roamed with my soul,
Of cypress, with Psyche my soul,
These were days when my heart was volcanic
As the scoriac rivers that roll—
As the lavas that restlessly roll
Their sulphurous currents down Yaanek
In the ultimate climb of the pole—
That groan as they roll down Mount Yaanek
In the realms of the boreal pole.

These lines protest too much (and with what a variety of voices!) that they are poetical, and, protesting, are therefore vulgar. To start with, the walloping dactylic metre is all too musical. Poetry ought to be musical, but musical with tact, subtly and variously. Metres whose rhythms, as in this case, are strong, insistent and practically invariable offer the poet a kind of short cut to musicality. They provide him (my subject calls for a mixture of metaphors) with a ready-made, reach-me-down music. He does not have to create a music appropriately modulated to his meaning; all he has to do is to shovel the meaning into the moving stream of the metre and allow the current to carry it along on waves that, like those of the best hairdressers, are guaranteed permanent.

Huxley recasts the dignified lines of Milton, where music and sense go together appropriately, into the flashy vulgarity of Poe's rhythm:

Milton

Not that fair field
O Enna, where Proserpine gathering flowers,
Herself a fairer flower, by gloomy Dis
Was gathered, which cost Ceres all that pain
To see her through the world. . . .

(*Paradise Lost*, IV, 268–272)

Poe

It was noon in the fair field of Enna,
Where Proserpina gathering flowers—
Herself the most fragrant of flowers,
Was gathered away to Gehenna
By the Prince of Plutonian powers;

Was borne down the windings of Brenner
To the gloom of his amorous bowers—
Down the tortuous highway of Brenner
To the god's agapemonous bowers.

It is important in the use of metrical forms that the emphasis in the writing grow *justly* from the expression. Inversions or unassimilated phrases to fill out the meter destroy the sincerity of the discourse.

CONTENT AND FORM

The critical tendency to regard a long or philosophical poem as a contradiction in terms has been fairly widespread. Edgar Allan Poe in his essay "The Philosophy of Composition" takes the view that *Paradise Lost* is a series of short poems connected by generous amounts of prose. Logan Pearsall Smith regarded *Paradise Lost* as a mixture of auditory delight and outmoded theology.[36] The "organ harmonies," he says, are all that is left of Milton. The content has to be disregarded; the form is disengageable.

The question arises whether, in *fact,* content and form *are* disengageable. One can think of form and content, it is true, as separate ideas. Content can be conceived as that which is contained; form as that which gives arrangement, coordination, structure to the contents. But only in the mind, and not in the actual work of art, can one have content without form, or form without content. The analogy that can be made between a work of art and a chemical compound breaks down in one important respect. A chemical compound can be broken down into its constituent elements, and the elements retain their own identities. But a work of art consists in the *actual* compound. Break down the compound of a work of art, and one does not have separate elements of content and form. One has nothing at all. One can make a synopsis of the content, but the work of art does not lie in the content. The artistic effect is missing, for it depends on the effect of art as a whole.

Form can, of course, appear in various ways in literature. An artist can arrange his material in terms of a preconceived form; or he can allow the form to develop from the dynamic process of the material itself. Coleridge liked to speak of mechanical form and organic form. Mechanical form is like a jar or mold into which material is poured; organic form is the form developed by living things as they grow, as, for example, a seed develops by stages into a flower. The word "mechanical" should not necessarily have a bad sense in relation to form. This is outward form particularly in the sense of *product.* We make biscuits in a biscuit tin. We make sonnets, so to speak, in a sonnet tin. The biscuit cannot develop any shape it pleases, nor can the sonnet. Milton makes an epic in an epic container. He did not write spontaneously in the sense that his spontaneous outpourings took the shape of an epic. But within the mechanical container, organic growth can also be present. The biscuits have to follow their own laws of development even within the biscuit tin; Milton's poetry has to burgeon like a flower within the epic form. The artist in selecting a preconceived form has in mind his ultimate product, but in reaching that product he also uses organic form, form as *growth,* as *process.*

It is possible for an artist to use a badly conceived tin, one not suited for his purpose or for his materials. The artist-cook, for example, would not make very excellent soup in a biscuit tin. Obviously in the art of literature a wide variety of forms are available, from the most simple to the subtlest, and they serve a wide variety of purposes. The reader's response to form in literature should be kept as flexible as possible. New forms and new idioms may trouble readers, and often a long struggle precedes acceptance of the form, as it did with free verse and the naturalistic novel. The current tendency is to stress the internal organic form rather than form in the sense of the containing structure. The classification of literature, through *genres,* types of classification in terms of organization or structure, is stressed less. As one critic says:

> The abandonment of distinction of species in the demand for universally desired qualities is one of the most interesting events in modern literary history. One aspect of it is the loss of distinctions between levels of style suited to different literary kinds. Auerbach shows in *Mimesis* that this breakdown of levels has occurred in literary history whenever "everyday reality," however defined, has come to be of major importance. It is also clearly related, as M. H. Abrams has shown, to the shift of critical emphasis, during the Romantic period, from poem to poet, from interest in the artistic product to theories of expression dealing with the artistic process. When critics are mainly interested in the author, and in his works largely as they are signs of certain qualities in

him, they are likely to look for the same qualities in all works. Objectivity, subjectivity, sincerity, insincerity, inspiration, imagination—these can be looked for or blamed whether the author is writing comedy, tragedy, epic, satire, or lyric.[37]

THE ARTIST'S INTENTION

Is the knowledge of an artist's intention, either directly stated in his work, or derived from comments external to it, helpful in getting to know the work? Will it help us to understand his particular union of content and form? Some contemporary criticism goes so far as to speak of such reliance on an artist's overt statement as the "Intentional Fallacy."[38]

Thomas Carlyle in his essay on Goethe argues that the critic's prime responsibility is to discover "what the poem's aim really and truly was, how the task he had to do stood before his eye, and how far, with such materials as were afforded him, he has fulfilled it."[39] Doubt has been cast on the possibility of knowing what the poem's aim is except by looking at the poem itself. How is the critic to find out what the artist tried to do? It has been argued that if the poet succeeds in his intention, the evidence lies in the work of art itself. If the artist does not succeed in whatever his intention was, the artist's intention is irrelevant to the work. It is probably an exaggerated statement to call the assumption of the artist's intention a fallacy. Artists' statements about the intentions of their work can be helpful guidelines. Milton's overt statement of his aim in *Paradise Lost* is to "justify the ways of God to men." Actually only a small part of Miltonic criticism has been devoted to determining whether Milton accomplishes this aim. In a multidimensional work of this sort, other leading themes are suggested besides that of justice—freedom, for example. Since the days of William Blake, who decided that Milton was of the devil's own party without knowing it, a great deal of criticism has ignored the stated aim of the work altogether. But, on the other hand, a good argument could be made that it is relevant to the interpretation of the work. Experience by this time, of course, has shown that an artist often consciously sets out to do one thing but unconsciously accomplishes another.

The skepticism about paying close attention to an artist's overtly stated aims has been increased in recent years by stress on the unconscious factors that enter creative work. The theory is that the author's will should be relaxed. W. B. Yeats goes so far as to insist on a state of trance, "in which the mind liberated from the pressure of the will is unfolded in symbols."[40] Northrop Frye takes a more moderate position along the same lines: "It takes a great deal of will power to write poetry, but part of that will power must be employed in trying to relax the will, so making a large part of one's writing involuntary."[41] The idea of a preconceived conscious formulation of a work, normal in neoclassical times, is out of fashion, and an adequate defense of it has not recently been made. Frye observes about intention: "And creation, whether of God, man or nature, seems to be an activity whose only intention is to abolish intention, to eliminate final dependence on or relation to something else, to destroy the shadow that falls between itself and the conception."[42]

RHETORIC AND PURE POETRY

For many generations, the art of rhetoric, a skill that had been developed in classical times and greatly reinforced during the renaissance, was held in high esteem. A Demosthenes or a Cicero knew how to sway audiences toward important decisions by cogent argumentation reinforced by strong emotional appeals that were carefully planned both artistically and psychologically. But those who strongly support the cause of pure *art* do not approve of the artist's having a primary concern with his effect upon the audience. In addition, various social developments in our era have lessened the effect of overt rhetorical appeal. Through news reports, commentary, inside information, the public has been habituated to regarding the political oratory of the past as outmoded. In 1863 Edward Everett spoke for two hours at Gettysburg and was much applauded. Lincoln's Gettysburg Address, short, direct, without traditional oratorical flourishes, created a very minor impression. Today we pay no attention to Everett's speech but highly prize Lincoln's. We tend to praise Lincoln for his lack of rhetoric. The more pertinent question, however, is whether the rhetoric of a piece is well or badly employed. In fact, Lincoln's speech is also rhetoric, but an effective rhetoric that has stood the test of time.

Rhetoric has nonetheless become a downgraded word in many

schools of contemporary criticism, in regard to both poetic and narrative prose structures.

To paraphrase Shakespeare, pure poetry must do away with the feigned touches that rhetoric can lend. The poet should be considered a pure craftsman rather than an unacknowledged legislator in the world of thought and morals, as Shelley imagined him. He must renounce rhetoric, moral judgments, and all other idols of the tribe. The symbolist movement (as in Mallarmé and Rimbaud in French, Rilke in German, Pound and Eliot in English) tends to stress the idea of *pure* poetry as exclusively verbal pattern of inward meaning. This rather narrow and exclusive view of poetry can be traced as far back as Longinus (A.D. ca. 213–273), who thinks of a poetic fragment as suddenly bursting upon the auditor "with an effect of intensity, shock and illumination" which, in its sublimity, scatters everything before it like a thunderbolt.[43] Longinus set the pattern of isolating the supremely poetic quality—*pure poetry*. It was the image or passage rather than the larger aspects of plot or design that were to be highly considered.

If this point of view is carried to extremes, we find a downgrading of assertive or substantive statement. Milton, for example, thinks of epic poetry as a *public* statement observing classical *decorum*. *Paradise Lost* is only occasionally and rarely a revelation of interior psychic conditions. The work is one of public rite and ritual. There is little that is *private* about it—not even in Milton's remarks about his blindness at the beginning of Book III. It is the office of the blind bard that is sung, not the person. The more ritualistic *Paradise Lost* becomes, "the more we are elevated to the rank of participants, precisely because the poet appears not as a private person but as a hierophant or Choregus."[44] C. S. Lewis observes "We are summoned not to hear what one particular man thought about the Fall but to take part under his leadership in a great mimetic dance of all Christendom, ourselves soaring and ruining from heaven, ourselves enacting Hell and Paradise, the Fall and the Repentance."[45] But many critics today are unsympathetic to Milton's epic, largely on the ground that it is not pure poetry. It is argued that Milton has a feeling for words, rather than a capacity for feeling *through* words. "The whole movement of Milton's work is not expressive but mechanical and ritualistic." It is alleged that the pattern, the stylized gesture and movement, has no particular expressive work to do, but functions by rote, of its momentum, in the manner of a ritual. One Milton scholar has stated that the whole modern critical problem regarding the epic poet arises from the theory of pure poetry that says a poem should *act out* rather than *state* its meaning. This assumption dominates a good deal of modern criticism, it is argued, and influences both our preference for the kind of language a poem should use and our expectations about the way language should be organized. The current tendency is to prefer a poetic imagery and diction which have sensuous immediacy and particularity, rather than the abstractness and generality of statement. It is maintained that many readers are no longer able to respond to literature of statement, suspecting it inevitably to be dogmatic or complacent or sentimental.

Since the nineteenth century there has been a strong movement away from rhetoric, which always had as its primary aim the molding of a work of art with a view to its emotional and psychological impact on an audience, toward thinking of the work as an aesthetic object entirely by itself. This concept of the work of art as an autonomous creation, existing for its own sake, has had a major effect upon the prose narrative as well as the poem, as we shall discuss later. A poem is thought to be disqualified if it is meant to produce effects on other men; it becomes rhetoric (often referred to as "mere" rhetoric) rather than poetry. As Archibald MacLeish puts it, "A poem should not mean/But be."

A poem should be palpable and mute
As a globed fruit.

Dumb
As old medallions to the thumb,

Silent as the sleeve-worn stone
Of casement ledges where the moss has grown—

A poem should be wordless
As the flight of birds.

("Ars Poetica," 1–8)

Obviously, pure poetry has a case. The question, however, is one of proportion. Does not a Milton have his place just as well as the imagist and symbolist? And does not rhetoric have an important and legitimate place?

One matter that the strong antirhetoricians overlook, particularly in the case of poetry, is that the meaning of words and images depends upon the work of many past authors. Although we may keep these influences offstage and in the wings, there are hundreds of ghosts of past authors hovering over every other word! A poem like Milton's "Lycidas," presenting "the ebb and flow of hostility in the universe,"[46] achieves its effect through an artifice based on the conventions and artificialities of many centuries. We have the rhetoric of a long literary tradition behind the poem. In this sense, a poem cannot just be by itself. Many others have secretly contributed to it.

Discussion Questions

1. Why is emotional response important in art?
2. What is the general purpose of the arts?
3. How do prose and poetry differ in the use of words?
4. Why are not *generalizations* characteristic of poetry?
5. What predominant characteristics are to be found in poetry?
6. What predominant characteristics are to be found in prose?
7. How would you explain the meaning of "intuition"?
8. What is characteristic of the *expression* of poetic intuition?
9. How do we use the word "imagination" in reference to the arts?
10. What is meant by a "synthesis" in regard to poetry?
11. Why is the paraphrasing of a poem unsatisfactory?
12. Can you illustrate how the mind works through mental association?
13. Why might it be said that mental association is the basis of *poetic vision*?
14. What else does the poet tell us about in addition to the actual object he sees?
15. Illustrate some of the conflicting views of poets in regard to *inspiration*.
16. What is the romantic view of the poet's function?
17. What assumptions are implied in "art for art's sake"?
18. What is meant by irony?
19. Why today is there an increased preoccupation with irony?
20. How is ambiguity used in literature?
21. What is meant by ambivalence?
22. Can you show why Satan in Milton's *Paradise Lost* might be considered an ambiguous figure?

23. Discuss the ambiguity of any other leading character you have met in literature.
24. How would you explain *climax of mood*?
25. What is meant by onomatopoeia?
26. Why is word order so important in poetry?
27. How would you distinguish free verse from blank verse?
28. What are some of the characteristics of effective free verse?
29. What are the dangers of poetry's being too *poetical*?
30. How would you distinguish between content and form?
31. How would you relate content to form?
32. What bearing does the artist's intention have on his work?
33. Has rhetoric a place in poetry?
34. How can it be shown that past tradition contributes a rhetoric to a new work?

PART THREE

Response to Prose

Prose is architecture, not interior decoration.

ERNEST HEMINGWAY

RESPONSE TO PROSE

Prose constitutes a much vaster and quite different area than that of poetry. Prose can take many forms and run through many moods—pathos, humor, fantasy, satire, excitement, curiosity, fear, hope, love—but its method is distinctly a step-by-step involvement and resolution. It expresses its content by demonstration rather than by intuition and symbolic imagery.

This fact is much more essential than any considerations of verse (meter and rhyme). While the difference between poetry and prose is difficult to pin down in a few words, certain things are obvious—the primary dependence in poetry on symbolism and mental association, in prose on explanation and reasoning discourse. Here are two statements, neither in meter or rhyme. One is good prose, the other poetry. Cannot the difference be seen at once?

This is a quotation from Rachel L. Carson's *The Sea around Us:*

> As the waves roll in towards Land's End on the westernmost tip of England they bring the feel of the distant places of the Atlantic. Moving shoreward above the steeply rising floor of the deep sea, from dark blue water into troubled green, they pass the edge of "soundings" and roll up over the continental shelf in confused ripplings and turbulence. Over the shoaling bottom they sweep landward, breaking on the Seven Stones of the channel between the Scilly Isles and Land's End, coming in over the sunken ledges and the rocks that roll out their glistening backs at low water. As they approach the rock tip of Land's End, they pass over a strange instrument lying on the sea bottom. By the fluctuating pressure of their rise and fall they tell this instrument many things of the distant Atlantic waters from which they have come, and their messages are translated by its mechanisms into symbols understandable to the human mind.[1]

While this passage makes an effective use of imagery, contrast it with the following which is dependent on imagery for its real meaning, as distinct from using imagery for demonstration and illustration. It is from Anne Morrow Lindbergh's *Gift from the Sea.*

> This is a snail shell, round, full and glossy as a horse chestnut. Comfortable and compact, it sits up like a cat in the hollow of my hand. Milky and opaque, it has the pinkish bloom of the sky on a summer evening, ripening to rain. On its smooth symmetrical face is pencilled with precision a perfect spiral, winding inward to the pinpoint center

of the shell, the tiny core of the apex, the pupil of the eye. It stares at me, this mysterious single eye—and I stare back. Now it is the moon, solitary in the sky, full and round, replete with power. Now it is the eye of a cat that brushes noiselessly through long grass at night. Now it is an island, set in ever widening circles of waves, alone, self-contained, serene.[2]

Let us take an abstract idea such as that of love, and contrast a philosophical with a poetic statement about it.

> The primary impulse by which our power of willing is set in motion, the impulse by which we are drawn towards objects which we perceive as good for us, is given the name of "love." Love is thus at the heart of our freedom; it is the mainspring of desire, so that the choices we make are the fruits of our love. *Pondus meum, amor meus,* says St. Augustine: My weight is my love—I gravitate toward what I love.[3]

And:

Let me not to the marriage of true minds
Admit impediments. Love is not love
Which alters when it alteration finds
Or bends with the remover to remove.
Oh no! It is an ever-fixed mark
That looks on tempests and is never shaken;
It is the star to every wand'ring bark,
Whose worth's unknown, although his height be taken.[4]

One statement is analytical definition; the other statement is imagistic assertion.

We are considering, here, of course, what we mean by *creative* prose. We are thinking of prose in the context of a work of art, to be enjoyed and contemplated for its own sake. There is a vast world of *functional* and scientific prose following what in grammar is called the method of exposition (answering the questions "what" and "how"—"What is the meaning of this?" "How does this thing work?") and the method of argumentation (answering the question "why"—"Why is this proposition true?"). Prose, as an art form distinct from a functional form, is not primarily interested in giving us information or in logically *convincing* us of some truth or other. It is primarily interested in giving us a picture of experience and moving us emotionally, or, as in the case of humor and satire, making our critical intelligence evaluate a described state of affairs. Always the distinguishing feature between prose and poetry is the predominance of the analytical faculty in contrast to the synthesizing and symbolizing faculty. As for drawing the line between creative prose and functional prose, the basic question is whether the given piece is geared to giving us an imitation of experience to contemplate or whether it is meant to inform us and convince us in an immediate and practical way. Most of the time such distinctions are easy to make. Occasionally, as in the case of some essays, particularly critical essays, there are borderline cases that are difficult to classify. Criticism, for example, has some of the features both of an art and a science.

NARRATIVE: FROM PUBLIC HERO TO PRIVATE ANALYSIS, FROM EPIC TO NOVEL

Of prime importance in the domain of creative prose is the narrative. The earliest great narratives, the epics, are normally classified as poetry. "Heroic" literature is normally predominantly imagistic; it even has a framework of such symbols, standardized epithets such as the "wine-dark sea" and the "rosy-fingered dawn" of Homer, that suggest a permanence of nature in contrast to the mutabilities and changing fortunes of men. There is constant emphasis on formal titles, modes of address, constant use of simile and metaphor, especially of extended descriptive metaphors.

By heroic literature is implied a literature in which the central focus, the central struggle, is that of man, seeking self-preservation against the forces of external nature. It is Odysseus alone on a wine-dark sea; it is the sailor home from the sea, the hunter home from the hill. It is the strength of the individual man pitted against forces ultimately too strong for him, which he faces squarely and honestly. Heroic literature is a literature of individual strength and resourcefulness. In war it is Hector against Achilles, Aeneas against Turnus; it is not the direction of massive machines against their opposites.

It is literature before the Enlightenment, before the industrial revolution. The great primary forces of nature stand undiluted in their strength and simplicity. If a classic writer speaks of standing by the banks of the Scamander or the Xanthus, we immediately envisage a stream of clear water unaccompanied by gas stations, four-lane highways, rubber tires, and tin cans. If we were to speak today of standing "by the banks of the Canarsie," or even of the Wabash, we have an almost humorous connotation. We are more likely to think of gas works than the sacred waters of a life-giving river.

It is almost impossible to recapture in modern literature the value of those universal and simple responses found in the great epics, which give us a mysterious kind of strength as if, like the Titan Antaeus, we had regained our pristine strength by touching the essential earth. Occasionally a more recent work, such as *Moby Dick,* recaptures some of this ancient spirit under very rare circumstances of special theme and of spiritual isolation from the prevailing contexts of our society. The nineteenth-century whaling industry, in terms of man against the sea, was still close in spirit to more primitive times. Such a spirit can, of course, be deliberately revived, as in the exciting experiment narrated in Heyerdahl's *Kon-Tiki.* Ernest Hemingway in *The Old Man and the Sea* (1952) chooses a typical situation and setting where an individual, as in *Moby Dick,* confronts nature (the sea) directly, and through his dignity and strength, seems to say that man is not made for defeat.

But the basic fact is that external nature has become much smaller and far less threatening than in the ancient classics. It is one thing to travel on a modern ocean liner or air jet and quite another to put to sea on a bark that is manually directed without motors or radio, dependent entirely on individual skills and teamwork and upon the mercy of winds and waves. As for danger from wild animals, we no longer even need our guns. We are making every effort to preserve the animals from biological extinction. There is a gulf between a man hunting his dangerous dinner with a bow and arrow and a housewife choosing her cellophaned meat in a supermarket.

There is also a major psychological difference between heroic and modern literature. Our struggles are turned from external nature inwards to our psyche and self-consciousness. Aeneas sought the Sibyl's advice on how to journey to Hades to visit his father. A modern man visits the psychiatrist to learn how he may live with his wife. Heroic man faced objectively dangers and monsters; modern man in some current fiction tends to explode with interior tensions and neuroses, often as a result of trying to learn to live with people. We may have lost an important relationship to life that the less self-conscious heroic past possessed. Anyhow, there are certain obvious differences that make heroic literature, as an understandable term, more or less restricted to the past. A profitable comparison could be made along these lines between the heroic *Odyssey* of Homer and James Joyce's *Ulysses,* which parallels the original in many ways but is written in a quite different psychological spirit.

Illustration: Ancient and Modern Odysseys

It is instructive to contrast Homer's handling of the story of Odysseus (the Greek name for the Latin Ulysses) with Joyce's adaptation in *Ulysses.* In Book IX of the *Odyssey* we are told of Odysseus's adventures in the land of the Cyclopaes: of how these giants have only one eye placed in the middle of the forehead, of how they dwell in dark caves, and of how some of Odysseus's sailors go to one of the caves in search of supplies. When the Cyclops returns, he responds to Odysseus's request for hospitality by picking up two of the sailors and dashing their brains out against the side of the cave; subsequently he devours them. The Cyclops then seals the entrance of the cave with a great rock, and, since Odysseus knows that his men lack strength to remove it, he has to refrain from attacking the monster while he sleeps. Next morning the Cyclops goes out, taking with him the flock he brings home with him every evening. In the meantime, Odysseus sharpens the end of a great staff, and, with the assistance of four of his men, thrusts the end of it into the Cyclops's one eye after he has fallen asleep on the completion of another cannibal meal. The blinded Cyclops feels his flock as they pass the entrance on the next morning. By sending out the rams in groups of three, and having one man attached to the belly of the middle ram, Odysseus manages to deceive the blinded monster and to engineer the escape of all the survivors.

Essentially this is a simple incident without any major overtones, a wondrous tall story telling us of the acumen of a primitive hero. In James Joyce, the basic material is redrafted to provide the most in the way of allegory, symbolism, and unlimited comedy. Leopold Bloom who, as a Hebrew Celt, symbolizes humanity and redemption, takes a trip to Barney Kiernan's pub. Everything he sees on the way is rather askew, reminding the reader of the one-eyed Cyclops; any remarks he makes are easily misunderstood. It is thought that he gives a tip on a horse, when he is talking about something quite different. The pub itself is the Cyclops's cave, symbolic of dark and one-eyed Irish nationalism, where all conversation misses its mark. Bloom is thought to have won a large bet (on the horse on which he has *not* given a tip). The customers wonder why he is not more hospitable. Among the numerous parallels to Homer's story William York Tindall mentions Mr. Bloom's cigar, that corresponds to the stake with which Odysseus blinded the one-eyed giant. It typifies Joyce's way of suggesting the reciprocal relationship between the ancient world and Dublin. "You don't grasp my point," says Homeric Mr. Bloom.[5]

The epic outline is used for more multitudinous purposes than would ever have occurred to the decorous Homer. *Ulysses* seems to combine everything, even suggestions and tones that would seem, on the surface, to be quite contradictory; intricate realism, parody (long series of questions and answers in the manner of a catechism or a review book for examinations), constant conflicts between real facts and equally real meaning, social satire, tenderness, intense seriousness, men thinking sublimely and trivially at the same time, spiritual exaltation and physical embarrassment, poetry, religious perception, all swept in a cataract of fierce and universal comedy. Not only is Joyce's canvas much more intricately organized than that of Homer, but certain important new techniques are used with mastery. He expertly explores both the conscious and the unconscious, the latter an emerging dimension in literature. He brings the interior monologue to a high degree of effectiveness. The interior monologue has been defined as the discourse without auditor, unspoken, by which a person expresses his inmost thought, the thought nearest to the unconscious and anterior to any logical organization, by means of sentences with a minimum of syntax. Written so as to give the impression that it is poured out, this slice of the interior life is presented without explanation or commentary. Molly Bloom's interior monologue about her past life and loves at the end of *Ulysses* is particularly famous and has had a wide influence on the technique of literature.

The Epic Narrative

A certain starkness and austerity characterize the early epic because man is pitted against natural forces that, collectively under the name of fate, win in the end, though man has proved that he can live and fight like a man. Christianity, with its concepts of Providence and the immortality of the soul, softens this particular kind of hardness with its special pathos, what Virgil had in mind with his oft quoted phrase "the tears of things" (*"lacrimae rerum"*). The medieval romance, the chivalric tale, found its main source of interest not in the dire conflict of man against nature but in the wondrous, with elements of sorrow, joy, and humor, always lightened and made hopeful by an implicit heavenly vision. Dante, in *The Divine Comedy,* bears hard upon the evil doer, but his vision of Heaven is inconceivable in the ancient pagan context. The basic drive toward a Christian optimism is even more pronounced in Milton's *Paradise Lost.* In that poem there is an increasing awareness of the complex relationship of good and evil, and a subtle attempt is made imaginatively to understand the devil of Christian theology.

But since the Enlightenment of the seventeenth and eighteenth centuries, and the industrial revolution coming down to our times, no major successes have been achieved in trying to recapture the spirit of the ancient epic. The heroic age, especially in its Hellenic aspect, had an idealizing quality. While in one sense it was realistic, in another sense it was highly selective about its details. Its plastic art, especially its sculpture, finds an eternal and immutable principle, something that is universal and generic, in forms that are still close to everyday life. Here is the strength of an athlete, the grace of a woman, suggested vividly by a casual twist or gesture of the body. But the extra detail that a lesser artist might introduce is carefully omitted. Economy was a great Greek ideal, not in the sense of penuriousness but of using the means at one's disposal with maximum impact, maximum emotional effect. Aristotle in *The Poetics* considered tragedy the highest form of art, higher than the epic, because it was the most *economic* in the means.[6] Epic is discursive, permitting many episodes and subordinate actions, but tragedy is closely unified, tense, and taut. The classical idea of art realized that too many *means* can get in one another's way, compromising the great impact that art should have.

The greatest contrast that can be made to the ancient epic art is the modern realism of the novel. While the classical epic stressed the conflict of the individual against nature, against fate, it always had a marked tendency to see something of what is universal about man in its individual hero. This is even more marked in the Virgilian epic, where Aeneas represents in his person the founding of Rome and the future of Roman history. Aeneas has to make a number of difficult personal decisions because of the symbolic character of his vocation; he must, for example, abandon the lovelorn Dido, Queen of Carthage, who befriended him in his hour of need. Milton, in his own great derivative from the Virgilian tradition, *Paradise Lost,* seeks an even larger canvas than Virgil. Adam represents in his person the origin and future history of the whole human race.

The Realistic Novel

The modern realistic novel is, in contrast to the traditional epics, almost the exact opposite in scope. It deals not with man in an idealized sense but in terms of what is thought to be a representative average.

Flaubert, in initiating the modern realistic novel in *Madame Bovary,* narrows the symbolism of the hero to the sociologically average and typical. The epic tradition was aristocratic; the epic was court poetry written by a court poet. The hero loomed larger than human on the hills, to paraphrase Tennyson. You were meant to admire him rather than to study and dissect him. Now the atypical is done away with; it is not the leader who is interesting but the most average member of the herd. It is what the French have called the *homme moyen,* the least common denominator, or to use Flaubert's own phrase "the bourgeois that is now all mankind."[7]

But Flaubert, like the great artists of the classical past, had a strong sense of surface form. He believed in what Aristotle meant by action. The celebrated nineteenth-century critic, Matthew Arnold, rated action as one of the chief requisites of great art. The artist should be telling us primarily about a given theme, a *story,* not primarily about himself and his interior psychic disturbances. Literature, according to Arnold, should "imitate actions" rather than be an "allegory" of one's state of mind.[8]

One characteristic of an action was that it had a beginning, a middle, and an end. But writers began to ask, "Is this really characteristic of life? Does real life have a beginning, a middle, and an end?" It is argued that life has no plot; to use an old American phrase, life is one damn thing after another. Things take place, begin and end, without connection. The realistic novel still believed in purpose, though purpose was infrequently fulfilled in the life of its characters. It could be said that the essential theme of all realistic novels is the "attempt to make life conform to one's youthful dreams, and after the vain attempt to make it conform, the renunciation of all dreams."[9]

The realistic novel could be, and sometimes was, depressing (depressing rather than tragic, for the tragic paradoxically has a certain exhilarating quality). The characters "could be duplicated in any town, village, or suburb, and none of them say or do anything that has not been said or done a million times before in the world."[10]

Such characters, unexciting in real life though not necessarily so as aesthetic creations, frequently met with frustration whenever they tried to break out of their encircling monotony. But the realistic novelist still subscribed to a sense of structure and a sense of purpose. Moreover, a novelist with a determined social consciousness could also use the methodology of the realistic novel to present a strongly implied social criticism, as, for example, Sinclair Lewis did in his portrait of Babbitt in his famous novel. The implication in such books was that things were so wrong that some remedy had to be searched for. Matters could not be left that bad, that pointless.

During the first half of our century, there have been numerous schools of thought about the function of the novel, schools of thought that would never have occurred to an Aristotelian with his sense of decorum, that is, his sense of what is suitable, what is fitting to a work of art.

The Naturalistic Novel

The novel has been considered by many to be a "study" of society, a testament of historic and documentary value. Viewed as such, the novel was to exhibit *scientifically* man's environment, his spatial and time relationships and his racial and psychological background. Man was to be objectively studied, as if he were simply a phenomenon of nature, without the emotional commitment of the writer or the reader.

The type of novel that has earned the label "naturalistic," unlike the "realistic" novel which may have a variety of values, seems to assume, on the surface, that man has no special place or special value in the world. He behaves according to preordained patterns that are all part of a *monistic* (Greek *mono* meaning "one") universe in which all things are leveled down. But frequently there is a kind of reversed sentimentality in the naturalistic novel. The traditional humanistic values that presume a special position and dignity about man may be so completely suppressed that such values, unconsciously, become conspicuous by their absence. The naturalistic novelist has frequently had a sentimental yen to take the worst aspects of the life of a man as typical of nature, so that violence, brutality, depravity, and disgust have sometimes been poured on so emphatically that the sincerity of the author has come into question. Under these conditions, a naturalistic novelist follows a similar pattern to that of the usual sentimental writer. Just as skepticism is aroused when the sentimental writer becomes too optimistic in a pat way about matters which experience shows are not readily solved just by "looking on the bright side," so does the naturalistic writing rouse skepticism when it paints a morbidity not characteristic of most people's experience.

A Change in Emphasis

As we have seen, the important shift in emphasis that took place through the development of realism and naturalism led to a focus upon the average man rather than the extraordinary one. Shakespeare's heroes, for example, are aristocrats, men of position and power, frequently with exotic backgrounds. An entirely different social world comes to the center of the picture in the works of Honoré de Balzac, Émile Zola, George Moore, Arnold Bennett, Sinclair Lewis, and Theodore Dreiser. The concept of what the literary art can deal with is enormously extended. The artist could now be expected to be concerned with the whole of human experience. He need not be restricted to the expression of what was traditionally considered to be the beautiful, the elegant, or the exceptional. In the special application of realistic method which goes under the label of naturalism, man was to be studied scientifically, as a naturalist might investigate fauna and flora. Literature should tell us about all that has been experienced in the world, *all* that has been thought and felt—not necessarily what was best or most striking.

Great artists, as a matter of fact, seldom stay within the boundaries of narrow aesthetic theory. Such great Russians as Tolstoi and Dostoievski are considered among the realists, and yet they present characters possessed of thought and passion well beyond the normal. New theories about literature do not seriously disturb the conditions that enter into all great art. But in realism and naturalism, we have new extensions of subject matter, new techniques. Although some novels, particularly of the naturalist school, concentrated on what seemed to many people the sordid and seamy side of life, there was a kind of concealed optimism about them, founded on the belief that the more knowledge we had of all kinds of experience, the better equipped we would be to deal with the problems of society. Many of these works were not interested in drawing a moral, even in a hidden way. The naturalistic novelist could often say, in effect: "Reader, I have drawn as accurately and as honestly as I can a certain slice of life that I have seen. There it is, reader. *You* can carry on from there."

As we move from the epic of the modern narrative, we witness a significant change in the terms of the reader's emotional response. Classical literature, the literature of the medieval and renaissance worlds, tends to think of the hero as a moral exemplar, someone whom we should at least admire in part and desire to emulate. The tendency in modern writing is to present characters whom we study and try to understand, whom we do not necessarily try to imitate in any way. We tend to look less for a pattern of excellence and more for the kind of psychological analysis that will enable us to understand the world around us. No one can deny the contribution of the great realistic novels to our understanding of the modern world. The naturalistic novel, which has been more in dispute because of its reluctance to deal with moral issues, has, at its best, given us works of art that go far beyond the status of poignant documentaries.

Later Developments of the Novel

The classical writer was not concerned with the statistical average but rather with gods and heroes. But, of course, certain areas were closed to him. He did not have the interior monologue, the stream of consciousness, the important findings of a Carl Jung or a Sigmund Freud, which have led to certain interesting, and probably important, developments in the modern novel. New themes and new points of view have emerged. We have a Franz Kafka challenging the image of a self-sufficient man in a self-sufficient universe by emphasizing the wonder, unpredictability, and apparent irrationality of the universe. We have writers who have become bored with incident and plot and want to concentrate on what they consider the *essentiality* of experience. For Marcel Proust, as one critic says, "the novel is an unrolling of life, revealing no crisis, no plot, only the poignant effects of Time on people who, day by day, are inevitably touched by Time, changed by Time, not only in themselves, but in their relation to each other. There is a rendering of an interior life that is not under the control of the intelligence, of an emotional life driven by a mechanism deep in the subconscious and not amenable to laws imposed by logic or rational ethics."[11]

In regard to some developments, it is sometimes easier for a person initiating a serious concern with literature to penetrate the classics than to understand some of the more "advanced" forms of modern writing. It is much easier, for example, for most people to understand Dante's thirteenth-century *Divine Comedy* than Joyce's twentieth-century *Finnegans Wake.*

In regard to the comparative importance of literary works, even a beginner should make some allowance for what may be called vested academic interests. A masterpiece, if it is simple and direct, does not lend itself to easy exploitation in the lecture hall. If you were to read a piece like Robert Herrick's "To Daffodils" aloud to a class, there would be little to say about it. The thing speaks for itself:

Fair daffodils, we weep to see
You haste away so soon;
As yet the early-rising sun
Has not attained his noon.
Stay, stay,
Until the hasting day
Has run
But to the evensong;
And, having prayed together, we
Will go with you along.

But a passage from James Joyce might open unlimited areas of speculation, interpretation, pro-and-counter symbolism. Quite frankly, Joyce can be academically "milked" in a way that Herrick cannot. We do not intend to disparage Joyce but only to point out that involuted forms of the literary art run the danger of being overrated for the simple reason that they afford so much material for a teacher to work with—while just as great, or even greater, works may undergo displacement, because they have an instantaneous directness. The teacher has little cause to add to it. Lewis Carroll's *Alice in Wonderland* might be included in literary art of a high order, but there is no way of making an academic career out of it in the same degree as Joyce's *Ulysses.* Teachers are sincere, but they may tend to an unconscious bias, in the sense that they favor those artists who provide the maximum material for points of departure and for academic publications.

It is a tribute to the novel form that it has such adaptability and flexibility. Modern literary art has shown the possibility for new extensions and conceptions of form. But there are, of course, limits. Too much in the way of idiosyncrasy and a false originality makes for a literature of the coterie and the cultist, who become increasingly sensitive within a narrowing area. Too much specialized private material in private idiosyncratic expression has also led to a certain amount of moral condemnation of current works.

Traditional literature, even when dealing with private and intimate themes, has always followed the conventions of *public* statement. Discussion of good taste often seems old-fashioned. But if the idea of good taste was ever valid, it remains so today. The problems of vulgarity and obscenity are not necessarily the same as those of morality. What is "obscene" is literally, by the etymology of the word, what is opposed to the public "scene" or "view." Many things that are not immoral, and that are even physically necessary, are not fit subjects of public perusal. Many things that are "vulgar" betray stupidity and insensitivity rather than immorality. In a kind of beatnik rejection of tradition, much that is vulgar and obscene is being negatively projected as art. Much that by its oddity and egocentricity is obviously private is being made public. Many people fail to be shocked by it as they should, and probably as the artist intended, because, like certain forms of contemporary abstract painting, the subject matter largely fails to *communicate* to a considerable number. The sensible point of view is that the acknowledged great works of the literary art, including modern ones, have so much to offer, and have increasingly more to offer as we prod in depth, that doubtful material may wisely be put to one side as curiosities.

After all, the great majority of readers, including the highly sophisticated, read narrative first of all for identification and excitement. Even the most sensitive readers of Joyce, Proust, or Kafka sometimes pick up a detective story to enjoy these characteristics alone. *Identification* implies imaginatively projecting oneself as the principal character in the story so that the imagined dangers that surround the hero also surround the reader. The reader, of course, has the enormous advantage that he can suspend these dangers at any point he chooses—he can suspend the gun duel, the hand on the door knob, the opening of the secret panel, while he goes to his own kitchen and makes a cup of coffee. He has the pleasure of identification and excitement together with the sense of comfort from knowing that it is all make-believe, that, unlike the hero in the novel, the reader can snap out of it at any time.

In the major works of literature, this elementary need for identification and excitement cannot be disregarded completely, though it may be subordinated to major consideration of characterization, of an emphasis on values and ideas (these also can be exciting), or of social criticism. The major passages of great narrative literature show things *happening* (including the developing of psychological states and of intellectual preoccupations) even when the novelist is greatly concerned with a background of ideas and values.

MODERN THEORIES OF FICTION

In recent years thought about the techniques of fiction has undergone many refinements. New emphasis is now placed on the most effective *point of view* from which to narrate a story, and on the wisdom of the narrator's *showing* rather than telling. In order for a narrative to make any sense it must have some focus, some point of view. A narrative must be told by somebody. It cannot come into being by itself. A narrator of some kind has to be assumed. But there are different theories of *how* such a narrator should be assumed. It has generally been regarded, since the impact of Henry James, that it is poor technique for a narrator to intrude directly into the novel, though the old masters such as Dante, Chaucer, and

Boccaccio did so very effectively. Often the secret of Chaucer's charm and humor is the pointed reminder of his presence through commentary and even through the apostrophe of direct address (apostrophe is generally in the form of an address to the reader, or to some deity or force not supposed to be physically present). The objection voiced by Henry James and others is that if the point of view is presented *directly* by the narrator, the discourse is deficient in dramatic intensity. When the author does not tell the story directly (the omniscient viewpoint), he may use a first- or third-person speaker (a character in the story) who plays the part of a disguised narrator while acting out his own part in the story. A more refined type of narrator is a third-person center of consciousness such as Gabriel in Joyce's "The Dead" (see p. 149). The reader is to see through his eyes what in the older-fashioned technique would be communicated by the author through his omiscient viewpoint. A narrator can also be created who is made deliberately unreliable (ironic) so that what he says has to be judged against the total context of the work.

Narrative as Showing Rather Than as Telling

Much modern criticism holds that any intrusion of the author by way of commentary, or even by any suggestion or reminder that there *is* an author behind the work, may be classified as *rhetorical.* The poem should simply be, and the novelist should *show* rather than *tell.* Actually there is a great deal of *disguised* rhetoric even in the most modernistic works. Nevertheless, the novelists and critics, who have deplored storytelling, have won for fiction the kind of standing as a major art form which, before Flaubert, was generally denied it. Just as assertive elements are viewed with suspicion in modern poetry, just as the poem's integrity as a structure of words should become what has been called a "contemplative stasis, a self-reflexive pattern," so the modern art-novel, such as Joyce's *Ulysses,* has sought to organize itself poetically (self-reflexively).[12]

The writer must show but not tell. For this reason, the obviously omniscient storyteller, the leisurely commentator often talking in his own right, has rapidly disappeared, though his form of authority was characteristic of most narrative until recent times. One critic observes that authors like Thackeray, or Balzac, or H. G. Wells are always telling the reader what happened instead of showing them the scene, telling them what to think of the characters rather than letting the reader judge for himself or letting the characters do the telling about one another. "I like to distinguish between novelists that *tell* and those (like Henry James) that show."[13] Henry James, of course, was an eminent practitioner of this principle, experimenting with various devices to show his material rather than to use a commentary. His subtlety as a craftsman is universally recognized. No one can skip passages in James as one could in Charles Dickens or Sir Walter Scott and still possess, so to speak, the artistic message (the new art does not like the word "message"). James is an intensely subtle writer who has to be read word for word almost in the manner of an imagistic poem. When one has arrived at the developed taste of the connoisseur, one may treasure Henry James above many others. But this does not necessarily give us a reason to part with some of the marvelous omniscient descriptions of place or character that we can find in Scott or Dickens. The fact is that a great work of narrative art develops such enormous energy that it can carry along in its onrushing stream a good deal that is irrelevant, even what might be considered debris. One would have to be very theoretical to object to a piece like that of the Grand Inquisitor, which is thrust into *The Brothers Karamazov,* or to Henry Fielding's commentary in *Tom Jones.* In all fairness, we are compelled to realize that there are different types of art. Purity and austerity mean certain gains, but diffused energy can also give us certain perspectives that subtlety must, by its interior laws, rule out. While a great deal can be said for the value of compressed and suggestive statement in narrative, where little things point to much greater wholes, we might also remember Gotthold Lessing's cautionary remark that many things would prove incontestable in theory, had not genius succeeded in proving the contrary in fact.[14]

The more extreme antirhetorical theoreticians would hurl the reader, in the words of Jean-Paul Sartre, "into the midst of a universe where there are no witnesses."[15] If this is so, it has been argued, the author must never summarize, never curtail a conversation, never telescope the events of three days in a paragraph. The artist must avoid terms like "moral" and "good." He must keep his judgment, indicative of his presence, out of his work.

It can be argued that rhetoric is important if for no other reason than to respect the rights and presence of an audience. If an appeal to an audience is a sign of artistic imperfection, where can perfect literature be found? "Any story will be unintelligible unless it includes, however subtly, the amount of telling necessary not only to make us aware of the value system which gives it its meaning, but, more important, to make us accept the value system at least temporarily."[16] Wayne Booth in *The Rhetoric of Fiction* gives a dramatic example. "Imagine a beautifully written tragedy with a convinced Nazi SS man as hero, his tragic error consisting of a contemporary, and fatal, toying with bourgeois democratic ideals. Is there any one of us, regardless of our commitment to objectivity, who could seriously claim that agreement or disagreement with the author's ideas in such a work should have nothing to do with our accepting or rejecting his art?"[17]

Obviously rhetoric has to have a restricted place in creative art, but this does not mean that it must be ruled out as superfluous or injurious. The rhetorical intrusion of the author can even be utterly essential to the work. Anne Davidson Ferry in *Milton's Epic Voice* points out in regard to *Paradise Lost* that the rhetorical condition of the epic is especially important to Milton's purposes: "His story, because it is 'invisible' to us, demanded not only a narrator but one endowed with unique powers of vision to make the impenetrable world of prehistory known to us. It is his voice, as we shall see, which interprets the story to us, and which is the principal device in the poem for expressing its *total* meaning."[18]

THE ROLE OF CONVENTION

The contemporary impatience with rhetoric causes one to inquire about the role of convention in art. Do some conventions pass away and die, never to be revived? Can there be breakthroughs in art?

Convention implies a previously agreed upon set of signs and signals accepted in common by the artist and his audience. When Milton wrote "Lycidas," he could presume upon the audience's acquaintance with a long tradition of the pastoral. He would not have to explain that the shepherds in the poem are really Edward King and John Milton himself. He would not have to remind his readers that a shepherd is also a pastor, a Christian ecclesiastical symbol. Milton's originality did not consist in creating new modes of communication but in using established conventions with new verve and power.

Milton studied classical forms in school; they were still the staple material of education. But who today will write a classical pastoral? W. H. Auden called his poem "The Age of Anxiety" an "eclogue for our times." Even though different in matter and manner from traditional pastorals, this piece is rather an exception. There is no sign anywhere of a desperate ambition to revive the classical epic. Conventions, still understood and admired, may not suit the interests and conditions of a different age. No one today would write a long didactic poem in the manner of Alexander Pope, Samuel Johnson, or Oliver Goldsmith.

Certain conventions lose their influence because of essential technical as well as social changes that take place. The development of photography made painstaking realistic detail far less valuable in painting and obviously helped bring about the emphasis on abstract painting. The modern breakthrough in psychology has created such new literary conventions as the interior monologue and the stream of consciousness. Some conventions pass; new ones are born. We have already analyzed the change from the emphasis on the public hero to that on private analysis, brought about, in large part, by the impact of the industrial revolution with the consequent loss of direct contact with nature. Changes in artistic conventions correspond in a rough way with historical changes. The open veranda on the American house prevailed when cities were smaller and had more open space; today we have ranch houses on small lots in which people gravitate to the television room rather than to the open porch. A technical invention like television can even affect architecture.

The Irish short-story writer, Sean O'Faolain, once observed that "the convention of realism depends for its success on our forgetting that realism is a convention. So does every other convention." He adds:

> The chief purpose of these conventions is, of course, the simple purpose of communication. Every art has its own hieroglyphics. These are its language, its technique, its conventions. In the short story the speaker of this language is the writer; he has to learn its conventions, know what can be done with them, understand their limitations, adapt them to his own purpose, and often add to them. The listener to the language is the reader, and he, also, if he wants to get the most out of the art before him, has to familiarize himself with its conventions. The

writer, however, must always presume that his reader is practiced in these essential conventions, otherwise there can be no artistic communication at all.[19]

It is obviously possible for the writer to break new ground. But it is important to remember that when we speak about a change in conventions we touch only a small number of the vast group of conventions that constitute art. The external aspects of a Homeric or a Miltonic epic would not be suitable for later literature, but a multitude of deeper conventions from the epic enter into such works as *Moby Dick* or *Ulysses.* Though an artist has to develop his own idiom, his own special way of saying things so that he does not merely echo the work of others, most of his resources have already been established—language itself, for example, which constitutes the most established body of conventions of all.

The tendency to underestimate convention has resulted from a lack of awareness of its basic universality. The theory of art for art's sake, without due regard for an audience, has also led to such underestimation.[20] Originality has been in this way opposed to convention. Convention does not necessarily imply dullness as in the phrase "a conventional work." Many of the greatest works of literature are conventional—*Anna Karenina,* for example. Innovations themselves shortly become conventions. The artistic question is whether effective use is made of the conventions that the artist chooses to employ.

THE GREAT SCENE IN NARRATIVE

Ultimately, after all the dust has sifted down from all the books in the library, after we have taken all the courses and given all the answers, after we have begun to forget what is irrelevant to us (though not necessarily to the examiner), what remains constantly with us from the pursuit of literature are the great scenes that move us deeply emotionally, that mysteriously exalt us, even if they cause pain.

Let us examine such a scene, see how relevant details are accumulated to give us a completeness of point of view and create emotional response, so that we keep saying to ourselves, "This is life or this is terribly possible in life. This is something I'm glad to know. This will enable me to see, to foresee, to understand . . . this is terrific!

I may be frightened by all this, but after reading such things I can never look on life indifferently as neuter or boring."

Illustration: The Death of Anna Karenina

Anna Karenina has had an increasingly uneasy alliance with her lover, Count Vronsky, for whom she has made severe sacrifices, leaving her husband, who is an egocentric, mediocre functionary concerned only with his own image and career, incapable of serious love. Under Russian law at the time, only the wronged party can ask for or obtain a divorce. This the husband will not do. Anna has had also to sacrifice her only son, for whom she has had real affection. But after her stormy romance with the Count, after various "escape" residences abroad with him, she has to face up to the basic insecurity of her situation. She is unable to "regularize" her position in society and she has not a sufficiently "tough" character to forget the society in which she has been born and bred, and to overlook that society which in subtle ways indicates to her that she has been rejected. Without the social contract of marriage or the approval of society (or at least its toleration), Anna becomes increasingly concerned about the stability of her relationship with the Count. Her tension takes the form of increasing irritability and jealousy, which promotes a corresponding reaction in her lover, consequently deepening Anna's original malady. A geometrical progression of a degenerating emotional relationship comes into play, though love between Anna and Count Vronsky is far from dead.

This is a picture of a human situation quite recognizable in modern life when a sexual relationship is not sustained by an overriding religious conviction or a strong sense of duty or the marriage contract itself, when the lovers are primarily seeking emotional and psychological unity without other means of support. Tolstoi probes the situation deeply and relentlessly.

The succession of episodes leading up to Anna Karenina's suicide are among the most poignant in literature. We *identify* with Anna, we are deeply sympathetic to her problems and hopes; at the same time we realize the moral issues at stake. In one sense she is admirable, for in the face of everything she seeks a real relationship in life in place of the correct but substanceless marriage. On the other hand, she is a tragic figure marred by what Aristotle referred to as the *tragic flaw*. Like every human being, she has a right to seek happiness, but not through pure subjectivity, selfishness, and immorality. We deeply understand her situation, though we cannot approve. In fact she cannot approve herself (and this is part of her total problem).

Anna's suicide may not be rational, but it is entirely explicable, and, in leading up to it, Tolstoi explores many *levels of meaning*.

As Anna comes near to suicide, she is ironically growing in self-awareness, but her deepened insights somehow miss the goal of wisdom.

> . . . "Well, if I get a divorce and become Vronsky's wife, will Kitty cease looking at me as she looked at me today? No. And will Serioja stop asking or thinking of my two husbands? What new sentiment will grow up between me and Vronsky? Can I possibly hope if not for happiness, at least for peace? No and no!" she replied to herself without the least hesitation. "Impossible! We diverge along different ways; I am the cause of his unhappiness and he of mine, and it is impossible to change either of us. Every attempt has been made. . . . There is a screw loose somewhere. There goes a beggar woman with her child. She thinks she ought to be pitied. Have we not all been put into the world for no other purpose than to hate and torment one another? There go some schoolboys, laughing. Serioja? I thought I loved him and used to be sentimental over my tenderness for him, but I exchanged him for another love and never complained so long as that love pleased me." She shuddered in disgust at what she called love. The clearness with which she saw her own life and that of other people gave her a sense of pleasure.[21]

That is a curious level of meaning—but how apt and just! She actually finds pleasure in her *pain*—the pleasure of seeing life clearly! And then almost immediately an ambiguity arises: is she *really* seeing life clearly? Or is she just thinking so? And even further, can life *be* seen clearly? What does Tolstoi's total novel have to say about that?

She had sent a note to Vronsky to meet her at a railroad station, but he had not received it. She was going to buy a train ticket and meet him once more before leaving him. "My love is growing more passionate and selfish and his is cooling off more and more," she had thought. She thought of how she still might have been happy, "of how terribly she loved and hated him, and how violently her heart was beating."

Tolstoi pours on the details of people and casual incidents at the railroad station. We share her excitement about whether Vronsky is going to show up. Finally a message comes that her note had not reached him in time, but that he would be "back at ten."

The cumulative details of Anna's emotional reactions to the things she sees and hears about her prepare us for, and help us to anticipate, what is to happen. She has learned everything but hope.

> She looked at the bottom of the carriages, at the linch-pins, the chains, and the iron wheels of the front carriage, and measuring with her eye, tried to determine the point midway between the front and hind wheels and the exact moment when it would be in front of her.

This precision, ironically enough, is the result of the *newfound* clarity of her thinking. The completely nihilistic act of suicide is thought of with all the *order* of an engineering problem!

And as in life itself, there is all the accidental "stumble-bumming" that trips the most carefully planned calculations.

> She wanted to drop down in the middle of the first carriage that came up, but the red bag, which she began to pull off from her arm, retarded her; it was too late, the middle had passed. She had to wait for the next one. A sensation, similar to the one she had always experienced when bathing, before she took her first plunge, came over her; she made the sign of the cross. The gesture called forth in her a whole series of girlish and childish memories, and suddenly the darkness that had enveloped everything lifted, and for a moment life presented itself to her with all its past joys. But she did not take her eyes off the wheels of the approaching carriage. And at the very moment when the middle was opposite her, she threw aside the red bag and, drawing in her shoulders, dropped down under the carriage on her hands, and with a light motion, as though preparing to rise at once, got on her knees. At that moment she became horrified at what she was doing. "Where am I? What am I doing? What for?" She wanted to get up, to throw herself back, but an enormous, relentless mass knocked her on the head and dragged her by the shoulders. "Lord, forgive me everything!", she murmured, feeling the futility of the struggle. A peasant, working on the line, was muttering some incomprehensible words. And the candle by which she had been reading the book filled with pain and sorrow, deceit and evil, flared up with a brighter light, illuminating for her everything that had been enshrouded in darkness, then flickered, grew dim, and went out forever.

Here is a passage of very great literature which, while following the overall analytic purpose of prose, is symbolic in the manner of great poetry. And it is amazing how many levels of irony are compressed into such a short passage by a master hand.

For the seconds preceding suicide, "she made the sign of the cross." In this dark moment, ironically, she imagines the joys of her young days. The image of paradoxical prayer continues in her rising and getting on her knees. The culmination of the religious movement lies in "Lord, forgive me everything!" The supernatural does not stop the mechanical forces of nature, yet the candle by which she had been reading "flared up with a brighter light." In the face of death has she revolutionized her values? Has she found the missing dimension in her clarity of thought? Or is the whole thing left ambiguous—"flickered, grew dim, and went out forever"?

At the back of our minds as we read these pages and the subsequent indirect portrayals of Vronsky's reactions to the news of Anna's death (this indirectness is here a sign of great art) is the underlying question of why love could not have been more adequate, more communicable, of why there wasn't some extra margin of patience, of fortitude—the sort of questions we ask about all of life's terrible and useless blunders. The Countess mother tells us that Vronsky rushed away to the station without a word. "I don't know what happened there, but they brought him home half dead." But the mother's evaluation—"It was a terrible time. Say what you please, but she was a bad woman. What is the use of these desperate passions?"—though it appears morally correct on the surface, is far from being adequate and inclusive. Anna Karenina was not a bad woman but one approaching maturity through the midst of confusions, gaining intense self-knowledge without learning hope (except perhaps in death?). Her passion did not remain "desperate" in the Countess's sense of the word. Her position might have been better had it done so. Her act of despair has much to do with her newly acquired ability for analysis. And, ultimately, we have the ambiguous question of whether Anna Karenina would have been a better woman had she not reached out toward the love that destroyed her. What we know emotionally, of course, is that we have a deep sense of pity and compassion for this overtly immoral woman. And we realize that the position of that wholly admirable and good man in the novel, Levin, does not compass everything, and that experience can be a hurricane, however rational and constructive in our best moments we may wish to be: "To live as his father and grandfathers had lived, to carry out their work so as to hand it on to his children, seemed to him a plain duty."

Neither Anna Karenina nor Count Vronsky is what we would normally call a "bad" person. What happened to them might conceivably happen to anybody. And the sheer suffering of Anna goes beyond any mere moral statement.

PITY AND FEAR

In a work like Tolstoi's *Anna Karenina* we experience the impact of *tragic* emotion—we experience *pity* and *compassion* for Anna herself and, having identified ourselves with her, we have *feared* for her. When her fate has been poignantly presented to us, we fear for the possibilities in human nature and in life itself. The emotions of pity and fear are those appropriate to a tragic sequence.

But there is a kind of work, important enough, though not as deep or searching as tragedy itself, which is distinguished by pathos. Pathos might be described as a feeling of sympathetic sadness, but it has special characteristics that distinguish it from tragic emotion. The essential difference between the pathetic and the tragic lies in the fact that the tragic situation has an *end*. And up to that very end the hero is an active agent. Anna chooses her fate and the incidents that lead up to it. And up to the last moment she could have chosen some alternative. In pathos, the hero is more sinned against than sinning; he is caught in the web of circumstances through which he cannot cut his way either triumphantly or unsuccessfully. We cannot really *fear* (as in tragedy) for what he will do, because basically he cannot do anything. The development of *conflict* so necessary to the tragic emotion cannot take place.

One of the most touching scenes in literature in this sense is the scene in which Sir Bedivere, the knight whom King Arthur had commanded to throw his sword Excalibur into the water, reluctantly takes leave of Arthur after having accomplished his mission.

> Then Sir Bedivere took the king upon his back, and so went with him to that water side. And when they were at the water side, even fast by the bank hoved a little barge with many fair ladies in it, and among them all was a queen, and all they had black hoods, and all they wept

> and shrieked when they saw King Arthur. Now put me into the barge, said the king. And so he did softly; and there received him three queens with great mourning; and so they set them down, and in one of their laps King Arthur laid his head. And then that queen said: Ah, dear brother, why have you tarried so long from me? alas, this wound on your head hath caught over-much cold. And so then they rowed from the land, and Sir Bedivere beheld all those ladies go from him. Then Sir Bedivere cried: Ah my Lord Arthur, what shall become of me, now ye go from me and leave me here alone among mine enemies? Comfort thyself, said the king, and do as well as thou mayest, for in me is no trust for to trust in; for I will into the vale of Avilion to heal me of my grievous wound: and if thou hear never more of me, pray for my soul. But ever the queens and ladies wept and shrieked, that it was pity to hear. And as soon as Sir Bedivere had lost sight of the barge, he wept and wailed, and so took the forest; and so he went all that night, and in the morning he was ware betwixt two holts hoar, of a chapel and an hermitage.[22]

This is extremely touching and we begin to share in the many tears of the various participants. "Why have you tarried so long?" is full of pathos—what can we do with the past except suffer its consequence? As for Sir Bedivere, there is nothing he can do about the situation. "Do as well as thou mayest" is a polite nothing. There is pathos in the showdown about a king's apparent power: ". . . for in me is no trust for to trust in." Sir Bedivere has to look for action in a sphere beyond his control—in the religious and supernatural—"pray for my soul"; "in the morning he was ware . . . of a chapel and an hermitage." He is left with his suffering, and he cannot do anything about it—and we pity him. But we cannot fear for what he will do, because he can do nothing but accept the situation.

HUMOR

We have been discussing the kind of prose narrative that causes the emotional response of shock and tears. But in the methods of humor and satire, we get quite different results. Here the reader is not emotionally involved as in the tragic and pathetic. He may laugh sympathetically or derisively, but his reaction is primarily that of the intelligence, weighing and measuring the absurd deviations from common sense so often frequent in real life.

Humor, as a literary method, has a specialized meaning and technique. The humorist deliberately plays levels of meaning against one another. He assumes a fundamental scale of values which he shares with his readers—some approximation to a universal moral code, some set of well-defined and accepted conventions. He then presents his narrative (or drama) in terms of a *surface* distortion of these values. The humorist does not intend to deceive anybody about his values; he assumes people have sense enough to perceive that his deliberate distortion is in a spirit of contrast and fun. In fact, by playing off his surface meaning against his real interior meaning, he employs a special kind of emphasis (in terms of contrast) to *drive home* his essential values.

If one of Sheridan's characters congratulates a member of *The School for Scandal* on the "delicacy of tint, and mellowness of sneer, which distinguish your ladyship's scandal,"[23] we are highly amused by the contrast of looking upon scandal as a work of consummate grace, when we really know it as dangerous and disgusting. If Chaucer tells us that the Pardoner, who delivers sermons against avarice and is the most avaricious of people himself, who lies, cheats, deceives, is "in church a noble ecclesiastic," we find the distortion deliciously cutting because, in fact, what Chaucer basically means in overt language is, "What a rogue and a scoundrel!" But, if he were to tell us this directly, it would not be nearly so interesting. He would not give us a certain pleasure of the intellect in seeing several things at once, of reading the concealed shorthand of Chaucer's real thought.

Humor is not necessarily allied to wit, once explained by Samuel Johnson as a "sudden and violent collision of ideas." This can be brought about by compressed epigrammatic statement, such as one finds in the writings of Alexander Pope, Oscar Wilde, or G. K. Chesterton. The essence of a pun, for example, is an accident of language where the same verbal sound stands for two different words, therefore two different ideas. Such ideas, though they may have been brought together by accident, may have unexpected but justifiable relationships and can be very funny. In wit there is no necessary contrast between surface statement and real interior meaning, as in humor. In fact, very often the distinguishing feature of wit is the conflict and contrast of two surface statements. If a participant in a dialogue suddenly advises an opponent to take Holy Orders, the mind reacts to his advice with the habitual routine of approval (normally a good thing)—at least momentarily. But when seventeenth-century critic John Dennis caps the advice with the statement "a pulpit sure is the only place where impertinence has privilege to be tedious, without interruption,"[24] the audience does a quick double-take in this lightning-like juxaposition of ideas. While wit can certainly enliven writing, it is not always suitable to the purpose of a humorous writer, because frequently he must build slowly for a lasting effect. Wit is generally swift, sharp, and brief.

Illustration: Humor in Gogol's *Dead Souls*

Nikolai Gogol's *Dead Souls* makes a good example of sustained humor. It is the story of what might be called a confidence man, outwitting a group of misers. While, as a reader, one does not give moral assent to chiselers, in this particular case the misers are so bad that one wishes Chichikov, the somewhat doubtful hero, all good luck. Gogol gives us a picture of a stagnant provincial life in Russia's nineteenth century, where practically no one does anything constructive or creative, but where misers and "close" traders abound, easy victims in certain directions because of their avarice. Chichikov is a crook, but an extremely controlled one, with an excellent sense of planning and timing.

Before embarking on his country tour to buy "dead souls," he has already been in trouble. He has worked his way up in the customs service by the most zealous and exaggerated ways of tracking down contraband. But when he reaches the top, he enters into a smuggling conspiracy on a wholesale level. Through a falling out with his partner, the conspiracy is discovered, and Chichikov disgraced. But Chichikov has some attractive qualities—he is resilient and optimistic, and soon he is pursuing another scheme.

In the province Chichikov ingratiates himself, or at least tries to, with various landowners and casually suggests the purchase of their "dead souls." Chichikov never lets on *why* he wants these dead souls, and the prospective sellers haven't the slightest idea of what he is up to. The author himself keeps the secret from the readers until the end of the book. But we know that somehow or other it must really be practical and have some possibilities of money in it. Actually, a dead soul is a male serf who has died since the last census but for whom the landowners are still compelled to pay a tax until a new census has been taken. By gaining title to these dead souls, Chichikov can get a large loan by mortgaging the paper transfers.

Part of the humor in the book arises from the fact that while Chichikov is a swindler, he has quite a *high* moral image of himself. He becomes quite indignant (at least inwardly, for outwardly he is a smooth operator) at other people's avarice, mendacity, and assorted insanities. And what a cast he has to work with!

Chichikov's public image is indicated by the type of statement he makes to one of his targets, "Do not treasure money; treasure the company of good men." In one case he deals with the ultimate among old crones and miserly women, one of the "petty landed proprietresses who are forever complaining tearfully about poor crops and their losses, as they keep their heads somewhat to one side, yet, who at the same time accumulate, bit by bit, their tidy little hoards of money, in little money-bags of bright ticking, tucked away in various bureaus."[25] This woman has no idea of what conceivable use dead souls could be, but after the closest bargaining, stalling, and deliberate diversions, not even equaled by the various negotiations of the USSR with the USA, and after Chichikov has offered her the bait of possessing special influence with the authorities that might do her some good, she eventually consents. But this horrible woman has her afterthoughts, and is soon found going into town making the incomprehensible inquiry, "What are dead souls fetching today?" Although Chichikov is in no position to be morally righteous, we fully share his indignation about this misshapen specimen of humanity.

In another case Chichikov deals with what must be the all-time male miser. Chichikov at least has a certain amount of vision, though generally exhibited in absurd context. Although unmarried, he has a terrible fear of "leaving no descendants, and bequeathing neither property nor an honored name to my future children!" He has a definite instinct for life, but, in contrast, listen to this piled-up description of the ultimate in absurdity and negation, in the person of the elderly Plushkin:

> But this was no beggar standing before him; standing before him was a landed proprietor. This landed proprietor owned a thousand serf-souls and more, and there would be no use in trying to find another who had so much wheat, in grain, in flour, or simply in stacks, or one whose store-rooms, warehouses, and drying sheds were cluttered with

such a world of linens, cloths, sheepskins (both dressed and raw), dried fish of all sorts, and all kinds of vegetables and salted meat. Had anyone peeped into his work-yard, where there was a reserve laid by of every sort of wood and wooden utensils, never used, it would seem to him that he must somehow have strayed into the famous Chip Fair in Moscow, whither the wide-awake matriarchs resort daily, with their cooks behind them, to put in supplies for their households, and where every sort of wood rises in mountains of white: nailed, turned, joined, to say nothing of wickerwork; there are barrels here, and chopping bowls, and tubs, and water-casks, and noggins, with spouts and without, and dippers, and bast baskets, and slop-pails, wherein to keep mops and suchlike, and hampers of thin, bent aspen wood, and cylindrical boxes of woven birch bark, and a great deal of all that goes to supply the needs of rich Russia and poor. What need, it seemed, had Plushkin of such a host of these wares? He would never have been able to use them up in his whole lifetime even if he owned two estates instead of only one, but even this accumulation seemed small to him. Not satisfied with this, he would also patrol the lanes and by-ways of his village every day, peering under small bridges, under planks, and in every nook and cranny, and everything that he came upon—an old sole, a woman's rag, an iron nail, a clay shard—everything would be dragged off to his place and piled on that heap which Chichikov had noticed in a corner of the room.

Plushkin, of course, was neurotic, and the really important aspects of his estate disappeared from his view. "All these goods, wares and produce were dumped into the store-rooms and all turned to rot and rents, and he himself had turned, at last, into a rent on the cloak of humanity." Plushkin goes into some very complicated bargaining with Chichikov, gets to the point of offering Chichikov a mouldy Easter cake, but then thinks better of it and has it put away again!

A humorous novel depends a great deal on the accumulation of vivid details, so that the best thing to say about it is "read it." Gogol is master of this genre. Chichikov is finally exposed and has to leave town. And though he is himself a distortion of humanity, he is the measure of sanity compared with the other humorous distortions in the book.

Humor of course can become quite complicated without losing any of its vitality. The humorist is distinguished by a sense of proportion, and it is this proper proportion that is always at the back of our minds as we perceive the various deliberate distortions.

But distortions can exist on many levels—you can have a distortion of an already existing distortion, or you can distort a situation in one direction, and then in another.

Lytton Strachey's biography of Queen Victoria offers an effective example of complicated dry humor, operating on many levels.

Illustration: Humor in Strachey's *Queen Victoria*

The humor in Gogol's *Dead Souls* stands out massively, like a giant caricature. Lytton Strachey's biography of Queen Victoria is a masterpiece of quiet statement and innuendo, of humorous distortion through minimization. He tells us of the efforts of the architect Gilbert Scott to build a suitable memorial for Prince Albert, Victoria's late husband. "My idea in designing the Memorial," Scott wrote, "was to erect a ciborium to protect a statue of the Prince; and its special characteristic was that the ciborium was designed in some degree on the principles of the ancient shrines. These shrines were models of imaginary buildings, such as had never in reality been erected; and my idea was to realize one of these imaginary structures with its precious materials, its inlaying, its enamels. . . ." Strachey comments on this (indicating by overtone just what he thinks of the value of the project): "His idea was particularly appropriate since it chanced that a similar concept, though in the reverse order of magnitude, had occurred to the Prince himself, who had designed and executed several silver cruet-stands upon the same model." The description of the finally accomplished edifice is utterly hilarious. The tip-off in terms of a climax of humor is contained in the last two lines of the last passage below.[26] We have the impression of a frantic and massive effort to accomplish something that was utterly stupid in conception and that only fools (Victorian, of course) could view with inane satisfaction.

> Gradually the edifice approached completion. The one hundred and seventieth life-size figure in the frieze was chiselled, the granite pillars arose, the mosaics were inserted in the allegorical pediments, the four colossal statues representing the greater Christian virtues, the four other colossal statues representing the greater moral virtues, were hoisted into their positions, the eight bronzes representing the greater sciences—Astronomy, Chemistry, Geology, Geometry, Rhetoric, Medicine, Philosophy, and Physiology—were fixed on their glittering pinnacles, high in air. The statue of Physiology was particularly admired. "On her left

arm," the official description informs us, "she bears a new-born infant, as a representation of the development of the highest and most perfect of the physiological forms; her hand points towards a microscope, the instrument which lends its assistance for the investigation of the minuter forms of animal and vegetable organisms." At last the gilded cross crowned the dwindling galaxies of super-imposed angels, the four continents in white marble stood at the four corners of the base, and, seven years after its inception, in July, 1872, the monument was thrown open to the public.

The reader is already experiencing the reaction Mr. Strachey anticipated—a sense of indigestible heaviness, in which every detail adds an extra absurdity. But more is to come.

But four more years were to elapse before the central figure was ready to be placed under its starry canopy. It was designed by Mr. Foley, though in one particular the sculptor's freedom was restricted by Mr. Scott. "I have chosen the sitting posture," Mr. Scott said, "as best conveying the idea of dignity befitting a royal personage." Mr. Foley ably carried out the conception of his principal. "In the attitude and expression," he said, "the aim has been, with the individuality of portraiture, to embody rank, character, and enlightenment, and to convey a sense of that responsive intelligence indicating an active rather than a passive interest in those pursuits of civilization illustrated in the surrounding figures, groups, and relievos. . . . To identify the figure with one of the most memorable undertakings of the public life of the Prince—the International Exhibition of 1851—a catalogue of the works collected in that first gathering of the industry of all nations is placed in the right hand.

Strachey lets the details show their innate absurdity. He deliberately employs a technique of detached narrative, in which the complacent quotations further distort by apparently accepting what the reader has inwardly rejected. The final touch, in which this gigantic grotesque of an edifice is distorted in the reverse direction, that of simplicity (a spurious one, of course, deliberately indicated by the relationship to *weight*) is now made.

The statue was of bronze gilt and weighed nearly ten tons. It was rightly supposed that the simple word "Albert," cast on the base, would be a sufficient means of identification.

SATIRE

The word "satire" comes from a Roman word meaning a "medley" and refers to the mingling of surface forms that characterized the classic satire. The satire was a form of literature, in the sense that we speak of the novel, the lyric, or the epic as a literary form. The satire as a distinct form was still imitated in seventeenth- and eighteenth-century literature. Today, however, it is more accurate to speak of satire as a literary method rather than as a form—you can have, for example, a satiric novel or a satiric essay. It would not be accurate, however, to speak of a "satiric" poem if you follow the distinctions in this book. Satire, of all the forms of creative discourse, is *analysis par excellence.* While it may be written in meter and rhyme, it does not possess the distinguishing characteristic of poetry—synthesis, imagistic statement.

Satire appeals specifically to the reader's intellect. As a method, as well as a *form,* it continues the original purpose of the classics—to attack folly and vice by making them ridiculous objects of *derision.* Like humor, to which it is in many ways allied, satire must continually suggest the norm by which the ridiculous is indicated. Humor does not necessarily have the same strong moral purpose as satire. The humorist may in fact be quite satisfied with the amusing contrasts and deviations of life and experience. He may not expect any judgment on our part. The satirist goes a step further—he *demands* our judgment. Ultimately we must say to ourselves, "This is right, or this is wrong." In its modern adaptations, satire generally plays off the surface meaning against the real interior meaning. Thus Gulliver in *Gulliver's Travels* gives an account of the progress of Europe to the King of Brobdingnag, an account which Swift, the author, supports with tongue in cheek. In Europe they have invented a cannon ball which can sink a ship and everyone on it. The king asks in effect, why do that? Gulliver is amazed by this manifestation of the king's ignorance. When Gulliver, with more patriotism than judgment, discusses the laws and institutions of England, the king asks many searching questions that destroy Gulliver's smugness. But it never occurs to Gulliver that he might be the real fool, nor does the author ever overtly suggest it. It is the king who is overtly wrong! Or again, in the work below, which is a remorseless attack on totalitarian society, no passage in the book indicates that the One State should have anything but support and respect.

Illustration: Satire in Zamiatin's *We*

A great modern satire that is becoming increasingly known to western readers, *We,* is a work of a Soviet writer (in this particular book very anti-Communist), Evgenii Ivanovich Zamiatin. It is the predecessor of such works as Aldous Huxley's *Brave New World* and George Orwell's *1984* but exceeds them considerably in depth and brilliance. No one has done a more destructive job on what many critics consider the increasing "dehumanization" of man in certain aspects of the modern world.

One of the most relentless probings of the interior contradictions to which man may be subject is to be found in Dostoievski's *Notes from Underground,* where various levels of meaning are played off against one another, where the rational aspect of man fails to tell the whole story, and where the irrational, though not utterly obvious, shows above the surface like an iceberg, with its main content below the surface. If, by some magic, one could take the relentless irony of Dostoievski's masterpiece and make it thoroughly comic, one would begin to approach the satire of Zamiatin's work. Human nature, Dostoievski shows, can be the result of willful choice. "You see, you gentlemen have, to the best to my knowledge, taken your whole register of human advantages from the averages of statistical figures and politico-economical formulas. Your advantages are prosperity, wealth, freedom, peace—and so on, and so on. . . . But, you know, this is what is surprising: why does it so happen that all these statisticians, sages and lovers of humanity, when they reckon up human advantages, invariably leave out *one?*"[27] And that *one* is the willful disregard of *reason.* According to Dostoievski, "man everywhere and at all times, whoever he may be, has preferred to act as he chose and not in the least as his reason and advantage dictated." Dostoievski has begun the attack of the "Crystal Palace" that Zamiatin finishes off. "Then—it is you who are saying all this—new economic relationships will be established, all ready-made and worked out with mathematical certitude, so that every possible question will vanish in the twinkling of an eye, because every possible answer to it will be provided. Then will the Palace of Crystal be built." Zamiatin shows us what happens when the Palace of Crystal *has* been built.

The hero of *We* is the director of the building of the Integral, which at one and the same time houses the community (the *One State* under the dictatorship of the *Benefactor,* assisted by the *Guardians*) and serves as a space ship which can take off from the ground. He is a mathematician, turning all of life's experiences into mathematics. In the One State "nobody is *one,* but *one of.*" All citizens wear the same costume, the *unif,* and they always walk in pairs. Their apartments are made of glass, so that no privacy is allowed except in one department. The State permits a social hour, at which time all the shades are drawn. Partners are carefully screened and adjusted to one another, and, instead of romance, State-issued coupons and stubs are exchanged. No one, of course, is permitted a child except through State authorization.

The State has issued a Table of Hourly Commandments, by which every human (?) unit in the State is controlled. Only two hours are left unassigned—apparently the State has not been yet organized to its maximum capacity, though this will surely be remedied. Guardians have the mechanical means of hearing and supervising everything that goes on or is said, and they benevolently correct and guide, for their own happiness and good, any citizens deviating from the straight and narrow path. As in the common method of satire (the role of Gulliver himself in *Gulliver's Travels,* for example), the author is apparently, but *only* apparently, supporting his hero's conscious position (in Zamiatin, the hero's *unconscious* position is very different from his *conscious* one). The hero is *involuntarily* reminded of what the ancients called an *icon* when he thinks of the beauty of the Table. "Ah, why am I not a poet, so that I might fittingly chant your praises? O, Tables of Hourly Commandments, O, you who are the heart and the pulse of The One State!" Everything is "simple, regular and limited—like a circle. "I'm not afraid of the word limitation," the hero says. "The work of the highest faculty man has, his reason, consists precisely of a ceaseless limitation of infinity into suitable, easily digestible portions—or differentials. That is precisely what the divine beauty of my element—mathematics—consists of."[28]

We is strongly antirationalistic in spite of its overt tributes to *reason.* Semantically a difference can be established between reason and rationalism: both use the surface methods of logic, but reason is in keeping with the facts and mystery of life whereas rationalism ignores them (and in this sense is not really reasonable). The hero asks, "How could it have come about that the ancients had not been struck by the whole preposterousness of their literature and poetry?" In the One State, poetry has sensibly become utility, producing such masterpieces as "Daily Odes to the Benefactor" or the immortal tragedy "He Who Came Late to Work." As Dostoievski's hero in *Notes from Underground* says, "I quite naturally want to live, in order to satisfy all my capacities for life, and not simply my capacity for reasoning, that is, not simply one-twentieth of my capacity for life." The hero of *We* (in the One State the pronoun *I* must never be used) finds he cannot bring his reaction to an attractive woman under any mathematical formula. "However, I don't know whether it was her eyes or her brows, but there was some sort of strange, irritating X about her, and no matter how I tried I could not capture it, could not give it a numerical formulation."

The hero gets into increasing trouble because of a developing attachment to a female member of the ancient races who have not been assimilated by the One State. The One State preserves a museum, the House of Antiquity, showing how such people formerly lived, although a few surviving members still lurk in the woods outside the Integral compound. Through his visits to the House of Antiquity the hero comes under the influence of this girl.

From contact with her he begins to develop a very dangerous disease. The hero himself is worried and tries everything in his power to stop the infection within himself. The Guardians extend him every courtesy and compassion. But he goes on developing a disease that seems to have been exterminated with the past. It is known as *a soul!*

A complicated action takes place in the story as the soul-disease spreads, endangering the finely wrought structure of the One State. Finally the Great Benefactor steps in, alerting the members of the Integral to the catastrophic danger they are in. All are asked to volunteer for a great brain operation, a "fantasiectomy" removing the sources of potential infection leading to the soul disease. Many have died and there is disorder, but the One State triumphs. Our hero is cured. He looks at his handwriting after the operations—it is the same, but there are no more absurd ideas. "There are no ravings whatsoever, no preposterous metaphors, no emotions whatever. Facts only."

As in its imitators, Huxley's *Brave New World* and Orwell's *1984,* the totalitarian state wins, the individual loses, in the end. This is part of the satiric method, because the author is sympathetic on the surface (but only on the surface) with the totalitarian idea. The underlying message, never overtly stated in the satiric formula in such books, concerns the absurd travesty of human nature exhibited in a dehumanizing and totalitarian society, and in the consequent interior vulnerability of totalitarianism, in spite of an imposing façade of invincibility. The indirect effect of such a book is to make us say to ourselves, "This sort of thing will not happen if I can possibly stop it." Zamiatin's *We* has attacked the folly and vice of a dehumanizing totalitarianism by making it an object of derision.

PROSE AS PERSONALITY AND REFLECTION

The essay has been an important and traditional form of prose, though of recent years it has been under a cloud. Joseph Wood Krutch has argued in *The Saturday Review* that marketable nonfiction is now either factual, controversial, or reportorial.[29] Anything resembling facts and statistics impresses the reader and makes him feel that he is being given the "lowdown." "Facts may be employed indiscriminately as long as the writer exudes self-confidence." It is desirable to seek for oddity in persons described, but self-revelation on the part of the writer is not permissible. The most successful magazines strive for anonymity of style. What seems to be desired is writing that might be produced by a machine rather than by a man.

This has not always been the case. The essay form dates from the sixteenth century and particularly from the work of Montaigne. An essay (associated with the French, *essayer,* meaning "to try," or "to attempt") was a form of writing, at least originally, the boundaries of which were determined by the author's personal point of view. The *news* value of the original essay lay in the writer's character, his personality. The reader was not only interested in a subject matter but also in a person. We must not think of an essay as a kind of unfinished book, an incompleted study. If we were to think of a book as a large oil painting, we might think of the essay as a work in miniature. A miniature is a work of art complete in itself; it is not an unfinished oil. But the form of a book is determined by a completed exposition of the questions and problems it presents. The form of an essay is thus determined by the originality, force, or charm of the writer's point of view on some segment of thought and experience. Of course, we must realize that the term "essay" has frequently been loosely applied to studies, to scientific papers, and so on, as in Locke's *Essay concerning Human Understanding*.

But the true essay derives its peculiar charm and power from the unusual processes of thought in the writer. We delight in the unusual, yet understandable, paths that the thought takes. This is prose made unique by the reflective process, the leisurely, controlled pace of a man who truly thinks for himself.

This is the type of essay Charles Lamb wrote. Here is an extract from "Mrs. Battle's Opinions on Whist," in which we see with new insight and humor a typical situation which we have nearly all shared at one time or other.[30]

> "A clear fire, a clean hearth, and the rigour of the game." This was the celebrated *wish* of old Sarah Battle (now with God), who, next to her devotions, loved a good game of whist. She was none of your lukewarm gamesters, your half-and-half players, who have no objection to take a hand, if you want one to make up a rubber; who affirm that they have no pleasure in winning; that they like to win one game and lose another; that they can while away an hour very agreeably at a card-table, but are indifferent whether they play or no; and will desire an adversary, who has slipped a wrong card, to take it up and play another. These insufferable triflers are the curse of a table. One of these flies will spoil a whole pot. Of such it may be said that they do not play at cards, but only play at playing at them.
>
> Sarah Battle was none of that breed. She detested them, as I do, from her heart and soul, and would not, save upon a striking emergency, willingly seat herself at the same table with them. She loved a thorough-paced partner, a determined enemy. She took, and gave, no concessions. She hated favours. She never made a revoke, nor ever passed it over in her adversary without exacting the utmost forfeiture. She fought a good fight: cut and thrust. She held not her good sword (her cards) "like a dancer." She sat bolt upright; and neither showed you her cards, nor desired to see yours. All people have their blind

side—their superstitions; and I have heard her declare, under the rose, that Hearts was her favourite suit.

I never in my life—and I knew Sarah Battle many of the best years of it—saw her take out her snuff-box when it was her turn to play; or snuff a candle in the middle of a game; or ring for a servant, till it was fairly over. She never introduced, or connived at, miscellaneous conversation during its process. As she emphatically observed, cards were cards; and if I ever saw unmingled distaste in her fine last-century countenance, it was at the airs of a young gentleman of a literary turn, who had been with difficulty persuaded to take a hand; and who, in his excess of candour, declared that he thought there was no harm in unbending the mind now and then, after serious studies, in recreations of that kind! She could not bear to have her noble occupation, to which she wound up her faculties, considered in that light. It was her business, her duty, the thing she came into the world to do,—and she did it. She unbent her mind afterwards—over a book.

One of the most stimulating practitioners of the reflective essay in modern times was G. K. Chesterton who, contrary to Joseph Wood Krutch's generally true observations, managed to get his material printed in popular publications. Who but Chesterton would undertake "A Defence of China Shepherdesses"? As usual, he used the symbol of the china shepherdess to point out some lack of insight in contemporary society.

Let us, then, consider in this light the old pastoral or Arcadian ideal. But first certainly one thing must be definitely recognized. This Arcadian art and literature is a lost enthusiasm. To study it is like fumbling in the love-letters of a dead man. To us its flowers seem as tawdry as cockades; the lambs that dance to the shepherd's pipe seem to dance with all the artificiality of a ballet. Even our own prosaic toil seems to us more joyous than that holiday. Where its ancient exuberance passed the bounds of wisdom and even of virtue, its caperings seem frozen into the stillness of an antique frieze. In those grey old pictures a bacchanal seems as dull as an archdeacon. Their very sins seem colder than our restraints.

All this may be frankly recognized: all the barren sentimentality of the Arcadian ideal and all its insolent optimism. But when all is said and done, something else remains.

Through ages in which the most arrogant and elaborate ideals of power and civilization held otherwise undisputed sway, the ideal of the perfect and healthy peasant did undoubtedly represent in some shape or form the conception that there was a dignity in simplicity and a dignity in labour. It was good for the ancient aristocrat, even if he could not attain to innocence and the wisdom of the earth, to believe that these things were the secrets of the priesthood of the poor. It was good for him to believe that even if heaven was not above him, heaven was below him. It was well that he should have amid all his flamboyant triumphs the never-extinguished sentiment that there was something better than his triumphs, the conception that "there remaineth a rest."

The conception of the Ideal Shepherd seems absurd to our modern ideas. But, after all, it was perhaps the only trade of the democracy which was equalized with the trades of the aristocracy even by the aristocracy itself. The shepherd of pastoral poetry was, without doubt, very different from the shepherd of actual fact. Where one innocently piped to his lambs, the other innocently swore at them; and their divergence in intellect and personal cleanliness was immense. But the difference between the ideal shepherd who danced with Amaryllis and the real shepherd who thrashed her is not a scrap greater than the difference between the ideal soldier who dies to capture the colours and the real soldier who lives to clean his accoutrements, between the ideal priest who is everlastingly by someone's bed and the real priest who is as glad as any one else to get to his own. There are ideal conceptions and real men in every calling; yet there are few who object to the ideal conceptions, and not many, after all, who object to the real men.

The fact, then, is this: So far from resenting the existence in art and literature of an ideal shepherd, I genuinely regret that the shepherd is the only democratic calling that has ever been raised to the level of the heroic callings conceived by an aristocratic age. So far from objecting to the Ideal Shepherd, I wish there were an Ideal Postman, an Ideal Grocer, and an Ideal Plumber. It is undoubtedly true that we should laugh at the idea of an Ideal Postman; it is true, and it proves that we are not genuine democrats.[31]

What we have in this passage, in addition to the thinking on the given subject, is the impression of a lively personality, who, wistfully and a trifle satirically, is telling us at least as much about ourselves as about china shepherdesses.

Of course, like a miniature, the essay may reach a high state of perfection. But just as a miniature cannot have the sweep and power of a great canvas, so, as fine as the essay can be, any number would have difficulty in equaling an *Anna Karenina* or a *Paradise Lost*.

A more extended use of prose as personality and reflection is to be found in the biography and autobiography. These are fields where the borderlines of literature and history become hard to define. In so far as such writing is meant to clarify the historical record, rather than emphasize a man's personality and general view of life (as in the autobiographies of General Eisenhower and General Montgomery), in so far as a scholar aims at a definitive authenticated life of his subject (as in David Masson's *Life of John Milton),* we tend to have history or scientific biography rather than literature. The degree of emphasis on human interest in a particular work offers a rough guideline. James Boswell's *Life of Samuel Johnson,* besides presenting the facts and incidents of Johnson's life, has the underlying literary theme of Boswell's hero worship (about which Boswell is humorously critical). It presents Johnson as a creative character, human in multidimensional ways, speculating on all sorts of matters beyond what a historical biography would demand. The biographer's choice of details affords an index to the biographer's own personality as well as to that of his subject. The literary biographer chooses not the details that are necessarily important in themselves but those that serve to make the character intriguing in terms of humor (Johnson's observations about Goldsmith), pathos (Johnson's melancholy), or surprise (Johnson's formidable way of expressing himself). Although Boswell gives us thorough and painstaking reporting, his work belongs definitely to literature. Some scholarly books, however, are hard to classify, for they contain many of the qualities of fine literature. Lytton Strachey's mordant biography of Queen Victoria or Ralph Roeder's interrelated biographical sketches in *Man of the Renaissance* are such books. In so far as the biographer or autobiographer himself maintains a highly personal view, he will tend toward literature; in so far as he is factual and writes with impartial detachment, he will tend toward scientific, historical writing.

THE SHORT STORY

Roughly, short stories can be classified into two groups: the short story without plot and the short story with plot.

Some of the greatest achievements in the modern short story are not based on formal plot narrative at all. The short story without plot is a method of writing in which a unity of impression, or a unity of mood, leads to a climax, or point of highest tension, and to the conclusion or *resolution* of this point. This climax is not necessarily related to a reversal of narrative situation, that is, to the turns, twists, and surprises that cause suspense in the short story with plot. Rather, it is related to the ironic or symbolic or intellectual overtone. By overtone we mean the essential implication beyond the surface meaning of the explicit situation. The short story without plot depends on irony; therefore, the writer of this type of story must master the use of overtone. In creating such overtone, he must be sensitive to the emotional power that can be achieved through *restraint*. In a short story with plot, details must often be explicitly clarified, whereas a short story without plot often succeeds for the reverse reason. It may leave the motive for an act uncertain. In fact, one way to create climax in this type of writing is to present the surface explanation as apparently acceptable while at the same time suggesting that the reverse, or submerged, explanation is really true. The reader's imagination and intelligence will be stimulated by this device.

This form, less unwieldy than that of the short story with plot, permits a greater freedom of approach, and often for this very reason leads to a production of great emotional force.

Favorite forms of the short story without plot are the thematic contrast—often ironic, humorous, or satiric—and the form dependent on pathos, an unresolved emotional situation.

Climax can often be indicated by repeating an initial pattern in relation to a growing seriousness of mood. Such a procedure is exemplified in the jingling of the bells in Edgar Allan Poe's well-known "The Cask of Amontillado." This short story has been regularly reproduced in anthologies largely because of its economy of style. It also possesses a perfectly studied irony in relation to the subject matter. The story is told in the first person by a murderer planning the perfect crime. His victim is dressed for the pre-Lenten carnival. "The man wore motley. He had on a tight-fitting parti-striped dress and his head was surmounted by a conical hat and bells. I was so pleased to see him that I thought I should never have done wringing his hands." The victim wears the fancy dress of a medieval jester. But the natural hilarity of the bells serves to mark a somber procession to doom. These bells jingle when the victim drinks his first glass of Medoc on his search for the Amontillado. The bells jingle again in death: "I thrust a torch through the remaining aperture and let it fall within. There came forth in return only a jingling of the bells." The murderer has walled up his victim alive, and with quiet, malicious irony he concludes: "Against the new masonry I re-erected the old rampart of bones. For the half of a century no mortal has disturbed them. *In pace requiescat.*"

The really powerful writer, however, does not have to seek for sensational, unusual, or garish situations. In fact, a story often is more powerful for its basic simplicity of situation—whether or not to open a closed door, to drop a letter in the mailbox, or to acknowledge or disregard an old acquaintance may be the basis of the most acute penetration into experience.

With the growth in psychological acuteness in modern writing, with a greater awareness in concrete particulars of the frustrations to which an individual may be subjected in an overmechanized society, writers on all levels have come to realize the value of symbolism in heightening tension. The symbol, as has been stated, is primarily an aesthetic device for carrying a burden of meaning in a compressed package. The writer need not expose this full burden of meaning, but any sensitive reader can follow in the train of his own thinking all the implications contained in the package.

The short story with plot differs from the short story without plot in the sense that it depends primarily for its emotional effect not on irony or overtone but on the resolution of a specific problem which the hero or protagonist faces. The solving of the conflict of circumstances is no less necessary than the psychological or intellectual evaluation of the circumstances themselves. Such an evaluation will often suffice for the short story without plot, but not for the short story with plot. The circumstances of the plot, therefore, must of themselves be of interest, be coherent and artistically acceptable.

A certain confusion has arisen about the question of the probability of the plot or action. It may be said that conditional probability is all that is necessary. There must be an internal consistency between the course of the action and the conditions under which the short-story writer has chosen to carry it out. The original hypothesis of the story need not be within the realm of our experience at all. We are willing to "suspend disbelief" in order to enter the conditions of artistic illusion. All creative writing is in a certain sense illusion. In this sense we must realize that art is distinct from real experience. In most cases this realization is so habitual that one is unconscious of the need for it. But within the conditions of illusion, we expect consistency.

Character in relation to situation spells conflict and change. Short stories of the highest literary merit most closely follow the principle that character makes action. Stephen Vincent Benét's "The Bishop's Beggar" is a story of the highest artistic quality because it preeminently presents character expressed through action. Benét's story has the high subtlety of showing an organic growth and change in character as it expresses itself through action and is in turn affected by action. The bishop, in befriending the cynical and ambitious beggar whom he had crippled as a youth in a coaching accident, learns a great deal about the life of privation and destitution which had been outside his elegant aristocratic experience. The beggar, once adopted, needles the bishop unmercifully, putting all his spiritual aspirations to the acid test. The bishop, though at first with great reluctance, gradually yields his polished and courtly values to the rugged insistence of a real Christianity. The beggar succeeds in making the bishop a saint. The more he tries to make him a bad man, the better he becomes. Through the interaction of these two basically tough characters, grace even reaches Luigi, the beggar. But even in death, he remains the symbol of a mocking and cogent criticism. "Of the tomb of Luigi, the beggar—that no man knows. They say that it was beside the bishop's but, in one war or another, it was destroyed, and there is no trace of it now. Yet Luigi was an arrogant spirit; perhaps he would have liked that best."

In so far as a storyteller emphasizes an unusual plot situation, he tends to make plot more important than character. But even here a minimum degree of correlation between character and plot is necessary. Nevertheless, novelty of interpretation—of "angle"—will often be sufficient to justify a story, though such a story will not be that of the highest artistic class. A recent story in a national magazine reinterpreted the dwarfs, the small creatures of folklore who live underground, as the survivors of a previous atomic age who had mutated to their present size and appearance. This angle alone, because of its analogy to contemporary circumstances, is sufficient for reader interest.

Every story, to be effective, must contain suspense. Suspense should not, of course, be restricted merely to the course of action.

Suspense can also be created by ambiguity, by the problem of how the reader is to evaluate the theme of the narrative, of what different kinds of meaning are to be derived from it. Suspense implies that the writer tells the reader in the course of the story enough to arouse his curiosity, but *not* enough to satisfy it. "Keep to the point of interest, but with a minimum of revelation." Always in the reader's mind must be the suggestion of possible alternatives—of plot solution as in the short story with plot, of contrasting evaluations as in the short story without plot.

RANGE AND VERSATILITY OF THE SHORT STORY

The short story can be a very great form of prose art. Within a limited space, it can create suspense and excitement. It can offer sharply defined insights into life and experience. Unlike the longer narrative of the novel, which can operate on a canvas as large as the energy and enthusiasm of the writer can sustain without causing the reader's interest to flag (we have only to think of what Tolstoi or Dostoievski, as exponents of the great realistic novel, achieved), the short story must accomplish its aim in miniature, in a short single focus. Short stories at their best have the economy and concentration which the classical Greeks so much admired in art. As for the range of emotional impact—humorous, satiric, pathetic, tragic—the short story knows no limitations.

Not only excitement but a high degree of symbolism, even of poetry, though subordinated to the analytical structure of narrative, frequently characterizes the short story.

The short story can bring creative wealth on many different levels, as a comparison of stories having a roughly comparable theme or image will reveal. Let us, for example, compare three short stories in which a bird is employed as an image. In all these stories we have real birds, but each bird is so interwoven in the psychological texture of the story that it is symbolic as well.

On a fairly direct level we have an ironic and satiric piece, "Alive—Alive, Oh!" by Osbert Sitwell, told in the first person by a narrator. The story offers a blistering comment on literary fashions and literary reputations. An English poet, struggling and impoverished, turns his attention to a favorite English preoccupation with bird lore. His book of poems is warmly received, and he becomes known as the Sussex bird poet. So far, so good. But the romantic tradition about poets is that they should succumb to declining health, emaciation, and an increasing paleness of countenance. But as the poet's royalties pour in, he, to the contrary, becomes ruddy and rotund, of exuberant good health. His publishers become worried; they talk to him privately about what is for them this unhealthy development. Some time later the narrator reads of the poet's surprising death. How could such a healthy man die so young? The obituary columns are compassionate and laudatory. The sales of his works zoom.

Years later the narrator is spending a holiday on the southern coast of Calabria, Italy, where he hears of a wealthy English recluse. Calabria is not a place where birds have been traditionally venerated, in the manner of Keats's nightingale or Shelley's skylark, but rather as inviting delicacies for the dining room table. He learns that this Englishman, so strange for one of his race, has ordered any bird on his property to be shot on sight. Rounding a stone wall, the narrator hears the excited Englishman shouting, "Another beastly Bullfinch, why hasn't it been shot?" Something strikes the narrator as familiar about that man's voice. Yes, you know who! It is his old acquaintance, the poet, whose death had been greatly "exaggerated," whose death had been fictional and literary to promote his books and suit the convenience of his publishers.

Here is a delightfully humorous story, containing an implicit exposé of the absurd aspects of literary tradition.

What delights the reader of a short story is not necessarily the tension and excitement (these, of course, may be psychological rather than plotted); it is also the writer's point of view, the impact of *his* personality. In this sense, the short story has capitalized on the charm that belonged to the personal essay. One enjoys the writer's point of view, even his prejudices. The particular effect of a short story is seldom lost because one disagrees with such views, for a story is always primarily an intriguing narrative rather than an ideological document.

G. K. Chesterton was famed as the writer of a special kind of plotted detective story. Though his Father Brown series is particularly well known, an even more brilliant and original collection is contained in *The Poet and the Lunatics* (1929). It is the custom of many short-story writers to have a common theme running through a series of stories. The theme may be one of characterization and locale (as in James Joyce's *Dubliners*), a predominant problem (for example, the relationship, often involving special types of frustration, between man and woman, as in the sensitive and penetrating studies of D. H. Lawrence), or an ideological approach as in G. K. Chesterton.

In *The Poet and the Lunatics* Chesterton is concerned with the dividing line between the great intuitions into reality demonstrated by the poetic imagination and the dementia of dangerous mental associations. A repeated point in this collection of stories is the difficulty most men find in distinguishing the poet from the lunatic. As Gabriel Gale, the poet, observes about the mad scientist in "The Yellow Bird," "Perhaps you think I am mad as he; and I have told you that I am at once like him and unlike him. . . . I am unlike him because, thank God, I can generally find my way home again. The lunatic is he who loses his way and cannot return."

"The Yellow Bird" has, as its ideological theme, the necessity of imposing certain limits to freedom, so that freedom itself can survive, so that it will not become self-destructive and injurious to others. The title "The Yellow Bird" derives from the incident in which Gabriel Gale, having accompanied a group of hiking friends to the top of a hill "overlooking a valley beautiful enough to be a vision," and having picnicked, lies on his back, and stares at the woods and the skies. He observes a lemon-yellow bird being attacked by the usual birds of the environment.

The group discuss an old manor house in the valley. Mallow loves Laura Verney, who lives there, but she has apparently lost interest in him. She is helping a Russian psychologist, her family's guest, to write an authoritative book. He had once escaped from a Siberian prison by blowing out a wall with a bomb of his own construction. Laura, under his influence, has begun to think of freedom in terms of "always going outwards" whereas Mallow thinks of it in terms of "always going inwards." "She says that even in her own valley, and in her own garden, the trees only grow because they radiate outwards, which is only the Latin for branching. She says the very word 'radiant' shows it is the secret of happiness. There is something in it, I suppose, but I radiate inwards, so to speak; that is why I paint all my pictures of this little corner of the world."

The party observes a window being opened in the house below—then another, and another, until they are all opened. The skylight is the last to open, and the scientist, with yellow hair and a light-colored garment, emerges on the roof. He is like the yellow bird.

The group visits the Verney house. Gale becomes agitated after he observes that a fish bowl has been broken and that the luminescent bodies of the fish are reflected from the table in the rising moonlight. He rushes Laura and his friends away from the house because he now knows that the scientist is really insane. Suddenly the house explodes: "For the instant that it lasted it was a standing glory, like a great sunrise. There rose to the surface of Mallow's memory one word for it, the word 'radiant.'" Chesterton points his moral which we enjoy along with the poetic descriptions, the sharp dialogue, and the suspense of the plot itself. "This man had made the great stride from liberty to lunacy. The man who opened the bird cage loved freedom, possibly too much, certainly very much. But the man who broke the bowl merely because he thought it a prison for the fish, when it was their only possible house of life—that man was already outside the world of reason, raging with a desire to be outside everything. In a most literal and living sense, he was out of his wits."

D. H. Lawrence is generally regarded as a master of the short story. His main concern, which he probes deeply, is the relationship between man and woman. Lawrence, as novelist Sigrid Undset has emphasized, had an important vision of what such a relationship should be. He saw the possibility that a developed self-awareness could unite with a full responsiveness to the other person, free from egoism and humiliation. As a realistic writer, he frequently shows that his creative relationship is not attained, and he arouses deep pity and compassion in the reader because of the contrast between the dream and the actuality. This holds true even when, as in "Two Blue Birds," he writes in a very cool and detached way.

"Two Blue Birds" gives an acute psychological analysis of the relationship of two women, one a wife and one a secretary (the "Two Blue Birds") to a writer whose main interest in life is his work, a man who relates far more closely to words than to people. The husband and the wife know each other more intimately than anyone else, but they cannot manage to live together. He has a secretary who adores him and on whom he completely relies. But he does not reciprocate her emotions. Everyone goes out of the way to make the wife welcome and comfortable when she visits her husband again. The secretary's family has moved into the writer's house. The mother is a good cook, and the sister an excellent maid. There is no detail of the writer's life that has not been anticipated and cared for. In this ideal situation he can work ten or eleven hours a day.

The wife knows her husband's weak point—his vanity.[32] "She knew he couldn't bear it if she mocked at his work for a moment." In her opinion, the husband is not really producing good work under these circumstances. She observes, "Perhaps it is not good for a man's work if he is too comfortable." She could not understand the secretary's slavish devotion to the man, for there was no corresponding return.

The main part of the story is centered in a garden scene. "He was dictating a magazine article about the modern novel. 'What the modern novel lacks is architecture.' Good God! Architecture! He might just as well say: What the modern novel lacks is whalebone, or a teaspoon, or a tooth stopped."

As in the stories of both Sitwell and Chesterton, the narrative introduces birds both as an actual reality and as a symbolic image. The wife observes a blue bird dashing

> . . . about the feet of the absorbed, short-hand scribbling little secretary. "The blue bird! The blue bird of happiness! Well, I'm blest," thought the wife. "Well, I'm blest." And as she was being blest, appeared another blue bird—that is, another blue tit—and began to wrestle with the first blue tit. A couple of blue birds of happiness, having a fight over it.

The blue birds in their fight symbolize the much subtler, much more catty struggle between the two women. In a short space, it is impossible to indicate the skill of D. H. Lawrence's dialogue, with its contrast between an undisturbed social surface and its inner pointed needling. Eventually the dialogue erupts into something rather fierce and direct. The wife tells the secretary: "On a soft, spring afternoon like this, you ought to have him dictating poems to you, about the blue birds of happiness fluttering round your dainty little feet. I know *I* would if I were his secretary." The wife, an accomplished needler, eventually suggests that the secretary is so efficient that it is really she who writes her husband's books.

But the wife also has a real knowledge of herself. "I tell you, I'm utterly incompetent. I never earn anything. I'm the parasite on the British oak, like the mistletoe. The blue bird doesn't flutter around my feet. Perhaps they're too big and trampling."

The secretary is shocked by the realism of the wife. No bridge can be thrown between the secretary's hero worship and the wife's knowledge both of her husband and of herself. The wife thanks God that she sees things differently from the secretary.

> "On whose behalf are you thanking God?" he asked sarcastically.
>
> "Everybody's, I suppose! Yours, because you get everything for nothing, and Miss Wrexall's, because she seems to like it, and mine because I'm well out of it all!"

The story, though somewhat enigmatic, contains a built-in theme of Lawrence's: the impossibility of a creative relationship when the man insists on being an egoist, when a woman (as in the case of the secretary) allows herself to be exploited and loses her dignity, when a wife cannot really love and give herself. There is a hidden irony in the fact that both husband and wife are very knowledgeable people, but this does not help them. In terms of what is ideally possible, the result is one of pathetic human failure.

These three stories exhibit the range and versatility of the short story. In Sitwell we have an entertaining and pointed satire; in Chesterton a closely-wrought detective story, with poetic flavor, containing an ideological message; in Lawrence a sharp and subtle psychological analysis. All of them (as is the contemporary manner) make extensive use of symbolism, as in the bird images. Artistically they all have certain qualities in common—economy, tension, climax, unity of mood and purpose.

NEW ART FORMS IN THE SHORT STORY

Developments in the short story parallel, or have anticipated, the new trends of contemporary art. The short story has not been able to go as "far out," let us say, as the Theater of the Absurd. By necessity, the short story cannot deny language as a means of communication or do without words. Since it has to make predicate statements, it cannot simply present a series of images as some modern poems do. But it has done nearly everything else. Its art forms have stretched all the way from the entertaining adventure story to the most symbolic and multidimensional statement, which may contain at one and the same time social criticism, comedy and tragedy, theme and countertheme, overt statement, suggestive statement, and no statement at all. It may resolve a tension at the end, or leave it unresolved, suggesting that the narrative just slips into life, life that goes on.

Obviously it requires a greater degree of sophistication to see the focus and unity of structure in a multidimensional story by Henry James or James Joyce than in a tale by G. K. Chesterton or Bret Harte or in the powerful, terse, economical, but utterly lucid movement of the masterly Hemingway. If our aim is a catholicity of taste, we should be able to enjoy the one-dimensional story as well as the multidimensional, for both can be excellent in their respective genres. When we speak of primitive art, we are not speaking of a lack of artistic skill—primitive art can be great art. We have, rather, in mind the effect such art has on an audience—a direct, uncomplicated effect. Sophisticated art satisfies the human desire to exercise special mental agility, for complexity confirms the reader's realization that life in actual fact often is complex. Such a story intrigues the reader into exercising many associative perceptions of his own. He is persuaded to think of life situations, of the problems of environment and psychological relationships, rather than of the excitement of the events narrated.

Illustration: Art Form in James Joyce's "The Dead"

James Joyce's "The Dead" is a representative example of this kind of art.[33] The environment is a segment of upper-middle-class Dublin life. An annual musical supper is given by two elderly spinster teachers of music. "Never once had it fallen flat. For years and years it had gone off in splendid style, as long as anyone could remember." Gabriel, their nephew, and his wife are among the principal guests. It is the Christmas season and some snow is falling. Gabriel gives the young maid a Christmas tip which she accepts ambiguously. Delicate and restless, Gabriel is superior in cultural attainment to the other guests. He is worried that he will have to make the speech of the evening, for he does not want to talk above people's heads. He suffers from other tensions as well; he is deputized to watch and head off one of the guests who is very likely to arrive drunk. He listens to a rendering on the piano of an academy piece by Mary Jane, a niece of the hostesses, with indifference. He talks with a Miss Ivors who had read one of his literary columns. She likes his reviews but not his politics. People talk about plans for their summer vacations—Aran Isles, France, Belgium, Galway. One guest has come from Glasgow. Gabriel goes over the topics of his speech in his mind: Irish hospitality, sad memories, the Three Graces, Paris, the quotation from Browning. He wonders whether Miss Ivors was sincere in praising his review. Gabriel carves the goose at the table, which is described in detail with its rich assortments. "Gabriel began to carve second helpings as soon as he had finished the first round without serving himself. Everyone protested loudly so that he compromised by taking a long draught of stout for he had found the carving hot work." The guests talk about opera and former stars. Miss Ivors has left, and Gabriel makes an elegant and successful speech. Gabriel converses with his aunts; the guests start leaving, and Gabriel helps to find cabs for them. He sees his wife leaning on the banister, listening to something. Someone is playing the piano, and a man is singing. "There was grace and mystery in her attitude as if she were a symbol of something. He asked himself what is a woman standing on the stairs in the shadows, listening to distant music, a symbol of." Mr. D'Arcy, the singer, has a cold, and everyone has told him to be careful of his throat in the night air. On the way home, Gabriel becomes amorous towards his wife, Gretta. "Moments of their secret life burst like stars upon his memory." His feelings increase when they are finally alone at home. But, surprisingly, she does not respond. The song that Mr. D'Arcy had rendered, "The Lass of Aughrim," has evoked some mysterious memories in her. It has reminded her of a boy she knew in Galway. Miss Ivors talked about Galway. The boy died for Gretta—a consumptive, shivering in the rain. Gabriel has prodded too deeply. "He saw himself a ludicrous figure, acting as a pennyboy for his aunts, a nervous, well-meaning sentimentalist, orating to vulgarians and idealizing his own clownish lusts, the pitiable fatuous fellow he had caught a glimpse of in the mirror."

Gabriel is deeply saddened rather than disillusioned. He thinks of how Gretta has lain beside him and how she has locked in her heart for so many years that image of her lover's eyes when he told her that he did not wish to live. "Generous tears filled Gabriel's eyes. He had never felt like that himself towards any woman, but he knew that such a feeling must be love."

> The tears gathered more thickly in his eyes and in the partial darkness he imagined he saw the form of a young man standing under a dripping tree. Other forms were near. His soul had approached that region where dwell the vast hordes of the dead. He was conscious of, but could not apprehend, their wayward and flickering existence. His own identity was fading out into a gray impalpable world: the solid world itself, which these dead had one time reared and lived in, was dissolving and dwindling.

Gabriel does not sleep but watches the snow falling. He thinks of how it falls everywhere, upon the living and the dead, upon every part of the lonely churchyard where the boy who was in love with his wife lies buried.

What do we make out of such a story? The interest does not lie in plot, in complications springing from a character's actions. The realistic details build up slowly and, at first, seem rather casual and disconnected. That many of these details are symbolic in some way or other is only perceived after the reader has grasped the whole work of art. Joyce was an almost self-conscious aesthetician. He stubbornly refused to use any propaganda. He shows, but he resolutely refuses overtly to evaluate. The title of the story is "The Dead." Are the characters dead? Is society dead? Is the story an attack on outmoded and stuffy middle-class life? One would not get Joyce to admit it. But some such criticism is evokable. Is Gabriel an ineffective mediocrity? Or is he heroic in a way—sensitive, protective, and loving in spite of his limitations? Ultimately, is Joyce telling us that this is the way life is, that humanity is troubled and tragic, yet that there is peace and reconciliation intertwined with pain? The story which started with slow-paced realism ends in poetry. We have to make what we can of it; emotionally it has done something to us. It has told us of real pain, real love under the smooth surface of social norms and forms.

In the manner common with Anton Chekhov, Joyce does not terminate anything. The conclusion of the story gives no hint of the future relationship of Gabriel and Gretta. But the ending indicates keys to the symbolic aspects of the story. The symbols are used for total meaning, not as indicators to light the road of the narrative line. An artist—Georges Bernanos, for example—may use symbols for a different purpose. In a terrifying scene in *Under the Sun of Satan* Father Donissan encounters a small dusky pedestrian on the road at night who, amid obvious remarks, says such things as "darkness brings people together. It's a good thing, a very good thing. When he can't see at all, the most standoffish chap has no pride"; or "I don't live anywhere, or the next thing to it." As the narrative develops, we are eased into accepting this stranger as the Devil himself, and all these quaint little remarks fit in. They have prepared us for the story line, at the same time that they are symbols in themselves. Joyce's method of symbolism is quite different.

Caroline Gordon and Allen Tate, in *The House of Fiction,* comment on Joyce's story as follows:

> In fact, from the beginning to the end of the story we are never told anything, we are shown everything. We are not told, for example, that the milieu of the story is the provincial, middle-class, "cultivated" society of Dublin at the turn of the century; we are not told that Gabriel represents its emotional sterility (as contrasted with the "peasant" richness of his wife Gretta). . . . All this we see dramatized; it is all made active. Nothing is given us from the externally omniscient point of view. . . . There is a brief description of Gabriel; but it is not Joyce's description; we see him as Lily sees him—or might see him if she had Joyce's superior command of the whole situation. This, in fact, is the method of "The Dead." From this point on we are never far from Gabriel's physical sight; yet we are constantly looking through his physical eyes at values and insights of which he is incapable. The significance of the milieu, the complacency of Gabriel's feeling for his wife, her romantic image of her lover Michael Furey . . . would have been put before us, in the pre-James era, as exposition and commentary through the direct intercession of the author; and it would have remained inert.[34]

Henry James, referred to in the criticism, was a *purist* in the sense of avoiding the storyteller's *assertive* statement or intervention through commentary. He went so far as to describe the novels of Tolstoi and Dostoievski as "great fluid puddings." Some readers may (and it is certainly their right) enjoy great fluid puddings rather than pure art. There is, of course, a place for both in the great house of fiction.

Discussion Questions

1. How would you distinguish poetry from prose?
2. What definition would you offer of "heroic" literature?
3. How does the presentation of external nature differ in ancient and modern literature?

4. Can you justify a major psychological difference between heroic and modern literature?
5. In what way did Christianity affect the course of literature?
6. How would you describe the "idealizing" quality of Greek art?
7. What contrasts could you make between the epic and the novel?
8. How did the realistic novel reject the classical idea of "action"?
9. What are some of the modern ideas about the function of the novel?
10. Can the naturalistic novel be said to underrate man?
11. What new areas have been opened by the modern novelist?
12. How would you distinguish vulgarity from immorality?
13. What are the generally popular attractions of narrative?
14. What arguments can be brought forward in support of a narrative's showing rather than telling?
15. What is the place of convention in art?
16. Describe and analyze a great scene from narrative literature of your own selection.
17. How would you distinguish the tragic from the pathetic?
18. What is the secret of creating humor in writing?
19. How would you distinguish humor from wit?
20. Describe and analyze a humorous passage from literature of your selection.
21. Why is "deliberate distortion" so important to the humorist?
22. What is the objective of satire?
23. Describe and analyze an effective satire of your own selection.
24. What is meant by the essay form?
25. What is attractive about the personal essay?
26. What are some of the characteristics of the short story without plot?
27. What are some of the new art forms in the short story?

PART FOUR

Response to Drama

The dramatic form is reached when the vitality which has flowered and eddied round each person fills every person with such vital force that he or she assumes a proper and intangible esthetic life. . . . The esthetic image in the dramatic form is life purified in and reproduced from the human imagination. The mystery of esthetic like that of material creation is accomplished. The artist, like the God of the creation, remains within or behind or beyond or above his handiwork, invisible, refined out of existence, indifferent, paring his fingernails.

JAMES JOYCE

RESPONSE TO DRAMA

The expectation with which we come to drama is a very special one. If we approach poetry primarily with a view to imaginative intuition, prose with a view to an analytical unfolding, we come to drama with the sense of men and women in *action* before our very eyes. It is this sense of action that takes precedence over everything else in drama. Drama may use either imagistic or analytical language, that is, it may be written in either poetry or prose, but *without* action drama does not exist. In fact, as long as there is action, words themselves are not absolutely essential to drama, as the famous French mime Marcel Marceau has shown.

We call such action "mimetic" from a Greek word meaning "imitation" as in our words "mimicry" and "*mimes* and mummers." Drama does not basically *talk* about something; it *shows* something through an action imitated. An actor *pretends* to be someone and pretends to be doing what the pretended person is imaginatively supposed to be doing. Actually in certain primitive dances (which are really dramas), such as those in Africa dealing with the hunt or in our own North American Indian war dance, language is either at a minimum or unimportant. The dance of the hunters presents a mimicry of the preparation for the hunt, of the conflict between the hunters and the hunted, and of the triumph of the hunters in achieving their quest.

We generally delight in any good imitation even if there is no story connected with it. How frequently have we found it highly amusing when someone catches the manner and tone of voice, the idiosyncrasies of someone we know. But such an imitation is limited for its effect to the special few who have knowledge of the person imitated. A good mimic can, of course, reach a wide audience if he imitates well-recognized types or well-known personalities. But for any prolonged mimetic effort that reaches people in general a story is almost indispensable.

Although current experimentation in the theater may modify the general principle (in such plays as Samuel Beckett's *Waiting for Godot* and Jean Giradoux's *The Madwoman of Chaillot*), drama, as it evolved, became dependent on a story line. That is, drama had a beginning, a middle, and an end; and the audience was kept in a state of suspense as to how things might end. The central character had to have at least the *apparent* choice of alternatives. Such suspense is generated, paradoxically enough, even if we know the end of the story ahead of time, as in the case of plays founded on history, legend, and well-known personalities. In this connection let us look at one of the earliest and one of the greatest plays in the history of Western theater, Sophocles' *Antigone.*

Illustration: Action of *Antigone*

You are sitting on a large stone horseshoe looking towards Athens in the afternoon sun. The sky is still a bright blue, the air is slightly chilly though you feel the exhilaration of spring. It is March in the year 450 B.C. It is the day of the religious festival of the Greater Dionysia.

You are looking down on a circular stone stage. To the right of your view is a magnificent and noble statue of the god Dionysus, his form looking placidly, yet alertly, at the open spaces beyond the audience, at the hillside, at the actors in their heroic masks. He is the god of death and resurrection, of the cycle of nature from winter to spring. He symbolizes a kind of religious awe permeating the scene. You feel, though you are sitting under the open sky with ten thousand other spectators, that you are in the midst of a religious ritual in some vast cathedral.

You have always known the story of Antigone, daughter of the ill-starred house of Labdacus. You have sometimes wondered what the story meant in terms of the immortal gods, mortal men, life here and on the other side of the grave where grows the immortal amaranth. Why do certain families stand out so, with their great gifts and ambitions, and yet manage to arouse some enmity from afar? Is it just the ordinary human plight magnified under heroic circumstances? Is it true of everyone that "no one should count his life as gain, until the full story is told. . . ."?[1] Is there any escape from fate? Nobility is to be admired, but sometimes you wonder whether nobility is enough.

And there the noble woman stands, statuesque, poised, self-confident, speaking in clear, ringing tones. Yet what she says, with scarcely a touch of emotion, is terribly sad and drastic. Speaking to her sister, Ismene, she states matter-of-factly: "Nothing painful is there, nothing fraught with ruin, no shame, no dishonor, that I have not seen in thy woes and mine."[2]

And then we remember the oft-told story of the fratricidal war between Eteocles and Polyneices, the sons of Oedipus through an incestuous marriage with his mother Jocasta—a fate which Oedipus had done everything humanly possible to avoid. Eteocles and Polyneices were to rule their heritage, Thebes, each year alternatively. But Eteocles refused to yield the rule when his turn was due. Polyneices, infuriated, returned with his in-laws from Argos (for he had married the daughter of the king of Argos during his year's wanderings) and attacked his native city. One's native city is a sacred place, sacred to one's ancestral gods and to all the gods. Polyneices, though unjustly treated, had committed the greatest of sins—sacrilege toward his own gods. The Argive host did not succeed. Champion against champion at the seven gates of the city were all killed. Eteocles and Polyneices killed each other in the slaughter.

Now Creon, their uncle and successor, inters the body of Eteocles with all public and religious rites but orders the body of Polyneices, the obvious traitor, to be left "unwept, unsepulchred," food for carrion dogs and birds to prey on at will.

This is the order that Antigone will resist. She will steal away from the city and perform the rites for her brother. Will her sister Ismene follow her or not? In short alternative lines the issue is joined. Ismene is timid and conservative, reluctant to defy authority and enter into public affairs. Ismene loves and fears for her sister, but she declines her support. Antigone is obsessed with the moral rather than the human aspects of her problem:

Ismene: Alas, unhappy one! How I fear for thee!
Antigone: Fear not for me: guide thine own fate aright.

The chorus, an integral part of a Greek play, sings and dances, patriotically telling us about the war that raged about the noble city of Thebes. The temples of the gods are to be visited with night-long dance and song—"and may Dionysus be our leader, whose dancing shakes the land of Thebé."

Creon, the king, enters. He has a vivid and rigid political philosophy: "No man can be fully known, in soul and spirit and mind, until he hath been seen versed in rule and law-giving." A messenger brings him news that his edict about leaving the corpse of Polyneices unburied has been defied. He is furious and orders that the culprit be discovered.

As is the custom in Greek plays, the chorus now sings about the status and nature of man:

> Cunning beyond fancy's dream is the fertile skill which brings him, now to evil, now to good. When he honors the laws of the land, and the justice which he hath sworn by the gods to uphold, proudly stands his city: no city hath he who, for his rashness, dwells with sin. Never may he share my hearth, never think my thoughts, who doth these things!

On her second attempt to bury her brother, Antigone is identified and brought into confrontation with the king. Creon gives her a chance to say that she did not know of the law. Her answer deliberately invites trouble: "I knew it: could I help it? It was public." Creon asks her, "And thou didst indeed dare to transgress that law?"

Antigone sets the terms of the conflict in the play. Which takes priority—the laws of the state, aiming at its welfare and military security, or the laws of conscience and religion, its duties transcending the purely temporal order? To Creon's question she responds:

> It was not Zeus that had published me that edict; not such are the laws set among men by the Justice who dwells with the gods below; nor deemed I that thy decrees were of such force, that a mortal could override the unwritten and unfailing statutes of heaven. For their life is not of today or yesterday, but from all time, and no man knows when they were first put forth.

Creon is angered by her open defiance; she has told him that he may be a foolish judge, and, having nothing to live for, she is not afraid of death. His vanity is deeply hurt also by the fact that a woman dares to oppose him. Ismene, after investigation, is absolved from blame. The chorus sings of the curse that has hung over the house of Labdacus for generations.

Haemon, Creon's son and Antigone's betrothed, now has a sharp and excited exchange with his father. Creon takes the totalitarian position—the prime responsibility of the ruler is to do everything for the military protection of the state, and it is the duty of the citizen to render the obedience to the ruler that makes such protection possible. His son has advised Creon that it does a ruler no harm to keep his ear to the ground and find out what the people are really thinking. On this particular case, they are saying that no one deserved her fate less than Antigone. Here again the ideological problem of the play comes into sharp focus:

CREON: Am I to rule this land by other judgment than mine own?
HAEMON: That is no city which belongs to one man.
CREON: Is not the city held to be the ruler?
HAEMON: Thou wouldst make a good monarch of a desert.

Creon condemns Antigone to a kind of death by ordeal. She is to be walled in alive in a rocky cavern with so much food as piety prescribes, and the gods may rescue her if they please. The chorus now sings of the power of love. No immortal can escape it, "nor any among men whose life is for a day." Love may have caused the present crisis—"victorious is the love-kindling light from the eyes of the fair bride; it is a power enthroned in sway beside the eternal laws; for there the goddess Aphrodite is working her unconquerable will."

Actually Antigone has not previously mentioned her betrothal to Haemon. But at this point Sophocles dramatizes the human, the womanly aspect of Antigone. She has seemed too much the woman of uncompromising principle, too much the suffragette, too much the earlier unmellowed Major Barbara of George Bernard Shaw's play. She, the courageous young woman who is looking her last on the sunlight, faces death while the chorus, composed of cautious old men holding on to life, freely advise her. The chorus ironically compliments her on her distinguished death; she will be grouped with goddesses and famous women of legend! Antigone suddenly sees the irony of the situation: "Must you taunt me to my face, O my city?" Our hearts are full of pity for this young woman who has had no song for the crowning of bridals. "Unwept, unfriended, without marriage-song, I am led forth in my sorrow on this journey that can be delayed no more. No longer, hopeless one, may I behold yon day-star's sacred eye; but for my fate no tear is shed, no friend makes moan."

Teiresias, the blind priest, a symbolic figure in a number of Greek plays, now appears. He is the blind man who *sees,* in contrast to the physically sound man who is *spiritually* blind. He warns Creon of how the religious rites are no longer functioning because of the dogs and birds that have tasted human flesh. It is Creon's responsibility because of his refusal to bury Polyneices. He must redress the error at once, for "self-will, we know, incurs the charge of folly." Creon's first response is to attack the priesthood, and he reaches the point of blasphemy when Teiresias prophesies the disasters that hang over Creon's head.

The leader of the chorus now advises Creon to go slowly and reconsider his decision. At last, Creon moves—but too little and too late.

The consequences that Teiresias foretold now occur. Antigone has hanged herself. Haemon rushes on his father, but failing, leans his full weight on his own sword. These events, reported to Eurydice, the wife of Creon, lead in turn to her suicide. Creon is left even more helplessly alone and desolate than was Antigone. "Lead me away, I pray you; a rash, foolish man. . . . I know not which way I should bend my gaze, or where I should seek support."

And the chorus winds up the play with the pronouncement: "Wisdom is the supreme part of happiness; and reverence towards the gods must be inviolate. Great words of prideful men are ever punished with great blows, and, in old age, teach the chastened to be wise."

A great hush falls on the audience at the conclusion of these solemn words. They are the culmination of what in many ways is a religious ritual. Some great thought, over which the audience can brood indefinitely, is the final contribution of the chorus. At the end of *Oedipus the King* we are told that "we must call no one happy who is of mortal race, until he has crossed life's border, free from pain." At the end of *Medea*, "oft do the gods bring things to pass beyond man's expectation; that, which we thought would be, is not fulfilled, while for the unlooked for, good finds out a way. . . ."

"Self-will leads to folly" is a constant underlying theme. Nothing disturbs the basic balance or harmony of life more than the failure to accept good counsel. Overweening self-confidence *(hubris)* leads to faulty judgments, and faulty judgments to a kind of madness *(ate)*. These plays, while saying great things about man, showing his potential nobility, emphasize the limitations he must observe. Men have weaknesses which in a state of *hubris* remain unchecked and are allowed to take over. Creon intended to be a just and good ruler but his personal vanity led him into rashness both with

Antigone and with Teiresias. And in crossing the path of Creon, Antigone might have more easily won her point by diplomacy than by obvious rebellion.

ARISTOTELIAN PRINCIPLES

This is the type of great play from which Aristotle educed the principles of drama in the famed *Poetics*. What are some of the conclusions that Aristotle reached?

First of all there must be *unity of action;* there must be a discernible chain of cause and effect between events in a play. The drama, especially tragedy, is a compressed form of art, and can permit very little of the discursive or the irrelevant. Aristotle, in this matter, considers tragedy a higher form of art than the epic because tragedy is the tensest, most tightly constructed of the arts.[3]

Such unity of action does not mean that the action must consist of one event, though in some rare examples it might do so. We could not say that the death of Antigone is the action of *Antigone*. It is merely one of several events. In later plays, dramatists employ subsidiary plots connected with the mainstream of the action. Nor does unity of action necessarily mean unity of hero. In the tragedy of Antigone it could reasonably be argued that we have two candidates for "hero," Antigone herself and Creon. Because of Antigone's death the focus of dramatic interest shifts to Creon.

Aristotle also thought of the *unities of place and time* as necessary for the drama. The Greek theater was in the open air, visible from an overlooking hillside, and did not have changes of scenery. It was almost inevitable that the unity of place would be observed, not only because of the physical limitations of the theater itself but because of the correlative unity of time. Unity of time meant that what was mimetically presented (events actually imitated by action—not conversational flashbacks or projections) did not exceed the time of a natural day. You could not travel far in one day in classical times, only as far as a horse or your feet could carry you. Unity of time grew out of the early history of the Greek theater. Tragedy developed from funeral orations over the grave of a dead man, and gradually mimetic features were added to it. So tragic action begins on the day of the hero's death; what he does on the last day of his life alone is mimetically presented.

Aristotle had only one kind of drama—the Greek—from which to draw inferences. If he had seen other plays, those of Shakespeare, for example, he would have modified his conclusions. We have many great works of the dramatic art that do not observe the unities of time and place, so we may conclude that they are not essential. On the other hand, unity of action is found in all great drama.

Dramatic Action

Dramatic action parallels the story line in narrative. It begins in a human decision which starts a chain reaction involving other people and their decisions. And normally, such a chain reaction ends in a climactic situation imitating those in real life—marriage (in comedy) or death (in tragedy). This is true of all drama up to the twentieth century, even in such *theme* theater as that of the comedy of ideas (as in Molière) and of the *problem* play (as in Ibsen and Pinero). Even George Bernard Shaw, who tends to subordinate his characters to the social criticism and definitions he wants to offer, is careful to have an amusing story. But in his theater, and in more recent plays, the *state of the question* becomes dramatically more important than the fate of individual characters. And though dramatic action has generally been well defined as a procedure from cause to effect in which the original problem (generally a human one) put forth by the dramatist is given some sort of answer (success or failure, life or death), we have also evolved a type of play which is somewhat like a Socratic discourse, a dialogue to which the dramatist has no definite answer to offer. In effect, he puts the problem in our laps asking, "And what do *you* think?" Though this may not seem obvious, this is also an answer to the dramatist's original problem—that he is unsure, or really doesn't know the answer. It might not satisfy a philosopher or a scientist, but it is sufficient to satisfy the story line of a play.

What are the important aspects of dramatic action as recognized in the history of the theater?

The dramatist, like the storyteller, must first of all identify the environment, the characters, and the general outline of the situation in which they are placed. But in a play this must be done quickly, and always, as far as possible, by action. Of course, some information has to be conveyed by verbal interchange among the characters. Thus it is better technique to *show* a man drunk on the stage, perhaps dropping a bottle or two, than to spend time in *describing* that he is a drunkard. But the widening implications of what the character's drunkenness may mean to his family or to his employer may be indicated in terms of a dramatic dialogue or *foreshadowing* about him.

This part of the play may be described as the *cause* or *exposition* of the action.

Drama, like the novel and the short story, is an *art of conflict.* The key character or characters must find themselves involved in difficulties and oppositions which they want to bend to their will. We, as the audience, become imaginatively identified with this beginning conflict, forming our desires as to the general direction and solution that should take place. This part of a play is called the *growth of the action* or the *rising action.*

Finally the issues are "jelled" and joined—the chips are down and we have the *climax,* the "show-down" of the play. Some decisive act takes place, some decision or final point of view is reached, the consequences of which may be foreseen, but not with absolute certainty. At this point the conflict hits us with the highest tension, with the greatest uncertainty, in which we are emotionally involved. We are gravely concerned as to what course of events may have been set in motion by the climactic act and decision.

Normally the dramatist prolongs this kind of uncertainty. The audience's interest will be deeply held as long as it continues to be actively worried about what may happen. Just as experience in life itself may temporarily dash or raise our hopes, so the dramatist will create a situation in which our fears for the central character or *protagonist* (literally "the one struggling on behalf of") may be temporarily increased, or our hopes diminished. This is known as a reversal of situation or, to use the Aristotelian word, a *peripeteia.* What the dramatist strives to avoid in this part of a play, known as the *falling action* or *consequences,* is any lessening of tension that might lead to *anticlimax,* a situation in which we are no longer sufficiently involved or emotionally concerned.

Eventually a conflict is given a final solution: the protagonist is married or dead, the dramatist has given us his final thought on the problem or thrown it into our laps. For this section of the play we customarily use the term *denouement* or *close of the action.*

These divisions of the dramatic action are present, at least in an informal sense, in any play, whether it is composed of five acts, three acts, or one act. Generally, the traditional five-act play corresponds in its respective acts to the five parts—exposition, growth of action, climax, falling action, denouement. But it is more interesting and instructive to consider the divisions of the dramatic action in terms of a one-act play.

John M. Synge's *Riders to the Sea* is short even for a one-act play, approximately 4,000 words, and fills about six printed pages of two columns. It is a tremendously compressed work of art possessing a stark, austere quality. The setting is extremely simple, the language economical, the characters terse. Yet the play is most poignant.

Illustration: Dramatic Analysis of *Riders to the Sea*

The *exposition* identifies Cathleen and Nora, sisters of Michael who is drowned off the coast of Donegal. They wonder whether a shirt that has been found is his or not. But the main concern of the brief exposition is in reference to an unidentified "she" and her potential reaction to the news. Almost at once the main dramatic interest is focused on the old mother who has lost six of her seven sons to the wild Atlantic, from which they had had to wrest a perilous living. What are her reactions going to be? This is the keynote of the exposition, and the rest of the play is concentrated on her reactions. We wonder whether, as Nora says, "she'll be getting her death . . . with crying and lamenting." The first sentence in the play has told us that she "*may* be sleeping, if she's *able*."

The other characters, however endowed with a compelling simplicity, and however logical, forthright, and drastic in their language, would aid but little in the creation of a great tragedy if the dramatist had not emphasized one character alone to bear the brunt of the conflict and to duel bravely with adversity. Maurya is the protagonist in the play and she pierces the depths of our hearts by her interior nobility. Her suffering becomes great and wins our compassion. But her tense self-control that only breaks momentarily through her sensitivity, her premonition, wins our admiring wonder. Our sympathy for this noble woman is intensified by the contrast between her practical language ("It's a hard thing they'll be saying below if the body is washed up and there's no man in it to make the coffin, and after I giving a big price for the finest white boards you'd find in Connemara.") and the depth of her emotions so rigidly confined within her soul.

Synge in the exposition had sharply conveyed the sense of impending doom awaiting Maurya. Now the *growth of the action* centers around the question whether Bartley, Maurya's last surviving son, will go to Connemara to sell a horse. Maurya asks the question that gets to the heart of the emotional problem in the play: "If it was a hundred horses, or a thousand horses you had itself, what is the price of a thousand horses against a son where there is one son only?" But Bartley's decision to go remains unaltered.

The *climax* of the play begins at the point when Maurya forgets to give Bartley her blessing and his "bit of bread" for the dangerous trip from Aran island to the mainland. "He's gone now, and when the black night is falling, I'll have no son left in the world." The climax terminates when Maurya, expressing unconcern over the identification of the clothes that have been found as Michael's, thinks only of the vision she had seen of the dead Michael following Bartley on the gray pony, of her inability to say "the blessing of God on you," because something choked the words in her throat.

The source of excitement in the falling action lies in the question of whether Maurya's prognostication about her son is going to be fulfilled. It is. "The gray pony knocked him into the sea, and he was washed out where there is a great surf on the white rocks."

In the denouement the body of Bartley is brought in. The craftsmanship of the play is emphasized by the fact that the tension of the play is at this point by no means over, because we still do not know for sure just what Maurya's emotional and psychological reaction will be. What will be her criticism of the lot that life has dealt her? Will she be resentful or deranged, or will her tragic experience enable her to see deeply into the truth of experience? The denouement of the play offers a tense situation in which the mental attitude of the mother is of poignant interest to us. "They are all gone now, and there isn't anything more that the sea can do to me. . . . It isn't that I haven't said prayers in the dark night till you wouldn't know what I would be saying; but it's a great rest I'll have now, and it's time surely."

Synge renders the effect more poignant by a sudden introduction of the practical, the commonplace, which jars and stabs our nerves, when Cathleen and the old man discuss the coffin. "It's a great wonder she wouldn't think of the nails, and all the coffins she's seen already."

This drama approaches heroic literature in the way in which the characters face nature directly. They are in a naked, barren environment, where the struggle for life is the least disguised, the least superficial. The mother's final attitude is one of realism, and yet it shows a universal religious sense similar to that sometimes found in the great Greek tragedies. "Michael has a clean burial in the far north, by the grace of the Almighty God. Bartley will have a fine coffin out of the white boards, and a deep grave surely. What more can we want than that? No man at all can be living forever, and we must be satisfied." This has the kind of tone found at the end of Sophocles' *Antigone:* "Wisdom is the supreme part of happiness; and reverence towards the gods must be inviolate." Defiance rarely arouses the deepest feeling; resignation (though not fatalism) and charity in the face of pitiless (or what appears pitiless) adversity win our souls by the strange power of sincerity.

THE EMOTIONAL POWER OF TRAGEDY

We have spoken elsewhere of Aristotle's theory of catharsis, particularly in relationship to the morality of art.[4] Here we refer to it in regard to certain characteristics of the tragic hero and to the special emotions that tragedy elicits from the audience.

Aristotle refers to the emotions of pity and fear. We have compassion for the hero of the tragedy because the fate that overtakes him is out of proportion, in terms of suffering inflicted, to any punishment he might be deemed to deserve. We experience fear through our identification with the hero; we fear for what may happen to him as the story unfolds; and, when fate has overtaken him, we fear for ourselves, because such a misfortune has overtaken the hero as a representative of all mankind. Perhaps we think that we might deserve a worse fate than the hero in terms of comparative moral attainments. Aristotle rules out the entirely good man as a fit subject for tragedy, because his disastrous end would not cause compassion in us, but rather indignation at the state of things, at the world in general. On the other hand, if the protagonist is a really evil person, we scarcely have any emotional reaction whatsoever. He simply deserved what he got. The personage suitable for tragic treatment is a person who, on the whole, is good but contributes to his own destruction by some fatal *flaw* or weakness. Thus

Aristotle says, "There remains, then, the intermediate kind of personage, a man not preeminently virtuous and just, whose misfortune, however, is brought upon him not by vice and depravity but by some error of judgment."[5]

Aristotle has a further concept, to which more attention should be paid and which helps to explain a certain characteristic of tragedy. A tragic artist, while preserving the *likeness* of a man, should *ennoble* him in the total picture he presents. It is a distinctive feature of tragedy that somehow it touches what is universal and exhilarates rather than depresses. What is destructive and painful seems immediate but passing, while wisdom and reverence remain inviolate and permanent.

Let us consider the character of Romeo in *Romeo and Juliet* in these terms. Romeo is young, enthusiastic, imaginative, and courageous. He is the man who leaps over the wall, defies the impossible, the family feud that now has the status of history. In terms of his own vision, death and danger mean nothing to him:

With love's light wings did I o'erperch these walls;
For stony limits cannot hold love out,
And what love can do, that dares love attempt.

(II, ii, 66–68)

When his circumstances permit him to be affirmative, he sees life in terms of grandeur, space, nobility:

. . . for thou art
As glorious to this night, being o'er my head,
As is a winged messenger of heaven
Unto the white-upturned wond'ring eyes
Of mortals that fall back to gaze on him
When he bestrides the lazy-pacing clouds
And sails upon the bosom of the air.

(II, ii, 26–32)

He is at once civilized and uninhibited, free and noble:

. . . wert thou as far
As that vast shore wash'd with the farthest sea,
I would adventure for such merchandise.

(II, ii, 133–135)

He has evoked a similar grandeur in Juliet, who expresses love in its grandest, most universal sense:

My bounty is as boundless as the sea,
My love as deep; the more I give to thee,
The more I have, for both are infinite.

(II, ii, 133–135)

Juliet expresses one of the great Greek perceptions about goodness (bounty), that goodness goes out of itself, freely gives, is creative without any diminution of its own vitality.

Romeo has the quality that medieval writers signified by "magnificence." If Shakespeare had not been careful to introduce another aspect into the characterization of Romeo, we would have a story of a completely noble person who comes to a disastrous end. We would not have had a tragedy. So Shakespeare almost goes out of his way to emphasize a tragic flaw in Romeo, a flaw that is inextricably mixed up and combined with his magnificence. Though Romeo tries to impose a tight control on himself, his recklessness breaks forth—a recklessness almost inseparable from his youth and drive. Ironically he tries to put a stop to the family feud when it breaks out again in the form of a duel between Mercutio and Tybalt. The intervention makes it physically possible for Tybalt to kill Mercutio. Then Romeo, in righteous indignation, kills Tybalt, and as a consequence he is banished from Verona. Given his temperament, only a superhuman control could have saved him in such a situation.

Apparently Shakespeare does not feel that the tragic flaw so dramatized is sufficiently convincing. So he presents Romeo in a hysterical interview with Friar Laurence. The Friar is an elderly man, a bachelor, a scientist, a man almost inevitably calm; whereas Romeo is young, newly married, a poet, a man now agitated and in torment. The Friar advises "Adversity's sweet milk, philosophy," and Romeo responds, "Hang up philosophy/Unless philosophy can make a Juliet." Romeo becomes so distraught with the idea of his banishment that he attempts suicide and is restrained by the Friar who calms him down by a fearful outbreak of indignation at his sudden immaturity ("Hold thy desperate hand. Art thou a man?"). This suicide attempt is a foreshadowing of what actually happens.

In Mantua Romeo buys poison from an apothecary on receiving the false news of Juliet's death. His recklessness is such that he does not notice anything strange about Juliet's death even when his own words might indicate it:

. . . Beauty's ensign yet
Is crimson in thy lips and in thy cheeks,
And death's pale flag is not advanced there.

(V, iii, 94–96)

Other elements enter the denouement besides Romeo's fatal flaw of recklessness. There is the fact of accident—Friar Laurence's inability to get a message through to Romeo in time. But even this obstacle could have been overcome had not Romeo already developed the propensity to suicide.

This is certainly a serious or fatal flaw, but the interesting thing is that it does not lessen our impression of Romeo's *nobility*. Romeo's permanent substratum of a great personality is only superficially compromised by waverings and psychological weaknesses. Romeo consigns himself to death—but what *is* death in the context of the drama? It is also an assertion of eternal love and fidelity:

. . . Shall I believe
That unsubstantial death is amorous,
And that the lean abhorred monster keeps
Thee here in dark to be his paramour?
For fear of that I still will stay with thee
And never from this palace of dim night
Depart again. Here, here will I remain
With worms that are thy chambermaids. O, here
Will I set up my everlasting rest
And shake the yoke of inauspicious stars
From this world-wearied flesh.

(V, iii, 102–112)

It is in this kind of conflict, or paradox, that the emotional power of tragedy lies. We pity and we fear, but we feel, however indirectly, that in spite of everything to the contrary, something noble and permanent has been established. Somehow, love of the quality that

Romeo and Juliet have exhibited is not really dead; it is not really in the hands of "unsubstantial" death. For love has the *substance,* not death. And, in Shakespeare's play, the first creative fruit of such *undying* love is the reconciliation of the two feuding houses. We, of course, say to ourselves at the end of *Romeo and Juliet,* "If we could only have changed things a bit, if we could only have given Romeo a better sense of balance when he needed it—if experience only had less misunderstandings, less accidents!" But we also instinctively feel that a precious universal value has been established.

THE WORLD OF COMEDY

English drama is particularly rich in humor, and satire is by no means uncommon to it.

Comedy appeals to our sense of the incongruous, to our perceiving emphatic deviations from what at any given time we consider normal, appropriate, or decorous.

In this sense, comedy primarily appeals to our evaluating sense, to our intelligence. As an audience we have a greater sense of detachment than in the case of tragedy; we identify less, we are less emotionally involved.

In medieval religious drama, our earliest English drama, the playwright felt freest when he dealt with the comic. Otherwise, he felt compelled to follow the literal dramatization of scripture. A typical situation is that of Noah persuading his wife to cooperate with him in the building of the Ark. Noah is a very serious, pious man deeply concerned with carrying out the Lord's instructions to the letter. But Noah's wife considers his whole plan preposterous. She wants nothing of it and prefers to tipple among her "gossips" in the local alehouse. Noah tries prayer, gentle persuasion, sweetness and light, but to no avail. Then we have the humorous deviation from the norm, the deviation from a convention suitable to Noah's personality and character. This pious, gentle man threatens his wife with physical violence; he will beat her up unless she hurries her fat self into the Ark. And now, as often in the method of humor, we have a deviation based upon a deviation. His wife says in effect, "All right, Noah, let's see you do it!" And the audience is under the impression that Noah may very well get the worse of it.

However, virtue wins in the end, and Mrs. Noah, with assorted children and in-laws, marches into the Ark along with the selected animals.

In the earlier history of the drama, what we call *situation* is basic—more important than wit and brilliant dialogue. The ancient dramatist who influenced renaissance comedy most was Plautus; in fact, his influence has never declined. Plautus's stock-in-trade is the theme of mistaken identity—the confusions generated by a known and unknown twin in the same city, as in *The Menaechmi* (imitated with further complications in Shakespeare's *Comedy of Errors*). An advantage of this kind of drama is that a denouement is readily available. Once the true relationship, previously unknown to the characters in the play, is revealed in a *recognition scene,* all the confusions and misunderstandings are understood and resolved. Once the twins appear simultaneously on the stage, everything is explained. Plautus is also the source of the *stock* characters that, varying with different cultural conditions at various times, have always been a staple of the comic theater. Plautus is not a romantic and he writes of moral standards in his own time, so the young woman in his plays is generally a courtesan. She is pursued by a lover who is somewhat witless and easily votable as "the man least likely to succeed." But he does win in the end, through the ingenuity of a very clever servant (the Messenio of *The Menaechmi,* the Dorine of Molière's *Tartuffe,* the Jeeves of the P. G. Wodehouse stories), a master of know-how and of intrigue. Other standard characters, prototypes of the *comedy of humors* of the renaissance, are the old man who is primarily funny because he has outlived his biological prowess (but what a gay young blade he has been), the parasite who lives at his master's expense and is jealous of his relationships with other people (Peniculus in *The Menaechmi,* Matthew Merrygreek in *Ralph Roister Doister,* Mosca in *Volpone,* who is also the smart servant), and other types such as the braggart, the miser, and the veteran.

This comedy of situation and of mistaken identity continues right through the history of the English stage, giving such brilliant productions as *She Stoops to Conquer* (where the mistaken identification scene concerns Miss Hardcastle in her dual role of a fine lady and a barmaid) and *The School for Scandal* (in spite of outward appearances, which is the decent brother—Charles or Joseph Surface?). In these plays a close correlation exists between actual types in English society and the original prototypes in Plautus—the good host (Mr. Hardcastle) with the old man; the faithful family retainer (Rowley) with the Plautine slave; the pompous poet (Sir Benjamin Backbite) with the braggart, and so on.

An important departure from the ancient classics lies in what is termed *romantic comedy*. This permits a serious and noble love affair often in terms of lofty poetic sentiment, which we meet in Shakespeare's plays such as *As You Like It, Twelfth Night,* and *The Winter's Tale.* The good and handsome young man seeking the hand of the virtuous maiden becomes a standard story line on which comedy is built, even satirical comedy as in the case of *The School for Scandal.* Many of Gilbert and Sullivan's operettas are outstanding satires, but running through them all is this basic story of pure and tender love.

Various forms of comedy have descriptive labels that indicate the theme of the play rather than any important difference in its structure. We thus speak of the "comedy of manners"—the sort of thing written in England by Congreve and Wycherley—which is concerned with deviations from standard norms of behavior, dress, and etiquette in a specific segment of society. We have the *comedy of humors* in Ben Jonson's day which basically deals with types in the fashion of Plautus but is also related to specific Elizabethan ideas about psychology. A humor is a kind of fixed mental attitude which may be determined by sex, age, or profession. While one is in "one's humor," nothing can be done to shake one out of it. A humor is an inflexible obsession, and therefore, a departure from common sense —therefore, basic material for comedy

The *comedy of ideas* is a comparatively recent development, although it had already been foreshadowed by the theater of Molière, to whom George Bernard Shaw, its outstanding practitioner, is greatly indebted for his comic techniques. In this case, a social thesis is driven home often by showing the ridiculous side of traditionally accepted ideas and conventions. George Bernard Shaw, not content with driving home his points in the actual plays, also writes long and interesting prefaces outlining his ideas. The remarkable thing about Shaw's plays is that they retain their liveliness in spite of the danger that his ideas may have become socially deemphasized and outmoded (a very real danger in this kind of theater).

He remains interesting and amusing even to those readers who disagree with the soundness of his assumptions.

THE PROBLEM OF TRAGICOMEDY

We have what we may call *pure* forms of drama in tragedy and comedy which are easily identifiable. But we can also have what may appear to be a mixed form, or even a distinct genre. A term frequently used for this kind of play is *tragicomedy.*

The phrase was at one time used to indicate the introduction of comical elements into a tragic situation, a practice common enough in the Elizabethan drama but contrary to the prescripts of classical Greek drama. Thus Samuel Johnson said that "Shakespeare's plays are not in the rigorous sense either tragedies or comedies, but compositions of a distinct kind; exhibiting the real state of sublunary nature, which partakes of good and evil, joy and sorrow, mingled with endless variety of proportion and innumerable modes of combination; and expressing the course of the world, in which the loss of one is the gain of another; in which at the same time, the reveller is hasting to his wine, and the mourner burying his friend. . . ."[6] This sort of thing has more frequently been called *comic relief*—a term deriving its reputation from Thomas De Quincey's famous essay, "On the Knocking at the Gate in *Macbeth,*" in which it is shown that the comic element does not lessen tragic tension but increases it. The episode of the drunken porter after Macbeth's murder of Duncan gives a momentary relief in the sense of a change of pace, but it is like a deceptive reassurance that has been found to be false. If we forget the seriousness of the murder for a moment, we then come back to it with an increased awareness of what it means because of the comic contrast itself.

In a more technical sense the word "tragicomedy" refers to a type of play in which there are two mingled plots, one of which ends unhappily, and one of which ends happily. Sometimes the relationship between the two plots is comparatively loose as in some of the plays of Beaumont and Fletcher, prominent practitioners of this form.

There is still another possible extension of the term. Some plays move in a tragic direction although they have a comic termination. If Molière had kept to the inherent logic of his play *Tartuffe,* the religious hypocrite Tartuffe would have ridden high in the saddle and the deceived Orgon and everyone else would have been under his thumb. At the last moment, the King's discovery of his duplicity, a *deus ex machina* device ("the god from the machine"—referring to an automatic windup of a dramatic situation by an outside agency, originally supernatural, independently of the interior logic of the play), foils Tartuffe. Similarly in *The Misanthrope,* the hero, who loves solitude and sincerity and maintains an uncompromising integrity away from the corrupting influence of the court, fails to persuade and win the girl he loves, who takes a less ideal and more realistic position. *The Misanthrope* is not a comedy in that it does not end joyfully in marriage; it would also stretch the term to call it a tragedy, for the hero is alive and kicking, pursuing his program of integrity.

Tragicomedy, as a rather loose and extended term, points to a dilemma that we inherited from Greek classical drama once it was adapted to a Judaic-Christian tradition. The Greek drama was written before the Christian concept of Providence had brought a certain kind of hope to the world. The fact of death seemed very final to the pagans. But the otherworldly view of Christianity brought a new dimension to the traditional conclusion of tragedy. Death is viewed less as a finality than as a transformation. A play, let us say, dealing with the death of Christ could hardly be classified as tragic, for, though the sufferings of Christ were real, his death meant the possibility of redemption for all. Actually, in a truly Christian civilization death would lose its terrors. On the other hand, we could scarcely classify such a play as a comedy. Or to take a subject matter on a smaller scale, how would we classify *Riders to the Sea?* The principal character, Maurya, suffers intensely, but she reconciles herself to the situation, and is calm and alive at the end of the play.

The force of tradition is these matters is very strong, but obviously classical tradition does not cover every possibility in the drama. In Christian tradition, death does not constitute a disaster. It is, rather, *moral evil* that constitutes disaster. A play dealing with Sir Thomas More could hardly be tragic, for Sir Thomas More joked about death and did not object to dying. If he didn't mind, we can scarcely worry about it. Should we call such a play a comedy because it reveals the joyousness of martyrdom? Conversely, a play in which moral evil retains the upper hand might be classified as tragic even if no one dies. Obviously, in this connection, there are still some open-ended problems about the drama.

OTHER FORMS OF DRAMA

Melodrama and farce, while they have often constituted very successful shows, have not really had a place in the serious study of the drama.

Melodrama is not basically good drama because it exploits the emotions of an unsophisticated audience by scenes of horror, pathos, and last-minute rescues, outside a convincing chain of cause and effect. A more sophisticated audience may find melodrama hilarious. The characters do not observe Aristotle's tragic-flaw principle. They are strictly black and white; the villain is all evil; the heroine all virtue. But melodrama would not have succeeded as it has without some positive merits. It may have strong, bold outlines of plot and action even if it is uncritically violent.

Farce is pure "situation." Custard pies fly in all directions. The whole universe concentrates in the bedroom or the Turkish bath; doors open in all directions; everybody is running down corridors; trousers split and dresses are torn. Like melodrama, it has the merit of vivid action. In the hands of capable performers, like Charlie Chaplin or Laurel and Hardy, it can become a kind of art. In many ways it resembles a form of comedy known in classical times as the *old* comedy.[7] The old comedy demands almost complete detachment on the part of the audience. We view the main character derisively, as a sharper, crook, or buffoon, though he may be set in conflict with even more objectionable specimens than himself. Ben Jonson's *Volpone* is something on this order, crook cheating and outwitting crook. We do not identify with anybody; our interest is restricted to the absurdity of the situation.

EXPRESSIONISM IN THE THEATER

Literary changes in the theater have paralleled other developments, particularly those of the novel. The development of realism as a literary theory, for example, affected the dramatist's choice of a central character. Thus the man of high station and power, the protagonist of Greek and Elizabethan drama, was replaced by the common man in everyday surroundings. Such is the emphasis in the theater of such playwrights as Henrik Ibsen or Anton Chekhov.

Stress is placed on logical and plausible plotting and on realistic stage settings. The naturalist, stressing documentary fidelity, obviously could not be as free on the stage as in the novel. He differed from the realist not so much in technique as in the type of his subject matter, in the exposure of depravity and the seamy side of life, as in Maxim Gorki's *The Lower Depths. Expressionism* was even more creative in its departure from previous convention.

The expressionist dramatist struggled with a special problem: how to get inside the mind of the protagonist and show *his* view of the world dramatically, making the stage and other characters reflect his own views. Thus on Shakespeare's stage a drunkard would see the other characters from his own point of view, but the characters themselves would retain their true identity before the audience. The problem in expressionism would be to conceive of a scene showing the other characters as the drunkard would see them while he is drunk—a chorus of pink elephants, perhaps! This means that the various characters in a play are no longer on the same dramatic level of presentation. Only the principal is a character in his own right; the other characters are at least partly projections of his own mind. The audience would see them only through the eyes of the drunkard seeing them. Famous examples of this kind of play are Eugene O'Neill's *The Emperor Jones* and Elmer Rice's *The Adding Machine.* Brutus Jones in O'Neill's play drives away each of his menacing visions with a revolver shot. The structure of the play is virtually a monologue set against the continuous throb of tom-toms. Brutus has saved a silver bullet with which to shoot himself, but he is ironically shot by others. In *The Adding Machine*, Elmer Rice depicts the vision of a mechanical world as seen by a carefully named entity in it, Mr. Zero. Such expressionistic techniques were useful in stressing a certain essentiality within a limited area of theme, but they did so at the cost of being one-dimensional. Expressionism attempted to do something very difficult to accomplish in the theater. The outward dramatization of a character's interior state of mind is difficult enough in the conventional theater. Shakespeare succeeded magnificently, in the more conservative norms of his times, in showing dramatically an inward psychological situation in the great scene in *Othello* where Iago comes to dominate and pervert Othello's mind (III, iii), but Shakespeare added to the resources of the theater the power of great poetry. His success is as largely verbal as it is strictly dramatic. The complexity of dramatizing outwardly on the stage *several* characters (not just a Brutus Jones or a Mr. Zero) who view the others through their own distorted lenses can hardly be imagined, even less mastered. Such an art, limited as it is to one principal character such as the Emperor Jones or the protagonist of *The Adding Machine,* is episodic, a series of incidents like that of dream sequences held in certain unity by the playwright's monolithic idea or message. It can be occasionally effective, but it is obviously a limited genre.

THE THEATER OF THE ABSURD

Expressionism has some technical affinity with what today has been called the Theater of the Absurd. The dramatist's psychological point of view in the Theater of the Absurd, however, differs essentially from that of the expressionist. The expressionist was intent on giving an overt message. The Theater of the Absurd rejects all messages, but often uses the technique of dramatizing outwardly one man's view of the world, everything on the stage merely reflecting that man's pair of eyes.

The Theater of the Absurd is a type of dramatic art that has come into prominence in recent years and has led to a good deal of discussion and controversy. Is it a major breakthrough in the dramatic art, or is it merely a sign of a certain contemporary malaise? Drama has traditionally been thought of in terms of moral choice—consequently, of free will, actual or supposed. It has been thought of in terms of a plausible chain of cause and effect. But the Absurdists ask whether there is any free will, any real chain of cause and effect in life. Are cause and effect simply projections of our wishful thinking? An Aristotelian is apt to be surprised that anyone would be bold enough to create ("construct" might not be the right word from the point of view of the Absurdists) a play, ignoring moral evaluation and causality. But the fact is that it has been done, and audiences have been responsive.

One critic has put his finger on what may be the central truth about the Theater of the Absurd.

> In the conventional theater the action always proceeds toward a definable end. The spectators do not know whether that end will be reached and how it will be reached. Hence, they are in suspense, eager

> to find out *what* will happen. In the Theater of the Absurd, on the other hand, the action does not proceed in the manner of a logical syllogism. It does not go from A to B but travels from an unknown preface X toward an unknowable conclusion Y.[8]

The audience, it is pointed out, cannot be in suspense about what is going to happen, because they have no idea of what the dramatist is driving at. What interests them is whether what happens next will add to, or make possible, their understanding of the play. The spectators are in suspense, not in regard to what will happen to the characters, but as to what the play may mean. Since the dramatist never lets them know, if *he* knows, the audience can carry their suspense home with them for further speculation.

This has been a tendency in certain forms of the modern novel, as illustrated by Franz Kafka (whose novels have also been dramatized), as well as in the theater. The phrase "Kafkaesque situation" has, at least temporarily, passed into the language. The meaning of *The Castle* was a standard topic of literary conversation for some years, and such a range of interpretations were offered over the years that the matter seems now in abeyance. Kafka succeeded in making us uneasy about prevailing rationalism. He stressed the sense of man's plight in what seemed to be an unpredictable and irrational environment and managed at the same time to create a sense of wonder as well as of the absurd. He could hardly be called a pessimist, though he cut the ground out from under all previous sentimentality. He succeeded in conveying the message that our happiness must have a far more mysterious meaning than anything that is suggested by our convenient categories.

The Theater of the Absurd has gone much farther, and not in the direction that Kafka would necessarily have taken. Samuel Beckett, Arthur Adamov, and Eugene Ionesco reject both realism and naturalism, not as conservative but as irrelevant. The naturalists felt that no literary picture could be real unless it did full justice to the unpleasant side of life; the Absurdists often find no meaning in life at all. Indeed it often seems a tale told by an idiot. They do not, like the naturalists, offer accuracy of description. They often doubt the possibility of any communication by language, and their plays often feature the bizarre and the fantastic. Often dialogue, because of its presumed essential meaninglessness, is at cross purposes and in direct contrast with what is going on in the play.

They make a case for their art as *pure* art. Like many contemporary novelists and poets, they do away with rhetoric, and, quite frequently, with any framework of conceptual rationality. A sympathetic interpreter argues that the Absurdists do not reject all meaning, that they mirror aspects of society as we know them today, the basic absurdity of most of our objectives.

> If the dialogue in these plays consist of meaningless clichés, circular repetition of stereotyped phrases—how many meaningless clichés and stereotyped phrases do we use in our day-to-day conversation? If the characters change their personality halfway through the action, how consistent and truly integrated are the people we meet in our real life? And if people appear in these plays as mere marionettes, helpless puppets without any will of their own, passively at the mercy of blind fate and meaningless circumstances, do we, in fact, in our over-organized world, still possess any genuine initiative or power to decide our own destiny? The spectators of the Theater of the Absurd are thus confronted with a grotesquely heightened picture of their own world: a world without faith, meaning, and genuine freedom of the will. In this sense, the Theater of the Absurd is the true theater of our time.[9]

As in the claims sometimes made for symbol and myth, it is asserted that this theater has meaning only in the sense that its meaning is what one wants to make it. One critic interprets Samuel Beckett's *Waiting for Godot* as an image of man searching for relationship—with himself, with his fellow men, and with his God—"only to shatter this image by questioning the validity of the quest. Is there, after all, any ultimate and objective truth? How can we know it? Is it possible that we may be wrong? Is it true for all of us? Prove it! Why bother? In short, what's the use of living anyway?"[10]

These are painful attitudes that may provoke sympathy, pity, or fear in an audience, but not catharsis. For implicit in catharsis is the idea of the possibility of the restoration of health, of a redemptive force. It is very possible that the Theater of the Absurd will not create great art (though it has provided a sensation), but rather, as many think, a new idiom and a new technique which may prove useful in other directions than that of themes of basic pessimism.

Discussion Questions

1. With what expectation do we come to drama?
2. What is essential to drama?
3. What are some characteristics of a Greek tragedy?
4. What is the relationship of *hubris* to *ate* in a Greek tragedy?
5. What are some of the main Aristotelian principles in regard to drama?
6. What was meant by the three unities?
7. What are the requirements of dramatic action?
8. What are the traditional divisions of the dramatic action?
9. Analyze the theme and development of one great play of your own selection.
10. Why are pity and fear appropriate emotional responses for the art of tragedy?
11. What requirements does Aristotle make for the tragic hero?
12. Present an analysis of the "tragic flaw" in any tragic hero of your own selection.
13. How does comedy differ in its emotional appeal from tragedy?
14. What is meant by the comedy of "situation"?
15. What is meant by romantic comedy?
16. What is characteristic of the following types of comedy: the comedy of manners, the comedy of humors, the comedy of ideas?
17. What is meant by tragicomedy?
18. What is meant by melodrama?
19. What characterizes farce?
20. Describe and analyze any play which you have seen recently that seems particularly effective to you.
21. What is meant by expressionism in the theater?
22. What characterizes the Theater of the Absurd?

PART FIVE

The Criticism of Literature

Criticism should not be querulous and wasting, all knife and root-puller, but guiding, instructive, inspiring, a south wind, not an east wind.

RALPH WALDO EMERSON

APPROACH TO CRITICISM

Criticism can be approached in a variety of ways. Different periods of literary history have been characterized by different emphases and presuppositions. Literature is to teach and delight; literature is to hold up the mirror to nature in different ways; literature is to reflect the generic and idealized norms of universal experience; literature is to excite us by ecstatic vision; literature is to reveal the intensity of the artist's inner psyche; literature is to tell us the facts of life within a controlled artistic form; literature is to give us a scientific account of man's behavior; literature is to be a slice of life itself without the personal intervention of the artist.

These are a few of the main views, and criticism itself reflects this range and variety. In this book we are particularly concerned with what the reader can obtain from literature for his own emotional and psychic growth. Literature is not viewed as a body of organized knowledge or primarily as an academic discipline. One critic argues that great works of art do not "improve" on one another. What improves with the passing of time is "the comprehension of them, and the refining of society which results from it. It is the consumer, not the producer, who benefits by culture, the consumer who becomes humanized and liberally educated." A book, in one sense, is simply a stack of paper, covered with hieroglyphic dots, standing stagnant between covers. Only a reader awakens it to life.

As far as the development of personal response is concerned, one has to start with what one sincerely feels and sees. This does not necessarily mean that one is going to do justice to the work; nor should this be alarming, for even the most sensitive criticism is not necessarily complete, and all criticism is subject to verification by others. As one writer comments,

> We still need to face up to the full consequences of the realization that criticism is not a physical, nor even a psychological, science. By setting out from and terminating in an appeal to the facts, any good aesthetic theory is, indeed, empirical in method. Its aim, however, is not to establish correlations between facts which will enable us to predict the future by reference to the past, but to establish principles enabling us to justify, order, and clarify our interpretation and appraisal of the aesthetic facts themselves.[1]

THE CRITIC: JUDGE OR INTERPRETER?

There have always been two main views concerning the function of a critic. One view would make the critic primarily a judge; the other would make him primarily an interpreter.

One point of view has roughly corresponded to the neoclassical approach, the other partly to the Romantic, in the formal or artistic sense of this word. The *New Criticism* in some respects resembles that of the major Romantic critics (such as Coleridge or Hazlitt) in that it concentrates on the individual work of art, but it places more emphasis on detailed examination and verification, less on the critic's personal feelings. However, these are only approximations, and it is best to think of these two types of criticism as the criticisms of *judgment* and the criticism of *interpretation*. Actually, of course, the neoclassicist approach has suffered in literary history from an overconservative outlook. Comparatively few classical critics (Matthew Arnold and Sainte-Beuve are exceptions) have had sufficient breadth of outlook to see the eternal principles of art as divorced from mechanical or conventional adaptations of these principles. A neoclassical critic could conceivably be sensitive to new techniques and methods and could see the permanent principles of art even in unfamiliar forms. But unfortunately such a type of critic has not often appeared.

The history of criticism reveals that it has been as difficult for the general reading public to recognize the significance of criticism, as it has been for the public to accept at once an entirely original work of art. It is not till quite recently that we have learned that it is misleading to apply preconceived rules to a new work of art. Too often in the past the critic completely misunderstood the spirit of a work of art as a whole if it were expressed in a form unfamiliar to him. Nowadays some of the neoclassical critics seem somewhat naïve, but their power once could drive Keats to say (he refers to the laws laid down by Boileau and Pope, Boileau's chief English representative):

Could all this be forgotten? Yes, a schism
Nurtured by foppery and barbarism,
Made great Apollo blush for this his land.
Men were thought wise who could not understand
His glories; with a puling infant's force

They sway'd about upon a rocking horse,
And thought it Pegasus. Ah dismal soul'd!
The winds of heaven blew, the ocean roll'd
Its gathering waves—ye felt it not. The blue
Bar'd its eternal bosom, and the dew
Of summer nights collected still to make
The morning precious: beauty was awake!
Why were ye not awake? But ye were dead
To things ye know not of,—were closely wed
To musty laws lined out with wretched rule
And compass vile: so that ye taught a school
Of dolts to smooth, inlay and clip and fit
Till, like the certain wands of Jacob's wit,
Their verse tallied. Easy was the task:
A thousand handicraftsmen wore the mask
Of Poesy. Ill-fated, impious race!
That blasphemed the bright Lyrist to his face,
And did not know it,—no, they went about,
Holding a poor, decrepit standard out,
Marked with most flimsy mottoes, and in large
The name of one Boileau!

("Sleep and Poetry," 181–206)

The neoclassical school obviously was offensive to a fresh and enthusiastic poet like Keats. Pope, for example, demanded in poetry the expression of only the general and the essential. He says, for example:

First follow Nature; and your judgment frame
By her just standard, which is still the same.[2]

By "nature" Pope meant what the French classical critic, Boileau, called *la nature raisonable* (reasonable nature). Often both in Boileau and Pope nature is made equivalent to reason, comprising on its positive side sequence and discipline, on its negative side impersonality and lack of passion. This kind of reason (more properly, rationalism) must have sovereign sway in every form of literature, according to the neoclassicist:

At once the source, and end, and test of art.[3]

Of course, the warfare between poets and critics is an antique heritage. Matthew Arnold's conception of the critical power as making "an intellectual situation of which the creative power can profitably avail itself"[4] has been realized only occasionally in the history of literature.

The old-fashioned neoclassical critics, critics of judgment, insisted on telling us what a work of art *should be*. They were not interested in looking at a work of art and seeing *what it was*. They insisted reasonably enough that poetry should afford pleasure, but they demanded what they themselves considered pleasure, and not necessarily the pleasure that a particular work of art itself provided. A poet, if he were to be accepted, had to abide by their preconceptions. The poet could not really be himself. The eighteenth century tended to regard Shakespeare as a barbarian even when it was granted that he possessed genius. And Shakespeare is only one of the more prominent victims of neoclassical criticism.

Historically, the critic of judgment has too seldom managed to escape the influence of the early educational training that led him to have too narrow a conception of form. He has tended to confuse, to use Coleridge's words, "mechanic" form with "organic" form:

> The form is mechanic, when on any given material we impress a pre-determined form, not necessarily arising out of the properties of the material;—as when to a mass of wet clay we give whatever shape we wish it to retain when hardened. The organic form, on the other hand, is innate; it shapes, as it develops, itself from within, and the fullness of its development is one and the same with the perfection of its outward form. Such as the life is, such is the form.[5]

The canons of the criticism of judgment depend on Horace's misconception of Aristotle's definition of art (Aristotle said that art is a heightened or a selective imitation of life). Horace advised the writer to keep to the norm of a class and not attempt a perhaps impossible and certainly dangerous individuality. George Saintsbury analyzes the contribution of Horace, the spiritual ancestor of Boileau and Pope, to literary criticism thus: "In short, the false mimesis—imitation of previous art—is mixing itself up more and more with the true mimesis, representation of nature."[6]

Now where we have the false mimesis we judge a work of art by predetermined rules. But if we have a true mimesis, it appears absurd to judge by such rules. In art it is the result that matters, and the method by which the result is obtained is irrelevant to the value of that result. Of course, the penetrating critic will always be interested in the mechanism of an artistic achievement, but his interest is dispassionate, impersonal, and scientific. He will not judge the mechanism of creation except in the light of the result.

What is overlooked in this criticism of judgment is that tradition is important, not for the purpose of imitation but as *analogy*. A writer can learn richly from the techniques of the past, but he has to incorporate his discoveries in the manner that suits his own sense of organic form.

THE DUAL CHARACTER OF CRITICISM

The function of criticism has often been misunderstood because criticism possesses a dual character. *It is both a science and an art.*

Viewed in this light, since literature is directly a mimesis of life, criticism should directly be a mimesis of *literature*. Criticism, therefore, should in this sense reflect the work of art with which it deals. This reflection is built up by a scientific analysis of particulars in a given work of art, but, *since a critic is also a creative artist,* he combines with his scholarly concentration on minute points the ability of an artist to make vivid the beauty in the reality he sees, which we may not always have the mental acumen to observe for ourselves. Great criticism owes much to the inner power peculiar to great artists that enables them to integrate outward things into finished wholes. This particular world, which the artist-critic creates in his criticism, is in itself complete. If we consider the subject matter of the critic as a macrocosm, or great world, we can legitimately call the critic's creation a microcosm, the minute and concentrated representation of the greater world. The microcosm is related to, yet independent of, the macrocosm.

The function of criticism, then, might be defined as the interpretation of art by *mimesis,* or the selective imitation of literature. A great critic will automatically reflect in his criticism the spirit of the work of art as a whole which he criticizes. Of course, much criticism has to be written concerning failures in art, in which there is little of value to reflect. A critic, even then, by following the method of scientific particulars, can reflect with appropriate effect the emptiness of the alleged work of art without assuming the function of a judge. The critic's judgment is implicit, to be inferred, rather than delivered as a pronouncement.

In the interpretation of a work of art, a critic should set himself certain questions that should be answered before undertaking the writing of his criticism. He should first try to answer the question: What *is* the work of art? As Walter Pater once said:

> "To see the object as in itself it really is," has been justly said to be the aim of all true criticism whatever; and in aesthetic criticism the first step towards seeing one's object as it really is, is to know one's own impression as it really is, to discriminate it, to realize it distinctly. The objects with which aesthetic criticism deals—music, poetry, artistic and accomplished forms of human life—are indeed receptacles of so many powers or forces; they possess, like the products of nature, so many virtues or qualities.[7]

Second, the critic, pursuing the method of a scientist, particularly should ask *how* the work of art (the novel, the poem) is what it is. He should check his first reaction to the question, *what* is the work of art, by the facts he uncovers in the investigation of the second question. In the course of such an investigation he may have to change, or in some way modify, the first impression he obtained of the work. Since any critic must start with a first impression, it is only fair both to himself and the artist that he regard this as tentative.

Although knowledge of the artist's actual intention as it is revealed through personal documents and letters is relevant, it should be viewed with reserve. An artist's original design may be considerably altered in the act of execution. Milton said that his objective in *Paradise Lost* was to "justify the ways of God to men." He achieved a great work of art, but it is debatable whether he succeeded in this overt purpose. Frequently an artist achieves something different from what he believes he has achieved. Sometimes the artist's judgment is wrong in regard to his own work. Milton preferred *Paradise Regained* to *Paradise Lost.*

The critic in conscientiously meeting these two questions proceeds empirically, and according to the method of interpretation. The critic should by this time have seen the work of art in its individuated light. Every great work of art is unique and does not submit to mechanical comparisons with other works of art. It is true that in a deep sense there are certain qualities present in all great works of art which give them a common bond, but a work of art is a creation in a concrete context and it has a vivid individuality that is never reproduced again in the same way.

Only after the critic has examined the work of art in this light should he proceed to the processes of judgment. Actually it is possible to write quite a satisfactory criticism without making a specific judgment, by merely letting the facts speak for themselves. But in some cases judgment may be required, and in this case the critic may have to decide whether an alleged work of art was worth creating in the first place and whether such a work exercises sound moral, political, and social influence.

It has also to be remembered in this context that literature is a relevant study even when its material can be considered artistically somewhat deficient. Literature provides material for the assessment of cultural forces and of historical perspective. The relationship of literature to cultural history involves a criticism of judgment as well as a criticism of interpretation. But this fact should be kept separable from the principle of criticism as applied to the disciplined study of an individual work of art.

MORAL CRITICISM

A certain subtlety is required on the part of the critic in determining the morality of a work of art. When an artist uses irony, he deliberately omits a criterion of moral judgment; in fact, makes it conspicuous by its absence. In following this method, the artist may continuously imply a standard which he never explicitly states. It is possible in following this method of irony to write a profoundly moral book in which, however, there is no surface statement of the moral principle. On the other hand, obvious moralization in literature may in itself be inartistic. Since literature reflects experience, it deals with both good and bad elements in life. The moral evaluations of literature seem, on the whole, more convincing where they are *implicit* rather than *explicit*. Obvious moralization is inartistic because morality is not absorbed into the unity of a work of art. It destroys the singleness of the pattern. When moral instruction is evident, a work of art has failed to that extent, but where moralization is fused with a mimesis of life constituting the work of art, then the work of art is uncorrupted and the moral element is properly fused into the unity of the work affected. Unfused moralization lessens the artistic value of a work of art. But this fact does not compromise the principle that art is responsible to truth. Art has a moral responsibility but must exercise that responsibility according to the nature of art.

VIVIDNESS IN CRITICISM

The critic's most important tasks are to understand the artist's real objective in a piece of work and to show in a carefully argued analysis how the artist achieves that objective. Vividness is as essential to the critic as it is to the artist. Since criticism is a mimesis of what is already a vivid mimesis of life, criticism should also have this vivid, concrete quality. The study of literature should be supported by the practice of criticism, which provides training in scientific perception in the elementary stage and opportunity for original observation and exact generalization in the advanced stage. Literature intellectually interpreted provides the finest possible training in intellectual acumen and sensitivity because in criticism we have embodied the exactitude of a science with the liberality of an art.

CRITICISM AND LITERARY LABELS

Both in literature and in history we should use labels with the greatest caution. The significance of a label should not be assumed but rather should be investigated. We have to realize that labels are used for purposes of convenience and also because complete exactitude of thought is not easily possible in the practical order. Before using a label we should ask ourselves whether the label is an adequate one. How far does it indicate the preconceived idea of the literary work or of the period to which it is attached? We should further check on the accuracy of the label by a study of those works of literature and history that have come to represent the meaning of the label.

THE READER AS CRITIC

Every man, in so far as he reacts to the book he reads, is in that measure a critic. The accuracy and maturity of his reaction determine how well-developed a critic he is. No one can be a critic simply by repeating the findings of others. You have to start with your own honest reaction to the work you read. It is very likely that as you read and weigh you will radically alter some of your first reactions. But your raw material, the beginning of your practice of criticism, is your own awareness of how you think and feel about a work.

But you might ask: What if I am mistaken or unjust about a work? Well, undoubtedly you will make mistakes, misjudgments. But you do have the responsibility to try to be accurate, and in time you will acquire greater accuracy—an accuracy that is *your own* based on your own perception and conviction. This does not mean that you should disregard competent and established critics about a given work. Reading them in conjunction with the work may give you insights that may enrich your reactions very much. But if you use established criticism as a body of law to be repeated and memorized, you will pay no attention to your own reactions and responses. It is better to make mistakes and grow rather than to become a passive and static transmitter of the thoughts of others.

In exercising the responsibility of criticism, there are certain questions that you should ask yourself.

1. *What* is the work that I have read? Surface considerations of form are easy to answer. Prose or poetry, novel, drama, epic, story, type of construction, techniques? More difficult to identify, but more important in a critical interpretation of the work, are the emotional and intellectual responses that the work has created. What are they, what do they tell me, what is their value?

2. Can I see and describe *how* these emotional and intellectual responses have been created? Can I locate an overriding idea or theme that holds the work together and gives it its particular quality or power? Does the work have tension or excitement of a special sort? What elements of evil and ugliness enter the work; how are they transcended and evaluated? To what characters, to what situations have I been particularly sympathetic or compassionate?

3. A characteristic of the beautiful lies in true proportion, in just measurement. How does the work under consideration reinforce a true scale of values, deepen our sense of what is fitting?

4. Are there any questions in the interpretation of character and situation that are left ambiguous? Is such ambiguity deliberate, part of an artistic design?

5. Are there any ways in which my own penetration into experience has been deepened by acquaintance with this work?

6. Are there loose ends in the work? Do they matter much? Is the current of the work sufficiently strong to carry along with it a certain amount of debris, of irrelevance?

CRITICISM OF SPECIFIC TYPES

In addition to the broad questions that relate to any work of art, there are specific considerations one must bear in mind in dealing with specific types.

What specific techniques are used in a particular narrative? What use is made of point of view, local color, dialogue, overtones, and symbolism? Is the theme aided by any special techniques such as interior monologue and stream of consciousness? How far does the narrator *show,* to what extent does he *tell?* Are there any special reasons, judging from the total effect, for doing what he does?

In regard to drama, we have a number of special technical considerations because a drama is what is specifically acted on the stage rather than what is read in a book. The Shakespearean critic Elmer Edgar Stoll, for example, became very impatient with critics who, working in their libraries, were able to demonstrate by minute analyses many minor inconsistencies and loose ends even in the dramatist's greatest works. He argued that a drama had to be evaluated in terms of the impact the work made when acted upon the stage. If, under such conditions, these inconsistencies went unnoticed, they were, in fact, artistically irrelevant, and in no way a valid object of adverse criticism. Obviously, in the criticism of a drama, some knowledge of the actual operative conditions of the theater—the stage and its peculiarities and its historical customs, the modes of acting—is highly relevant. Often the full import of what is read in the text does not unfold completely until one sees it acted. Since the drama, like the short story, is a very compressed form of art, the use of structure, such as complication, climax, resolution, must be carefully considered—are they deftly and effectively done?

Illustration: Criticism of a Poem

We are illustrating the criticism of a poem for three reasons: first, it can be treated within the limits of the present book; second, a poem, while limited in length, presents in miniature some of the major problems of criticism; third, many of the new major critical theories have been applied with specific reference to poetry.

Northrop Frye says in *Anatomy of Criticism:*

> Formal criticism begins with an examination of the imagery of a poem, with a view to bringing out its distinctive pattern. The recurring or most frequently repeated images form the tonality, so to speak, and the modulating, episodic and isolated images relate themselves to this in an hierarchic structure which is the critical analogy to the proportions of the poem itself. Every poem has its peculiar spectroscopic band of imagery, caused by the requirements of its genre, the predilections of its author, and countless other factors.[8]

We outline below how these principles can be carried out through a practical critical method. We show how a distinctive pattern can be ascertained, how a poem has its peculiar spectroscopic band of imagery, and how the images epitomize "the critical analogy to the proportions of the poem itself."

We start by carefully noting what may be called the syntheses of the poem. Synthesis (see page 59) means a union, a cohesion—a state by which elements are integrated into new substances.

The synthetic power of poetry is its pivotal characteristic. Synthesis basically implies a "uniting or bringing together." In chemistry we synthesize separate elements so that they form a new substance, a compound, which is radically different from the elements that enter into it. In poetry, for example, image-bearing words can be fused together to form a unique and untranslatable expression which carries so individuated a meaning that no other equivalent can be found for it. This synthesis, the outstanding achievement of poetry, involves a "bringing together"—a fusion that enables the reader to see many levels of reality at once.

The synthesis unites the abstract idea and the concrete setting or circumstance, a union that reflects the fact that the creative mind works on two levels. On one level it perceives the external world as it is. On another level it perceives the internal world of the mind as it also is, possessed of emotional and intellectual values, in the act of reaction to the external world. The creative artist unites in his work the difference between reality as the eye sees it and the world of action as the mind perceives it.

Note the effect of uniting the concrete "green" with "thought" and with "shade," in extract from Marvell's "The Garden":

Meanwhile the mind, from pleasure less,
Withdraws into its happiness;
The mind, that ocean where each kind
Does straight its own resemblance find;
Yet it creates, transcending these,
Far other worlds, and other seas,
Annihilating all that's made
To a green thought in a green shade.

(41–48)

Notice the successful impact of the abstract "death" with the concrete "village lights" in Humbert Wolfe's lines:

. . . For one lost life that finds in death
The village lights of Nazareth . . .

(*The Uncelestial City*, p. 94, 3–4)

The meaningful symbol—the unique picture—is more vital in poetry than the actual denotation of words. Horace, in his *Ars Poetica,* spoke of the *callida junctura* (the skillful junction or fortunate blending of words). The *callida junctura* is the indissoluble union between the word and the image, brought about by mental association. It is this combination of words and images that is the basis of all poetry.

Herbert Read uses the word "synthesis" for this type of combination, this powerful and unique form of expression in which individual words are lost in the combination of which they are a part. Not one word can be altered or taken away without destroying the synthesis. The point in any given verse where the poetry is most distilled constitutes the synthesis—the artistic union of one word, image, and sound with one or more words, images, and sounds.

Consider the use of language in Francis Thompson's "The Hound of Heaven." A metaphor featuring a horse—symbol of speed—has been used throughout the poem ("clung to the whistling mane of every wind") to signify the soul's mad, unavailing flight from the pursuer. Eventually, with an intensifying power of suggestion created by the interrelated imagery, a synthesis emerges:

I knew how the clouds arise
Spumed of the wild sea-snortings.

(78–79)

The expression "sea-snortings" is an excellent synthesis, because in it one can see the miniature crystallization of the poem's whole artistic development, in the sense that the image of the speeding horse is now symbolically infused throughout the language, carrying its overtone of the relentlessly pursuing God.

It sometimes happens that a line or two will express the entire poignancy of a poem, as in Milton's description of Adam in *Paradise Lost* (IX, 892–893) when he learns of Eve's sin:

From his slack hand the garland wreathed for Eve
Down dropped, and all the faded roses shed.

The roses have faded with the conscious knowledge of sin. The poet achieves a clever use of the pathetic fallacy (the assumption that nonhuman nature is capable of sharing the moods and thoughts of man).

But syntheses are not all on a level in regard to their depths of meaning, though all are concrete, compressed, symbolic statements. The general discourse or context of the poem, however, will tend to determine the intellectual depth of the synthesis. In Keats's "Isabella," the two brothers who have determined to kill Isabella's lover are thus described:

So the two brothers and their murder'd man
Rode past fair Florence . . .

(209–210)

The use of the word "murder'd" here is distinctly poetic and synthetic, but it is a descriptive compression rather than a penetrating symbol. In the same stanza the word "quiet" forms an effective synthesis with "slaughter":

... They pass'd the water
Into a forest quiet for the slaughter.

(215–216)

The word "quiet" is uniquely adapted and united to slaughter. Keats is not giving us any cosmic meaning, but he is giving us dramatic and ironic overtone. "Murder'd" is a compression of the situation—"whom they intend to murder."

Syntheses might logically be written as one expression. Poets frequently coin words, without hesitation and without apology to the dictionary. Note Keats's invention of "deep-damask'd" in these lines from "The Eve of St. Agnes":

Innumerable of stains and splendid dyes
As are the tiger-moth's deep-damask'd wings ...

(212–213)

"Damask," a noun, is given the form of a past participle, and is then blended with the adverb, "deep." Keats uses language very freely here. A beginner should be more discreet. But this tendency toward synthesis, even in word coinage, is natural in poetry.

The syntheses in poetry vary according to the work they perform. Some are purely decorative, some intuitive, and others symbolic. Also, syntheses may be predominantly emotional, predominantly intellectual, or predominantly musical and pictorial. Other types of classification may occur to you. What are presented here are not meant by any means to be inclusive.

It will be helpful for you to realize that the discovery and classification of syntheses is a useful step in understanding, appreciating, and criticizing a poem. In classifying syntheses, you are forced to examine particulars.

In order to illustrate how you may collect and label syntheses, let us assume that you are going to interpret Keats's "The Eve of St. Agnes." First of all, read the poem stanza by stanza. At the conclusion of each step in the reading, put down in your notebook what you consider to be the syntheses in each stanza. Also put down any pertinent remarks or observations about the syntheses that may occur to you.

After you have collected the syntheses, your next step is to label each synthesis according to kind: decorative, intuitive, or symbolic; emotional, intellectual, or musical. You will now have made the tentative beginning of critical analysis. The syntheses you have gathered constitute a heightened selection of the content of the whole poem; they are the basis of your artistic criticism. By this procedure you are making a heightened imitation of the poem, just as the poet was making a heightened imitation of life.

Here is a possible list of syntheses from the poem:

The hare limp'd trembling—pictorial

(3)

Note the double exaggeration. Not only was it so cold that the "hare limp'd." He was also trembling.

The sculptured dead, on each side, seem to freeze,
Emprisoned in black, purgatorial rails—pictorial

(14–15)

Again note exaggeration. Even the "sculptured" dead "freeze."

The silver, snarling trumpets—musical

(31)

Notice also the symbolism of the music as inimical, "snarling." Sound and music are the symbols of the outside "revelry" that threatens the safety of the lovers.

The music, yearning like a god in pain—musical

(56)

The music yearns not only "like a god," but "a god in pain."

. . . Beside the portal doors
Buttress'd from moonlight, stands he—musical and pictorial

(76–77)

Notice the contrast between labial and nasal consonants and the harsh separating "buttress'd."

He found him in a little moonlight room
Pale, lattic'd, chill and silent as a tomb—musical

(112–113)

Feebly she laughed in the languid moon—musical

(127)

Notice the contrast between shrill trochaic foot, "feebly" and long vowels, resonant iambics.

Sudden a thought comes like a full-blown rose—intellectual

(136)

Note the brilliant image of thought flashing upon the mind as a luxurious rose would hit the sense of sight.

Innumerable of stains and splendid dyes
As are the tiger-moth's deep damask'd wings—pictorial

(212–213)

Note music and tone-color.

Rose-bloom fell on her hands—pictorial

(220)

Here the poet particularizes color in the manner of a painter.

As though a rose should shut, and be a bud again—pictorial and intellectual

(243)

Note the brilliance of the image and its perfect appropriateness.

These delicates he heap'd with glowing hand—pictorial

(271)

"Glowing hand" crystallizes the poet's love of color and light.

. . . sumptuous they stand
In the retired quiet of the night—pictorial

(273–274)

These lines crystallize the poet's love of contrasting colors.

. . . he arose
Ethereal, flush'd and like a throbbing star—pictorial

(317–318)

The image suggests the energy of fast-moving color.

Into her dream he melted, as the rose
Blendeth its odour with the violet—emotional and pictorial

(320–321)

Note the symbolic use of color to present action.

When you have made your list of syntheses and labeled them, you may no longer regard "The Eve of St. Agnes" primarily as a story. (Actually it may lack some of the elements of a good story—character interest, fast-moving action, and suspense—or it may be deficient in them in some degree.)

In going over your list of syntheses, you will be immediately struck by the importance of color in the poem and the conscious use of color by the poet to achieve his desired effects. This will enable you to understand Keats's main purpose in the poem—to present a picture of rich and varied tone, to create atmosphere even more than to recount a narrative.

This collection of syntheses will not only give you immediate insight into a poem but will also serve the useful purpose of helping you remember the poem. With each of the syntheses, you will be able to recall the circumstances with which it is associated. For example, the synthesis "the hare limp'd trembling" will recall to you the whole winter scene and its attendant circumstances. Or "as the rose blendeth its odour with the violet" might indicate to you the situation of lovers as well as their respective characters. You can discipline yourself to reconstruct the story and its connecting links from keys such as these. As you come to recognize that all syntheses are not equally great or effective, you will consider the quality of the syntheses with special attention.

The value of this method of criticism is, of course, limited. The structure of the poem, the influence of previous works upon it, and its purpose must also be given attention. In combination with these other factors—and not regarded merely by itself—this classification of syntheses is very helpful, especially when you first attempt to analyze and criticize poetry.

In criticism, your objective is to see the work as it really is. It is possible to give other people's reports of what the work really is without your ever having seen the work in its concrete individual aspect. The following guide (in this specific sense—in regard to a poem) will help you to write an honest, direct criticism. Such criticism will be specific and concentrated on the one work you are actually looking at.

1. Look at the work of art before you (the actual poem). For the purpose of this experiment do not consult reference books or works of literary criticism. Look at the work of art in its own light.

2. Read the poem through (aloud, if possible). Mark off the syntheses as you go along.

3. Enter the syntheses individually on separate sheets of paper. This will permit you to reshuffle them for purposes of classification.

4. Examine and classify the syntheses.

5. See what leads they give to the specific nature of the poem.

6. With the syntheses and leads organized, begin the writing of a critical essay, answering the following points.

a. What do the syntheses indicate about the poem? What do they tell you about the use of color, of sound, of intellectual overtone? What do they suggest about the predominant motifs, the predominant ideas?

b. How are these syntheses used in building up the poem?

c. What is the total effect of the poem? Can you define the essential characteristics of the poem from the results of your analysis?

d. Estimate the general value and importance of the poem on the basis of your answer to *c*.

7. Aim for integration in your critical point of view. Try to see the work as a whole.

Discussion Questions

1. What are the two main views concerning the function of the critic?
2. What was assumed by neoclassical criticism?
3. How do Aristotle and Horace differ in their concepts of mimesis?
4. Why may criticism be said to have a dual character?

5. Why should criticism be a mimesis of literature?
6. What is Walter Pater's concept of the objective of criticism?
7. How should a critic check his first impressions of a work?
8. In what way may a literary work be valuable, even if it does not attain artistic excellence?
9. Why may overt moralization be inartistic?
10. Why does the practice of criticism lead to valuable intellectual training?
11. Why should we be cautious in the use of literary labels?
12. Why is it necessary to develop your own powers of criticism?
13. What are some good questions to ask yourself in preparing your own criticism of a work?

EPILOGUE

The Power of the Imagination

In this freeing of our personality from its separation and isolation, in this uniting of it with others, lies the chief characteristic and the great attractive force of art.

Leo Tolstoi

We have considered many things in this book: what literature is in terms of a work of art; what distinguishes poetry, prose, drama, and criticism as literary forms; why literature is a great human document. We cannot do better in terms of a conclusion than to speak of the imaginative power that underlies all literature but goes beyond it into all the highest achievements of man.

Imagination does not falsify experience; rather it enables us to see experience vividly in terms of a great vision, of full excitement and response. Thomas De Quincey wrote that

> . . . there is, first, the literature of *knowledge;* and, secondly, the literature of *power.* The function of the first is—to *teach;* the function of the second is to *move:* the first is the rudder; the second, an oar or sail. . . . What do you learn from *Paradise Lost?* Nothing at all. . . . What you owe to Milton is not any knowledge, of which a million separate items are still but a million of advancing steps on the same earthly level; what you owe is *power*—that is, exercise and expansion, to your own latent capacity, of sympathy with the infinite, where every pulse and each separate influx is a step upwards, a step ascending as upon a Jacob's ladder from earth to mysterious altitudes above the earth.[1]

We have spoken previously, in discussing the response to poetry, of the prime importance of the image. We want to go farther here and to think of the imagination in the widest sense, not only of what it does for literature, but what it does for man and the life of man.

This is not the place to criticize still-prevalent, though old-fashioned, educational practices. But too many of us have experienced scholastic knowledge as something *arid.* We have often kept on learning facts and operative procedures without *feeling* anything, or gaining much insight into ourselves or others. We sometimes have had no clear picture of what we really *know* and really *feel.* The deep training of the emotions which literature provides is not reflected in the examination system, which tends to form an educational pattern of its own. A student may take as many as 140 examinations in college, including midterms. The situation is about the same in high school. But as far as literature is concerned, these examinations frequently involve routine, factual questions—identifications, true-false, brief recapitulations of other people's thinking (the so-called "established" critics). To many students the reading of material that might not turn up in examinations is a doubtful gamble. Such an experience is, at the least, narrowing, and often, especially where there is no extensive effort in writing and written expression, it succeeds in doing the impossible—in making the great imaginative statements of the literature of *power* arid and lifeless. The Scottish peasant who daily read his Bible in his moorland croft had more capacity for expression and for feeling, though he went only to elementary school, than some of our own college graduates. His reading was noble, sincere, really part of his life. He received no "credits" for it, but he got a deep and wise human experience. Wise education can be of great help, but it is also possible to approach the imagination unimaginatively and, in the process, knock all the rungs from beneath "Jacob's ladder."

If we were to respond fully to the literature of power, we would enormously decrease the dangers of neurosis, immorality, and vulgarity. The fact is that men have to respond to something. If they have not been trained, either through environment or wise formal education, to respond to the highest, they will unquestionably respond to low-level emotional and value appeals. As a brilliant English artist once observed:

> "Where there is no vision the people perish." And in a sort of spiritual death men carry on as automatons, "hands," employees. . . . But as no means have yet been devised by which men and women can be doped and put on shelves during the hours when they are neither working nor sleeping (for human beings cannot sleep more than eight hours a day or work more than ten or twelve, and so there are about four hours of what we call "leisure" to be provided for), so we have to cater for those hours during which, while neither working nor sleeping, they tend to break away from the automatic and let their imaginations "rip," imaginations entirely undisciplined and untrained because entirely unused.[2]

"Cute chicks" moving through luxury motels, with shining convertibles speeding against Hawaiian breezes, handing banter back to well-dressed young men who have no other interest than deftly solving murder and blackmail cases: this is the staple material of popular television programs. Harmless enough, one might say, for, after all, the more decent people win in the end. But the underlying value is the image of easy comfort, of prestige based upon expensive restaurants, much casual liquor, a good figure, and a handsome smirk. Where is there a "Jacob's ladder" here to mysterious altitudes above the earth; how do we rise to a spiritual magnanimity or compassion by forever following cops and robbers?

When we think in terms of what people might attain in contrast to the level for which they settle, the "ripping" of the untrained imagination does not seem such a minor thing. Art has tended to become a form of distraction; it has lost the seriousness of ritual and religion that accompanied it in classical Greece, in medieval and renaissance times, that is still present in the great moderns, though not, perhaps in an overt sense. The sense of a presence in which all men stand, of the beauty and miracle of nature (the self-sustaining independence of a mountain, of a flower, a forest), the sense of wonder, the sense of the internal dialogue between man and his own conscience, all the ideas and inspirations which enable men to face the crises of their private and public lives, tend to be sacrificed to the most banal entertainment. Where the imagination has not been guided, people do not really mature (however much they "know"); they do not realize the depth or complexity of emotion; they lack what old-fashioned people called *taste* and *discrimination*.

The great novelist Tolstoi made a number of points in *What Is Art?* that have not always been fully appreciated. He said that "art is a human activity having for its purpose the transmission to others of the highest and best feelings to which men have risen."[3] His main standards for a literary work are sincerity and "infectiousness." The writer must be emotionally true (rather than contrived, or playing flattering tricks on the audience), and his skill lies in making his readers have a similar emotional experience to his own. Art for Tolstoi is a great unitive and "religious" force in the world, for what is deeply felt about what is profoundly human is shared by all men, and has a religious value, in the general sense that we realize the solidarity of the human family, and that human life is guided by purpose to a purpose.[4] Because Tolstoi sees so vividly the possible impacts of great literature on society, he is equally deeply distressed by the low-level values encouraged by low-level "art."

For the well-known English critic and educator Herbert Read, imaginative training is no less essential in education than the intellectual and the abstract. In fact, he argues that the intellectual is enriched and deepened by its relationship to the imaginative. Read says:

> Children, like savages, like animals, experience life directly, not at a mental distance. In due time they must lose this primal innocence, put childish things away. But what are they going to put in place of the unified consciousness they have enjoyed? That is the fundamental question, and the only answer that modern civilization and its pedagogues can give us is: a split consciousness, a world made up of discordant forces, a world of images divorced from reality, of concepts divorced from sensation, a logic divorced from life.[5]

For Read, training in creative and imagistic expression is a mode of "integration"—the most natural mode for children—and as such, its material is the whole of experience. "It is the only mode that can fully integrate perception and feeling."[6]

The crux in the matter of training the imagination lies in the fact that, if we properly take the leap from childhood to adult perception, we have to learn the process of abstraction. Obviously, if the most a person can do in the way of adult reading is the popular "picture" magazines, he has failed to mature to the easy grasp of abstractions. On the other hand, he may make this transition to abstractionism at altogether too high and needless a cost—he may lose the instantaneous and vivid image perception he may have had as a child. It has been argued that knowledge originates in sense perception, and it is a sign of wisdom to bring our most acute abstractions back into relation with our senses. That is what the artist and, in particular, the poet does. The concrete and the abstract, instead of being antithetical, reinforce one another. We have to realize that there is a field of knowledge and experience that does not fall primarily within the conceptual-logical field. It is one thing to say: "It was a beautiful sunset"; it is quite another thing to *transfer* your experience of the sunset so that another person can really share it. Such a statement is purely on a conceptual level; it communicates *ideas,* but not *experience.* Henley's lines about a sunset are expressed on a different level—the imagistic:

. . . The sun,
Closing his benediction,
Sinks, and the darkening air
Thrills with a sense of the triumphant night.

You might perceive intensely the beauty of a flower; you might desire to communicate the experience of that perception. How is this communication to take place? The physical reaction, the peculiar color, the fragrance are, as such, incommunicable in words. Words cannot transfer the exact experience; yet the artist is determined as a creator and communicator of experience to do this very thing. He has no concepts in the usual sense of the word, if by a concept we mean a clear perception that can be expressed in any of several choices of adequate vocabulary. Now, when a sudden analogy (metaphor, simile) comes to him intuitively, he is able to express his experience of the flower. This analogy is the result of creative act, of making an imagistic statement. It is imagistic knowledge. It is not the result of choosing to illustrate a concept through a choice of suitable similitudes (rhetoric). Take, for example, these lines from Humbert Wolfe's *The Uncelestial City:*

> *. . . snowdrops, nun-like, flawless, crisp,*
> *Less flowers, than a little gasp*
> *Of white astonishment.*

(p. 92, 23–25)

Flawless, crisp are adjectives applied in a subordinate conceptual way, but suddenly the experience is born and transferred into art by a symbolic image:

> *Less flowers, than a little gasp*
> *Of white astonishment.*

Paradoxically, in spite of the statement that they are "less flowers," they are, in fact, *more* flowers to us than ever before—when they cease to be snowdrops and become a "gasp of white astonishment."

We may say that we really know the flower experience of the artist once we see it as *something else.* That is why mental association becomes so important in creative expression. Mental association provides us with that *something else.* The flower has also become a symbol of the transcendent values that illustrate it—the "nun-like, flawless, crisp," the mystic wonderment of universal innocence.

The artist in expressing an experienced knowledge of an object must present it in terms of something else, and in so doing he touches, by a catalytic agency,[7] the world of intuition, the world of universals, so that the transcendent values are expressed in the snowdrop and yet the snowdrop is even more flowerlike than before.

Strangely, the transcendent values actually enable us to see the concreteness of the flower. We see its "itness," if you like, when our minds have glimpsed the universals connected with it.

The catalytic agency in imagistic statement is an amazing thing, and it is not easy to explain it in rationalistic terms. The thing beheld, the image of the snowdrops, remains unchanged, yet it has brought about the great synthesis of meaning that we have described. This is truly the function of a catalyst which, we are told in science, may be recovered intact at the end of a reaction.

What we actually see here—to use De Quincey's figure—is a "Jacob's ladder" that not only goes to a perceived heaven but can also bring us back to see the beauty of earth with a fresh intensity. It is a two-way ladder of the concrete and abstract.

We can do much on our own to deepen our powers of imagination. We should practice the creation of our own images based on our own experience. What universal ideas do we associate with such great natural images as dawn, ocean, waterfall, spring, flowers, forest, night? What visual images do we associate with such great abstractions as love, courage, hope? Frequently we can combine such associations verbally to form our own private nuggets of poetry, such as "quiet solitude of dawn reawakening over the untouched city"; "tranquility of promise in the wonder of the dawn." We will develop phrases in which the universal and the concrete are united according to the laws of imagination. By this practice we will not only give ourselves pleasure but gain enormous insight into great literary art. Frequently, without being professional writers, we can get intriguing and exciting results. We create our own *epiphanies,* or revelations, derived from images and symbols embedded in our own sense experience. If we can see how we can use our own mental associations in fresh and dramatic ways, we learn a great deal about the secrets of a great creative artist.

By the exercising of imagination, both in terms of art and of direct experience of life, we escape the passivity that has been exploited by the "hidden persuaders" and commercial "image makers." We can develop an awareness, a maturity about what our own images mean. We cannot be prompted against our will; we become conscious of the things that really make us happy, the things we ourselves have chosen. We enter more fully into the perception of life; we can *make* experience! Wordsworth once illustrated this theme in a very simple but convincing way, in a piece describing the delight he experienced when, "wandering lonely as a cloud," he suddenly came across a crowd, "a host of golden daffodils"

Continuous as the stars that shine
And twinkle on the milky way.

("The Daffodils," 7–8)

At first he did not realize the wealth that the "show" had brought to him. Later he realized that this scene would remain a permanent image in his mind, always available to give him refreshment and enthusiasm:

For oft, when on my couch I lie
In vacant or in pensive mood,
They flash upon that inward eye
Which is the bliss of solitude;
And then my heart with pleasure fills,
And dances with the daffodils.

(19–24)

Intensity and sincerity of response—they are the great gifts of the perceptive imagination. For the fullness and completeness of our own private lives, we cannot afford the neglect of imagination—not to mention what the creative imagination could do for mankind as a whole, in Tolstoi's unitive and religious sense of the term "art."

Discussion Questions

1. Why is imaginative power so important?
2. What distinction does De Quincey make between the literature of knowledge and the literature of power?
3. Why, in the course of education, is the literature of power sometimes made to appear arid?
4. What are some of the advantages of knowing the literature of power?
5. What evil effects arise from the untrained imagination?
6. How does Tolstoi evaluate literature?
7. On what grounds does Herbert Read criticize certain educational procedures?
8. How does a poet use the imagination in communicating experience?

Glossary of Common Terms

Abstract and concrete. All language is symbolic in the sense that it depends upon agreed conventions whereby certain sound arrangements are signs for certain ranges of meanings, denotative and connotative. But within such ranges we speak of *abstract* language, in the sense of generalized ideas perceived intellectually, and *concrete* language, which denotes the actual physical objects through which we recapture a mental picture. Thus "the danger of fire" is an abstract statement, a generalized concept. "John's house on fire" is a concrete statement in which we visualize mentally a particular house belonging to a particular person in relation to a particular fire. The language of philosophy, seeking definitions and universality of terms, will tend toward the abstract, in which the meaning of a new concept will be based on the arrived-at meaning of preceding concepts. The language of poetry will tend toward the con-

An asterisk before a word indicates a reference to that word as an item in the glossary.

crete, in which the associations of the new image will be determined in part by the range of associations created by the preceding images. This distinction, of course, must not be pressed too far, for Plato illustrates ideas through imagery and myth, and a poet, through symbolism, indicates a wide range of implicit intellectual meaning.

Action implies a real given theme, such as a myth, a story line, a complication of incidents, as distinct from an expression of a state of mind. It can, of course, be argued that a state of mind, if sufficiently penetrated, can be an action, as in much lyric poetry. In such a case it would be better to speak of *theme* rather than action, though action is also theme, or part of theme. The relative importance of action, in the sense of plot and story development, varies in different genres. It is of prime importance in the epic and drama, less necessary in the novel or in the lyric.

Action, falling. See page 164.

Action, rising. See page 164.

Aesthetic distance is a term for a certain objectivity and disinterestedness that art itself demands. Art is a heightened imitation of experience. It is not just the actual world of experience but experience viewed selectively, emphatically, at a certain distance. A work fails when it does not have the appropriate aesthetic distance. Compare, in this respect, a crooning love song with a sonnet of Shakespeare. The first tends to give the few basic emotions in terms of the prevailing clichés of the adolescent world. The sonnet, on the other hand, expresses the emotion of love in terms of an adult world, comprising many related insights and values, and gives a *public* statement to a private emotion. The work lacking aesthetic distance remains self-conscious and private; it is without universality. If we accept the Aristotelian approach of art as *mimesis,* the term already includes the concept of aesthetic distance, since Aristotle meant a heightened rather than a direct imitation. The term is implicit in the idea of *catharsis* as well. Catharsis implies the detachment of the spectator, both from the work of art itself and from the author. There may be degrees of aesthetic distance. The greater the use of rhetoric, the less will be aesthetic distance in certain kinds of literature. Aesthetic distance should not be viewed as an end in itself. As one critic puts it, "Distance along one axis is sought for the sake of the reader's involvement on some other axis." Thus, for example, in the realistic novel, the closeness of the narrative to external realities may serve the purpose of involving the reader more deeply in a social criticism and a social awareness. Realistic detail, in turn, has to be selected with care; that is, it must be significant, detail that suggests not merely a part of life but a whole experience. "Realistic detail . . . is a bore," say Sean O'Faolain, "if it merely gives us idle verisimilitude: its function is to be part of this general revelation by suggestion. It is fruitful realism when external reality releases the imagination. . . ."

Aesthetics is a science concerned with the principles of art. It is particularly concerned with the relationship of art to the beautiful (an aesthete in Greek means one who perceives).

Affective fallacy. See *fallacy, affective.

Allegory is a method of symbolism (see page 29) suitable either for poetry or for prose. Allegory, however, in itself is a piece of constructive projection, and, while using imagery, does not necessarily use imagery in the manner of poetry. "The dark conceit," as Edmund Spenser calls it, indicates a planned, logical discourse by which spiritual forces and abstract ideas are presented by *figures* and *images.* The character Everyman in the medieval play has an intellectual denotation, as do such figures as Knowledge and Good Deeds. This constitutes a very different use of the image than, let us say, a statement such as "My love is like a red, red rose." "Love" is a *direct* idea, standing for itself alone and not for something else, whereas "Everyman" is an allegorical idea, apparently symbolizing a character of that name but essentially symbolizing all mankind. Allegory has sometimes been described as the treatment of one subject under the disguise of another. This is true of Spenser's *The Faerie Queene,* where twelve different knights represent twelve different virtues, all embraced in the person of King Arthur, the sum and union of all the virtues. Spenser obtains double service from his characters—as individuals in a story and as symbols in a vaster construction. Gloriana is "figured forth" by different women, Britomart, Belphoebe, and others, symbolizing aspects of her total personality. Gloriana is also Queen Elizabeth.

Characteristic of allegory is the presentation of abstract and spiritual forces in concrete forms. Allegory is a distinct feature of medieval and renaissance literature. Allegorical discourse was as native to the culture of those times as factual and reportorial discourse is to ours. The whole of nature was viewed in allegorical terms—the pelican, the lion, the whale, the flower of the field. It has been said of medieval thought that it tended to move from symbol to symbol, and from symbolical significance to related symbolical significance, and often to treat a symbol as if it were the fact that was symbolized. Actually, medieval and renaissance writers attained, by the dexterous use of allegory, effects equal to those of the subtlest modern novelists. A good example is that of the *Roman de la Rose,* translated by Chaucer. It describes how a young man walks along by the River of Life until he comes to a walled orchard. Inside the wall exists the world of courtly leisure and amusement. Since the young man is well-bred, polite, and cheerful, the portress (Idleness) admits him to the orchard. After seeing various people in the garden, he walks off on his own, but is followed by the God of Love. Suddenly he comes upon the Well of Narcissus, bearing an inscription forbidding one to look into it. But the young man does this very thing and sees the whole garden reflected in the well, especially one particular rosebud which deeply affects him. The Well of Narcissus is a typical medieval allegory. The Well stands for the eyes of the lady; the grass represents her eyelashes. The Rose represents the possession of the lady's love. As the hero approaches the rose garden he is shot by the arrows of Cupid and surrenders to love. But he discovers that he cannot enter the rose garden because it is protected by a thorny hedge. The figure Bialacoil, who represents the Friendship of the Lady, leads him inside the hedge. The hero boldly asks for the rosebud. Bialacoil has no direct objection to the request, but she is embarrassed, for she realizes that Danger, Wicked Tongue, and Shame are lurking by. Danger, symbolizing lordliness or reserve, leaps up and drives the lover outside the garden, frightening Bialacoil into fits. Then Reason descends to the youth and tell him he is making a fool of himself. The lover does not argue but reaffirms his loyalty to the God of Love. Eventually Danger gives the hero permission to love but forbids him to approach the rosebud. However, Franchise, meaning the quality of a great person—his liberality, a virtue the opposite of suspiciousness, something between courage and innocence—cajoles Danger into allowing Bialacoil to return.

Danger yields sulkily, and Bialacoil duly returns. The story then repeats itself with a difference; for the young man is less presumptuous. He now asks only to kiss the rose. Bialacoil is still afraid of Jealousy, Danger, and Shame. Matters stand still until Venus appears. She touches the face of Bialacoil and the heroine falls in love. Thus friendship is subjected to love, and the lover kisses the rose. Here is a good illustration of the allegorical method skillfully used. A delicate psychological love story is told with only one overtly human character.

Alliteration is the repetition of the same initial sound in two or more words:

> *When the sun sets the air* d*oth* d*rizzle* d*ew,*
> *But for the* sunset *of my brother's* son
> *It rains* d*ownright.*

(*Romeo and Juliet*, III, v, 126–128)

Allusion consists of an incidental reference to some historical or literary figure or event outside the *essential* statement of the work. It is used for decorative and sometimes humorous purposes, as in Pyramus's statement in *A Midsummer Night's Dream* (V, i, 201), "Not Shafalus to Procrus was so true." In no way, by way of metaphor or background, do these two names enter otherwise into the structure of the work.

Ambiguity frequently has been used to indicate doubtfulness or uncertainty of meaning. But as a term applied to literature it has come to mean a work possessing at one and the same time a variety of meanings—or levels of meaning. William Empson in *Seven Types of Ambiguity* (revised, 1947) uses the word "ambiguity" in an extended sense, "any verbal nuance, however slight, which gives room for alternative reactions to the same piece of language." " 'Ambiguity' itself can mean an indecision as to what you mean, an intention to mean several things, a probability that one or other or both of two things has been meant, and the fact that a statement has several meanings." The seven types of ambiguity listed are: (1) ambiguity arising when a detail is effective in several ways at once; (2) ambiguity arising when two or more alternative meanings are resolved into one; (3) ambiguity related to the rendering of two apparently unconnected meanings given simultaneously; (4) ambiguity dependent upon two alternative meanings that make clear the complicated mind of the author; (5) "a fortunate confusion," as when the author is discovering his idea in the act of writing or not holding it all in his mind at once; (6) an ambiguity arising from contradictory or irrelevant expression; (7) an ambiguity of full contradiction, marking a division in the author's mind. William Empson thinks of ambiguities *artistically* as revealing mental and emotional experiences. Ambiguities are a nuisance in scientific discourse; they would not be desired, let us say, in a contract. But in art they are used as indexes of the complicated way in which the mind often really works. "An ambiguity . . . is not satisfying in itself, nor is it, considered as a device on its own, a thing to be attempted; it must in each case arise from and be justified by, the peculiar requirements of the situation."

Ambivalence indicates the presence in a work of art of two values which frequently excite opposite and conflicting values in the audience. Thus Satan in Milton's *Paradise Lost* might be both admired and hated, pitied and feared. Ambivalence as a psychological term implies the coexistence of opposite and conflicting feelings about the same person or object. Thus Hamlet could be said to have ambivalent feelings toward his mother Gertrude, for he seems both to love and hate her simultaneously. We can speak of a work of art as being ambivalent in the sense that the values it offers may be so open-ended as to face in opposite directions. This may result from the possibility that the artist's conscious point of view and his unconscious drives may not be in alignment. Thus from the point of view of some critics *Paradise Lost* could be considered ambivalent. On the conscious side, Milton, it is argued, wants to make Satan the villain of the piece, but unconsciously he is in sympathy with him.

Anagogic suggests, through its etymology, a bringing up, an elevation. It is used in reference to certain types of allegorical interpretation, particularly in scriptural tradition. Thus events in the Old Testament are viewed as prefigurings of what happened later in the New Testament. Jonah's three days in the whale's belly are regarded as a figure of Christ's descent into hell after his death and before his resurrection.

Analogy points up an indirect likeness between otherwise dissimilar things. A bird is like an opera star in that they both sing, though under very different conditions and for very different purposes. Every being has something in common by the very fact that everything is being. Analogy, coming from a Greek word meaning proportion, refers to a likeness of one thing to another in terms of some proportion or other. A man is heavy like a stone. A man is godlike in his generosity. Man, stone, and God have being. They have similarities to one another; they are also very different. In popular speech, we generally answer "what is its nature?" by describing what it is *like*. As M. H. Abrams points out, "We tend to describe the nature of something in similes and metaphors, and the vehicles of these recurrent images, when analyzed, often turn out to be the attributes of an implicit analogue through which we are viewing the object we describe." Art might be considered a gigantic analogy for experience itself, yet it has its own being different from the being of life. Metaphor, symbol, and myth contain implicit analogy (often several analogies). "In my heart some late lark singing" offers implicit analogies for love and joy and the evening of life. "My love is like a rose" offers an explicit analogy between the beloved and a flower. Both love and rose have utterly separate identities, but they are alike in their youth, freshness, and beauty.

Anapest. See *metrical feet.

Antithesis implies one statement (the thesis) rapidly followed by a modifying or contrasting statement (strictly speaking the *anti*thesis, what goes against the *thesis*). An antithetical statement in literature comprises both statements in one assertion, as in Jonathan Swift's observation: "We have just enough religion to make us hate, but not enough to make us love one another."

Apostrophe in literature is a form of direct invocation of a person or force not present *within the terms of the discourse*. In this sense, it is an apparent digression (though often serving an overall artistic purpose) as in Milton's invocation to Heavenly Light at the beginning of Book III of *Paradise Lost*.

Apron stage, sometimes called the "projecting stage," is characteristic of the English renaissance theater. This stage thrusts into the audience, allowing spectators on all sides, unlike the proscenium stage, which is demarcated from the audience by the footlights and a curtain. The apron stage has an extra dimension compared with the proscenium stage. The proscenium stage is like a painting, the apron stage like a piece of sculpture. The apron stage made great demands on the personality, versatility, and vocal powers of the actor, who had a more personal contact with his audience, with corresponding opportunities and risks. The projecting stage had no curtain and this fact resulted in several conventions peculiar to renaissance drama.

Archetype. See page 36.

Art of conflict. Most literature consists in an art of conflict. The novel, the short story, the epic, and the drama fall within this category. Such art demands conflict in which the reader identifies with one of the characters, hoping for his success in his struggle with circumstances. A villain, though not necessarily an evil one, is normally essential to this kind of art, though an impersonal force inimical to man's wishes, such as fate, may serve the purpose. Such art must present evil and ugliness as well as goodness and beauty, falsehood as well as truth, to set the pattern of conflict. No great work of art has shown the significant victory of evil in such conflict. Though tragedy shows the hero brought to disaster, moral values are not denied.

Assonance is sometimes a substitute for rhyme. It uses the same vowel sounds but different consonants in the terminal words of lines. In a more general sense it is the repetition of the same vowel sounds in a line, without regard to surrounding consonants:

> *At the* sea-*down's edge between windward and l*ea.

Autobiography. See page 138.

Autotelic is a term used in opposition to *didactic*. *Didactic* is applied to a work which has an overt message to deliver. An *autotelic* work contains its ultimate purpose within itself. An autotelic work, in the terms of the New Criticism, is nonrhetorical (see rhetoric).

Ballad is a simple narrative poem. It is composed of short stanzas generally suitable for singing. A number of ballads have a stark dramatic quality, such as "Sir Patrick Spens," "The Twa Corbies," and "Edward." Scholars debate about whether the older ballad was a result of personal or communal authorship, or some mixture of both. Even the excellent adaptations of the form in the English Romantic period preserve the elliptic and enigmatic features of the ballad as in Coleridge's "Rime of the Ancient Mariner," and Keats's "La Belle Dame sans Merci." It is a feature of the ballad to hit the highlights of a longer story but to omit the connecting links and explanation. A powerful mood often results, but the story line often remains suggestive rather than coherent.

Baroque, as applied to literature, is used chiefly in regard to the seventeenth century. Its most technical application is to the architecture and painting immediately following the renaissance. Renaissance art emphasized surface symmetry and balance, visual clarity, while baroque art was interested in open forms, emphasizing the light and color that modified the sharp outlines of objects. The high achievement of baroque architecture, as exemplified in the work of Giovanni Bernini, was its use of space. While any architect must, in fact, enclose space, the baroque artist was able to create the suggestion of free and unlimited space within the building. John Milton is, in many ways, a baroque artist. The cosmology of *Paradise Lost* would not serve the purpose of creating the illusion of freedom and space any more than raw bricks and mortar. Milton's baroque achievement is poetic; his images constantly symbolize a space that is free and unconfined, but not limitless or chaotic. "Lycidas" itself offers in miniature what Milton carries out on a vast scale in *Paradise Lost*. In this pastoral elegy all is open and free as the swift Hebrus coursing to the Lesbian shore; yet the ocean itself has limits, and the whole world is circumscribed, in spite of its uncircumscribed movements, by the idea of *home,* the great unifying center to which all the complex movements return—just as the baroque church is utterly free and yet intimately the house of God.

. . . whilst thee the shores and sounding seas
Wash far away, where'er thy bones are hurl'd,

Whether beyond the stormy Hebrides
Where thou perhaps under the whelming tide
Visit'st the bottom of the monstrous world;
Or whether thou to our moist vows denied,
Sleep'st by the fable of Bellerus old,
Where the great vision of the guarded mount
Looks towards Namancos and Bayona's hold;
  Look homeward *Angel now . . .*

(154–163)

As an extended term, the baroque is associated with certain religious and emotional attitudes, particularly derived from the counter-reformation. St. Ignatius Loyola in his *Spiritual Exercises* had particularly stressed the use of the senses and of the imagination as a means toward achieving spiritual knowledge and higher contemplation. The baroque movement was given further stress and strength by the Spanish mystics, St. Theresa of Avila and St. John of the Cross. Certain key seventeenth-century words, particularly "ecstasy," and numerous images of the metaphysical school of poetry are connected with this tradition. Milton in "Il Penseroso" calls upon Contemplation as a "pensive nun, devout and pure," and we come close to the image of a Spanish painting, such as an El Greco, in his presentation of a saint whose eyes are rapt heavenward:

Come, but keep thy wonted state,
With ev'n step, and musing gait,
And looks commercing with the skies,
Thy rapt soul sitting in thine eyes:
There held in holy passion still,
Forget thyself to marble, till
With a sad leaden downward cast,
Thou fix them on the earth as fast.

(37–44)

Bathos is a sudden shift in a statement from the elevated to the trite. If not intended for the deliberate effect of humor, the result is inartistic, destroying the whole mood of a piece and exposing a writer's incapacity to maintain consistency of value. A humorous example is found in *A Midsummer Night's Dream* (V, i, 334–339): Thisbe sees the corpse of Pyramus:

Speak, speak! Quite dumb?
Dead, Dead?

The situation normally calls for a deep, emotional response. Shakespeare, parodying some of the mechanical and insensitive forms of art before his genius came upon the scene, deliberately creates an effect of humorous bathos in the ensuing lines:

. . . a tomb
Must cover thy sweet eyes,
These lily lips, this cherry nose,
These yellow cowslip cheeks. . . .

For an example of how unpremeditated bathos can destroy the effect of elevated statement, we have the following lines of Marlowe suddenly destroyed by the contrast between the poetic buildup and the disillusioning object that constitutes their climax:

Our souls, whose faculties can comprehend
The wondrous architecture of the world,
And measure every wandering planet's course,
Still climbing after knowledge infinite,
And always moving as the restless spheres,
Will us to wear ourselves, and never rest,
Until we reach the ripest fruit of all—

At this point we are all prepared for an *epiphany at least the equal of Hamlet's "What a piece of work is a man!" Instead, we are completely disenchanted by the presentation of a value much below the suggestion of the previous lines:

The perfect bliss and sole felicity,
The sweet fruition of an earthly crown. (I *Tamburlaine*, II, vii, 21–29)

While bathos includes *anticlimax,* anticlimax may involve a gradual rather than abrupt declension in expectation, interest, and value.

Beauty, concepts of. See page 16.

Biography. See page 138.

Blank verse is unrhymed iambic pentameter (see* metrical feet). Great blank verse (as in Milton and Shakespeare) permits many modulations of this basic pattern. A *feminine* ending permits an extra unstressed syllable at the end of lines. There may be an extra unstressed syllable before the caesura. A monosyllabic foot or a trochee may be substituted for an iamb under certain conditions. Blank verse was an important innovation in the English renaissance theater. Blank verse is near enough to ordinary speech so that it can be understood in the theater. On the other hand, it is sufficiently remote from ordinary speech to lend a certain dignity and *aesthetic distance to the drama.

Caesura is a pause in a verse line, normally near the middle. Depending on the requirements of good oral delivery, a line may or may not have a caesura. It is denoted in scansion by a double vertical line.

> *They glide,// like phantoms, // into the wide hall;//*
> *Like phantoms// to the iron porch they glide//*

Canto is a word derived from the Latin *cantus,* meaning a song. Originally it indicated such part of a narrative poem as could be sung by one voice at one time.

Catachresis is a term applied to the use of an apparently farfetched and strained image. If the synthesizing power of the poetic structure is great enough, a catachresis can be very effective. Certain kinds of *conceits make effective use of surprising and unconventional images of this sort.

Catharsis is a term occurring in a passage from *The Poetics* in which Aristotle describes tragedy as an imitation of a serious and complete action, presented by those who act and not by narrative, exciting pity and fear, bringing about the catharsis (purgation) of such emotions. While Aristotle does not explore the meaning of catharsis, the word has become a key one in the examination of the moral and psychological implications of the role of art in general. Aristotle believes that the emotions are rendered healthy through their exercise in response to art. See page 23.

Centripetal is an adjective applied by some of the new critics to the inward-directed meaning of poetic discourse. The *sign, the *centrifugal* or outward meaning, is relatively of less importance in poetry. The *icon is an image of which the main meaning depends upon its centripetal relationships in the poetic structure.

Characterization. The creation of character in a short story, novel, or drama, must be determined in part by the total direction of the work of art. A novel of adventure cannot permit as much character analysis as the psychological novel. Robert Louis Stevenson, by the very fact that he is writing an adventure story and therefore stressing the turns and surprises of action, cannot afford to penetrate a character in the way that Henry James or Virginia Woolf can. In so far as a character is presented as one-dimensional, in so far as he is unchanging or uncomplicated, he is sometimes said to be a flat character; in so far as he is presented in terms of complexity and growth, he is said to be *round.* Within the same kind of art, there may be quite a range from flat to round. Contrast, let us say, a humorous character like Shakespeare's multidimensional Sir John Falstaff with a humorous character from Ben Jonson.

Chorus. While surviving in minor forms in later plays and occasionally revived in terms of its early power as in Milton's *Samson Agonistes,* the chorus is an essential feature of Greek tragedy. By interpretative dancing and singing it helps both to set and to register the mood of a play. Its song duets, or *commi* deal with a variety of subjects, the theme of *hubris* (pride) and *ate* (insanity), universal themes of truth, obedience, respect for the gods, human love, the nature of the state, and the duties of ruler and subject. It often gives background expository material about the hero's situation and the history of his family. In the spoken parts, as distinct from the sung parts, the chorus leader often asks questions and gives advice to the principal character.

Christian humanism, tradition of. This is a term often used in regard to the study of medieval and renaissance literature. This tradition, like that of humanism in general, stresses the dignity and importance of man. But it goes beyond the natural level, and finds additional sanction in theology and the supernatural. The humanist tradition stems from Greek and Latin sources, but there is a specific way in which we may speak of Christian humanism and the culture of Christian humanism. The cardinal principle here is that "the Word was made flesh and dwelt amongst us." This is the basis of the "wonderfully reformed" nature of man, his kinship with Christ. Jacques Maritain has characterized Christian humanists in these words: "They respect human dignity in each concrete and existing person, in the flesh and blood, in the historic context of life." In Christian humanism the central motivating fact is that God so loved man that he sent his only Son to redeem man. While Christian humanism does not overlook the universal and transcendent, it avoids the attitudes of idealistic philosophy (maintaining that the idea is the only reality) by stressing the incalculable value of the individual person. Individual men must not be sacrificed to the overriding idea of *man*. In interpreting the destiny of man, the Christian humanist takes the view that in its essential condition man's nature remains constant. He neither assumes, as did the renaissance pessimists, that man automatically becomes worse with the passage of time, nor that man's destiny is one of automatic progress, as did the evolutionary enthusiasts of the nineteenth century. On the other hand, he has grounds for optimism in the Christian concept of Providence. In spite of man's major spiritual deviations, the future is under Divine Providence. Views that would be alien to the tradition of Christian humanism would be a pessimistic naturalism or an uncommitted realism. The Christian humanist believes that, though man is capable of grave sin, he has been redeemed, and possesses autonomy, intelligence, and free will, and is not at the mercy of his environment. For the Christian humanist, charity is the first and greatest of the virtues, and it is only through the eyes of love in this sense that the created universe, including man, can be properly discerned. Christian humanism is in contrast to such other forms of Christianity as assume man's essential depravity, deny the value of the natural world, or assume postures of determinism.

Chronicle play. See *history plays.

Classicism. See *romanticism and classicism.

Cliché. See *stock epithets.

Climax in a play refers to the point of highest complication in which the course of future events is foreshadowed and the issues are joined in final terms. Climax is often used in another sense, particularly in oratory, as the culmination of strong emotional appeal after the initial argumentation has been completed.

Comedy. See page 171.

Comedy of ideas. See page 173.

Comedy of manners. See page 173.

Comedy, romantic. See page 173.

Comic relief refers to the introduction of comic elements within tragedy. This was forbidden by classical *decorum which maintained that it was disruptive and undignified. Thomas De Quincey's famous essay "On the Knocking at the Gate in *Macbeth*" was one of the first criticisms to show that an artful intrusion of comic elements deepened the emotional power of tragedy through ironic effect. The gravediggers in *Hamlet,* for example, show the broad practical world where even gravediggers have to make a living and be cheerful about their work. The effect of this scene is to reinforce our impression of the spiritual isolation of Hamlet himself who has been tortured by brooding on death and suicide. The comic aspect offers only a temporary and illusionary respite. When its reassurance is found to be deceptive, the tragic aspect seems deeper and more far-reaching than before.

Commedia dell' arte is the comedy of the professional actors. The word *arte* corresponds in meaning to the Middle English word *mystery,* a trade or a guild. It is sometimes called *commedia improvisa,* improvised comedy, because the actors spoke ad-lib. They could afford to do so because this theater was so highly conventionalized, using stock situations, stock characters, and stock epithets. It is contrasted with the *commedia erudita* (learned and polished comedy) which was carefully written, in which poetical and rhetorical effects were carefully prepared, in which stage business was carefully subordinated to literary considerations. The commedia dell' arte influenced Shakespeare to some extent in his choice of the pairs of lovers in *A Midsummer Night's Dream,* in Shylock, who is reminiscent of Pantaloon, in the pedant Holofernes, and in various types of zanies (clowns). The masked Harlequin derives from this comedy (see Allardyce Nicoll, *The World of Harlequin,* 1964).

Comparative literature in a broad sense means the comparing of two or more literary works. In a narrower sense it means the comparison of works drawn from more than one national literature. Works may be compared from many points of view and from a combination of them. They may be compared on the basis of a common theme, a common aesthetic form, the environment that helped to mold and shape them, including previous literary tradition, and their importance in the *history of ideas.

Complication is equivalent in meaning to the rising action in a drama (see page 164).

Conceit is the term applied to a complex type of imagery particularly to be found in the literature of the renaissance. It has often been alleged that such figures of speech are strained and far-fetched. In actual practice, they are often used with artistic success. Shakespeare in much of the poetry of *Romeo and Juliet* manages to bring about an organic unity of very simple and ingenuous statement with complex conceits so that he conveys simultaneously a sense of baroque grandeur and sincere spontaneous feeling.

Two of the fairest stars in all the heaven,
Having some business, do entreat her eyes
To twinkle in their spheres till they return.
What if her eyes were there, they in her head?
The brightness of her cheek would shame those stars
As daylight doth a lamp; her eyes in heaven
Would through the airy region stream so bright
That birds would sing and think it were not night.
See how she leans her cheek upon her hand!
O that I were a glove upon that hand,
That I might touch that cheek!

(II, ii, 15–25)

The image of the exchange of eyes and stars is extreme; the thought of Juliet's cheek putting the stars in her head to shame is extravagant. Yet the whole poetic passage reveals tremendous space, spiritual power, and physical intimacy. The last three lines would be too bald without the conceit preceding them. Through union with the conceit, they carry dignified and sincere conviction. Unlike the stereotyped conceits of his time, Shakespeare's image is entirely original.

Concrete. See *abstract and concrete.

Conflict in a drama refers to the opposed relationships of different characters which result in action and intrigue, the complications forming the plot. Conflict begins with the rising action and is resolved in the denouement (see *art of conflict).

Connotation. See *mental association.

Content and form. See page 91.

Context is the written continuity from which a statement is extracted or emphasized. Reading in context implies the relating of such a statement to what goes before and to what follows. A statement's meaning is only complete, in its overtones and other relationships, in context. That is why "quoting out of context" can be misleading.

Conventions in art are similar to ground rules in sports. They enable the game, the work of art, to function. They make possible the "let's pretend it's true" assumption basic to all drama and fiction. Typical conventions are stock characters, stock situations, as in the comedies of Plautus or a movie western. But more subtle techniques may also be conventions, as, for example, Ophelia's flower scene in *Hamlet,* or the play within a play in the same work. In the broadest sense of all, the stage itself, the novel itself, are conventions. "Convention" etymologically denotes what "comes together with," indicating a tacit assumption between an artist and the audience for the purposes of "make-believe."

Couplet is composed of two lines which have identical rhymes. The heroic couplet is always in iambic pentameter.

Criticism, Freudian. Sigmund Freud himself illustrated a number of his theories by reference to literature, particularly to Shakespeare. Freud was a brilliant diagnostician, and his theories were closely related to his empirical practice. His theories have been challenged and modified in various ways. The matter is too complicated for analysis here, but, in regard to literature, he opened new possibilities of interpretation. Because of Freud, symbol and myth assumed new dimensions for many critics. The major artists have always been sensitive to the ironic difference between appearance and reality, to the possibility that a man's image of himself may not correspond closely to the reality, or that the motives by which a man *thinks* he acts are not his real motives as seen by an external observer. Freud, in placing the sex drive as the central experience in human life, was, nevertheless, a strict moralist. The sex drive should be directed creatively so as to become the basis of great human achievement through *sublimation,* the transference into art and social activity of an instinct so powerful that it could never be satiated simply in terms of sex. The negative approach to sex, through inhibition, Freud regards as destructive and the cause of many mental illnesses. Freud's stress on the unconscious and conscious aspects of mind afforded a new vocabulary and a new refinement for what already was part of literary experience. A writer like James Joyce even makes use of the verbal slip (which Freud stressed) as revelatory of the unconscious. Freud's emphasis on the meaning and importance of dreams has played an important role in modern literature, particularly in combination with Carl Jung's stress on the archetype (see page 36) of the collective unconscious, the racial memory—a development that has led to the contemporary concern with the meaning of myth. It has been argued that an artist "sheds his sickness" in his works, that "the critic then becomes the analyst, taking the art as the symptom, by interpretation of which he can discover the unconscious repressions and drives of the artist." This assumption has to be viewed with caution, for an artist is always in control of his material; a poet, for example, draws on his storehouse of mental associations but he submits them to the demanding line and structure of art. The psychiatrist deals with what is sick in specific human behavior; the artist deals with human life as a whole.

Criticism, the New. John Crowe Ransom, in *The New Criticism* (1941), formulated some of the basic concepts of the New Criticism. Ransom was concerned with studying a poem as a poem, seeking its particular ontology or being, separable from historic, moral, psychological, or sociological relationships. Poetry, he said, has an order of objectivity to offer which should not be treated as scientific discourse. "Poetry intends to recover the denser and more refractory original world which we know loosely through our perceptions and memories. By this supposition it is a kind of knowledge which is radically or ontologically distinct." Poetry has a framework of stability: within that framework there may well be an unpredictability of meaning, something that may have a very personal interpretation for each reader, something that is indefinite, not in the sense of lacking in meaning, but rather as not having fixed and ascertainable limits. "Art," Ransom said, "seems to permit us to predict only some order of unpredictability."

> The world of predictability, for example, is a restricted world of scientific discourse. Its restrictive rule is: one value at a time. The world of art is the actual world which does not bear restrictions; or at least is sufficiently defiant of the restrictiveness of science, and offers enough fullness of content, to give us the sense of the actual objects. A qualitative density, or value-density, such as is unknown in scientific understanding, marks the world of the actual objects. The discourse which tries systematically to record this world is art.

The New Criticism approached a work of art as a thing in itself, and its form and content were to be examined and analyzed not separately but together. The restriction of criticism to the ontology of the work, however, seemed too narrow to some of the new critics themselves. Literature appeals on other grounds as well as that of aesthetic form. T. S. Eliot, finding a middle way, has argued that the ontological approach can determine the *literary quality* of a work of art but that its *greatness* depends upon other values as well. Among better known names in the New Criticism are William Empson, Richard P. Blackmur, Allan Tate, John Crowe Ransom, Cleanth Brooks, Robert Penn Warren, and W. K. Wimsatt, Jr.

Criticism, objective. The objective approach to poetry, as M. H. Abrams has pointed out, has become "one of the most prominent elements in the innovative criticism of the last two or three decades." The poem should be regarded as containing its own autonomy. As Northrop Frye puts it, such an approach "studies the symbolism of a poem as an ambiguous structure of interlocking motifs." The critic, according to this theory, must avoid the intentional fallacy and the affective fallacy (see *fallacy, affective).

Criticism, types of. The nomenclature of types of criticism varies, and it is possible for a critic to use several types of criticism or to make a general synthesis of several of them. The *moral* approach emphasizes the relationship of the work of art to moral and religious insights, makes clear the evaluation of society's manners and moral standards implicit in the work. The *historical* approach, working on the periphery of the work of art itself, deals with the facts of the author's times and life. The *formal* approach, especially emphasized in the New Criticism, stresses the value of the work in terms of its structure and aesthetic parts, normally without other consideration. It may study the place of a work of art in a *genre* or it may classify literary types, but some new critics reject such classification as going too much outside the individual work of art itself. This has also sometimes been called the *analytical* or *objective* approach. The *impressionistic* approach, particularly characteristic of the Romantic critics, stresses the personal effect of the work of art upon the critic. *Sociological* criticism looks upon works of art as revelations of society. This can be undertaken in an impartial spirit—the social life of ancient Athens, for example, as revealed through its literature. It may also be hitched to an ideological kite as in Marxist criticism, where the experience of literature is adduced as evidence in support of a preconceived ideology about society. *Psychological* criticism has become increasingly important in recent years through the impact of Sigmund Freud and Carl Jung. Literature is interpreted as a study of the human psyche, with particular stress on its unconscious aspects. *Archetypal* or *mythic* criticism is, in part, an outgrowth of a preoccupation with psychology, but it also owes a good deal to anthropology and the scholarship dealing with ancient myth. It stresses the kinship of man to his prehistoric past. We may also think of criticism in terms of method, as well as of focus. *Textual* criticism is concerned not with art as art but with the authenticity, variant readings, accuracy of the text. *Exegesis* attempts by scholarship to state the literal meaning of a text as it would be understood by a reader at the time the work was composed. *Explication of the text* offers a variety of commentary on the consecutive portions of the text. These various types of criticism could be considered to fall under the more general headings of criticism of judgment and criticism of interpretation. Comparative criticism is generally accepted to mean the comparison of works of different national literatures. The comparison may be based on some common element of theme, genre, technique, ideas, and may employ one or more of several critical approaches.

Dactyl. See *metrical feet.

Decorum is a Latin word signifying what is suitable, what is fitting. As applied to literature, it assumes that certain styles and conventions should go with certain subject matters. Thus, there is a style suitable to the epic, a style suitable to the pastoral. It is a key word in criticism from the renaissance through the neoclassical period. Sir Philip Sidney in his *Apology for Poetry* particularly commended the old-fashioned Senecan play, *Gorboduc,* for its decorum. A schoolbook of the late classical period, *Donatus on Terence,* sets out the basic premises of decorum as applied to the drama. Tragedy and comedy, being considered precise contraries, should not be mingled; tragic characters must be great, that is, of high rank; the direction of an action in tragedy is from order to disorder, the reverse in comedy; the plot of a tragedy is commonly historical and true, not feigned (hence the fusion of chronicle play and tragedy in Elizabethan drama); tragedy must be presented with a certain elegance of language. Decorum has other derivative implications. It assumes that there ought to be a special kind of congruity between a character and the type he represents. Decorum assumes that a man has a regular, settled condition, and that what a man is is largely determined by his place in life. Thomas Rymer, the eighteenth-century critic, objects to the character of Iago because he departs from the traditional delineation of a soldier. Iago thus violates decorum. Menenius in *Coriolanus* is not acceptable as a senator because he is not grave and dignified. Voltaire's conviction that Shakespeare wrote barbarously was based on the violation of decorum, a principle much reinforced by the neoclassicists.

Denotation. See *mental association.

Denouement is the section of the play in which a final disentanglement of the plot takes place.

Deus ex machina (literally, "the god from the machine") refers to the physical propelling from a stage structure ("the machine") of a god or supernatural force to remedy a dramatic situation which could not be solved within the terms of the logical structure of the play. This device appeared in the later history of the Greek drama and it is unanimously agreed that such a practice is a violation of good art.

Didacticism. Didactic literature has an overt instructional (generally moral) message to deliver, as in Oliver Goldsmith's "The Deserted Village":

Princes and lords may flourish, or may fade;
A breath can make them, as a breath has made;
But a bold peasantry, their country's pride,
When once destroyed, can never be supplied.

(53–56)

Much of the literature of the past was obviously meant to be didactic, for it was meant to teach as well as to delight. Modern theories of art tend to be strongly antididactic. James Joyce, for example, insists that art should never be propaganda. In a broad sense, however, all art teaches, just as we say that experience teaches. We cannot read a novel by Tolstoi without knowing more than we did before. The question is not whether art teaches, but what is the appropriate way in which art should teach. Such teaching must be organically united to the total structure of the work; it should not stand to one side or outside of it. Literature is broad enough to include a structure which is entirely and obviously didactic, such as Goldsmith's "The Deserted Village," where there is an organic didactic unity of didactic elements. Such work, of course, has its own special limitations. It obviously cannot do the same things as a nondidactic work. Furthermore, what is being taught may easily become dated because it is not sufficiently universal to affect later generations. The contemporary audience would find it difficult, for example, to see the need of a peasantry in Goldsmith's terms.

Dissociation of sensibility. *Sensibility* implies capacity for emotional response to works of art. It is often used as a generic term to denote the general taste, the themes and modes which evoke response in a given literary group or period. Thus we may speak of the *Romantic* sensibility or Victorian sensibility. "Dissociation of sensibility" is a phrase based on an essay by T. S. Eliot, "The Metaphysical Poets." Eliot praises the best work in metaphysical poetry, the work of such men as John Donne, Henry Vaughan, Richard Crashaw, and Andrew Marvell, on the ground that, while it was analytic, and in this sense dissociative, the metaphysical poets brought their material together again in a new unity. He finds that they were distinguished by a "direct, sensuous apprehension of thought, a recreation of thought into feeling." Such poets, he contends, were in the mainstream of poetic tradition and possessed a mechanism of sensibility which could devour any kind of experience. Eliot believes that this union of thought and feeling was not maintained by Milton and Dryden, that, while their language became more refined, feeling became more crude. They encouraged, in spite of their great achievements, dissociation of sensibility.

Drama, divisions of. See page 164.

Dramatic unities. See page 162.

Eclogue is a form of poetry developed by such classicists as Theocritus (Milton's "O fountain Arethuse" of the "Sicilian Muse") and Virgil ("Smooth-sliding Mincius crowned with vocal reeds"). Originally it dealt with dialogues between shepherds (hence the use of the word "pastoral"), in which through some competition, vocal or physical, one shepherd would win the favor or regard of a shepherdess. Sometimes the form is genuinely and honestly restricted to the rural life. Virgil's *Georgics,* for example, give sound advice on farming procedures. But in Roman times, the use of the form of allegory for giving serious or trenchant criticism under a surface of harmless innocence was developed. This explains the not-so-disguised attack on the Church of England in our outstanding English eclogue, Milton's "Lycidas." The use of shepherds' names for real people is part of the developed eclogue convention, as "Lycidas" for Edward King, "Damaetas" for Milton's tutor. The eclogue is one of the freest of classical forms. It can use terms that would not be considered to meet the *decorum of the epic or of tragedy. Thus Milton can speak of the *"taint worm* to the weanling herds that graze." Such a word would be below the dignity of epic or tragedy.

"Pastoral" is an extended term that goes well beyond the meaning of "eclogue." This term refers to a view of nature and of the countryside suitable to a sophisticated urbanite who genuinely loves nature but in an artistic and contemplative sense rather than through any active practical contact with rusticity. A working farmer is about the last person in the world to write a pastoral in this sense, though he might express his love of nature ably in other forms. Though hard to define, the pastoral must have at least some artificial quality like the china shepherds and shepherdesses of the eighteenth century and the country festivals *(fêtes champêtres)* of the French painter Watteau. The pastoral is an escape literature; it is a sophisticated literature making an art of following apparently guileless conventions.

Elegy is a song for the dead. The word comes from the Greek, originally meaning "a lament." The meaning has been extended to denote contemplative poems distinguished by a mood of sadness. Milton's "Lycidas" is properly a classical "lament." But we also refer to Gray's "Elegy in a Country Churchyard" as an elegy, although there is no lament for a specific individual.

Emblem refers particularly to the use of pictorial allegory, often in combination with verbal mottoes, in the baroque era. Where the traditional coat of arms served principally as an identifying sign of family background and relationships, the emblem often symbolized a complex set of values and relationships.

Empathy refers to our mental capacity for entering into the feelings and situations of another person (including, of course, a fictional or dramatic character). In the popular phrase, "we put ourselves in someone else's shoes." In literature, empathy enables the reader to understand a character's feelings and reactions, though empathy does not necessarily indicate moral approval. A reader can have empathy for Macbeth, without having sympathy for him in the sense of entering into wholehearted emotional approval of him. Empathy for Macbeth cannot be complete because what he does shocks our moral sense.

Epic is a complex narrative poem with a beginning, middle, and end. It is complex in the sense that numerous characters are involved, and subordinate actions and events are connected with the main story. An epic belongs to the classification of aristocratic literature. It was court poetry, sung to a lyre by a court poet. The court poet was also a historian who had committed to memory the great events of his people, who knew their genealogy and family background. The epic poet frequently alludes to other stories and events which he can safely assume that his audience knows without elaborating them or explaining them. Because the epic is written for an aristocratic and sophisticated audience, it is also concerned with court etiquette and propriety, and with statecraft and political techniques suitable to a ruler. Edmund Spenser, in a famous letter to Sir Walter Raleigh outlining the purpose of *The Faerie Queene,* says that his purpose is to fashion a noble gentleman as Virgil did in his Aeneas, Homer in his Odysseus. The hero is disciplined in all the virtues, both private and public.

Even *Beowulf,* which, in its structure, falls short of the classical prototypes its original clerical adapter must have had in mind, observes these conventions. As in the *Odyssey* and the *Aeneid* we are actually given an account of a court poet at work, in this case singing of the creation of the world. In the renaissance the epic was also an aid in the political training of princelings. Through these works, a young man destined for rule could be shown the prudent, tactful, and successful thing to do. Thus Odysseus finds an ingenious way to rescue his men from the cave of the Cyclops without a loss. *Beowulf* provides no less interesting, if less familiar, examples. It was always a touchy matter when a crew came from a foreign land. Did they come as friends, as marauders, or as dangerous exiles? The shore guard in *Beowulf* is very tactful but firm. He congratulates Beowulf's men on their appearance, welcomes them to Hrothgar's land, but gently informs them that he will look after their ship, place guards on it until they return. Without insulting anyone, the shore guard has achieved the proper political precaution. If the crew is bent on trouble, they will never get hold of their ship again.

Now this is the way a young prince should deal diplomatically with a touchy subject of this sort. We have another example where Beowulf and his men are warmly welcomed in Hrothgar's court at the same time that they are cautioned to leave their battle gear outside of the hall in which they meet the king for the first time.

A famous convention of epic structure is to begin in the middle of the action *(in medias res)*. The narrative should not be told in chronological order (as in a history). But the audience should be introduced at once into a suspenseful conflict *now* going on, as, for example, Aeneas already in the court of Dido, Satan already in Hell. The artist then works backward by allusions and conversations, forward by the developing action itself. This convention is not just a surface one; it is a basic device for creating excitement in the reader.

The epic has traditionally been distinguished by a great and noble style. As C. S. Lewis has pointed out in *Preface to Paradise Lost,* the epic is *solemn,* not in the sense of pompous, but in the sense of a dignified public statement. An epic has to be read slowly and ceremonially. C. S. Lewis makes relevant distinction between the *primary* epic (like the *Odyssey*), in which the individual, as an individual man, is fighting external danger and adversity, and the *secondary* epic (such as the *Aeneid* and *Paradise Lost*), in which the hero not only represents himself but also shows a relationship transcending his private concerns. Aeneas symbolizes the whole course of Roman history; Adam, the history of all mankind. Aeneas, for example, constantly has to go against his own desires because the gods insist upon his vocation as the future founder of Rome. He must leave Dido to die on her funeral pyre as his ship disappears over the horizon.

Epilogue is a speech delivered, generally by one of the actors, after the conclusion of a play. It may state a theme, pay compliments to the audience, congratulate an actor or a playwright, generally serving for propaganda and "public relations." In the epilogue of Sheridan's *The School for Scandal* we have an amusing parody of a famous speech of Shakespeare's *Othello:*

Farewell all quality of high renown,
Pride, pomp, and circumstance of glorious Town!
Farewell! Your revels I partake no more,
And Lady Teazle's occupation's o'er!

Sheridan pursues the theme of satire, found in his play, on another level in the epilogue. The epilogue, while consistent with the spirit of the play, is, of course, not essentially part of it.

Epiphany originally meant manifestation and was applied to the manifestation of Christ to the Gentiles in the persons of the Magi (the Feast of the Epiphany). As a literary term it originates in James Joyce's *A Portrait of the Artist as a Young Man.* Joyce has in mind the sudden shining forth, the bright illumination that a work of literary art gives us. It is not necessarily a climax in the rhetorical sense; it is something more illusive and transcendent, the birth of a great new symbol from the matrix of the work of art, dependent upon the work of art for its birth but also having a vibrant life of its own.

Episode is generally considered an incident in a series of events. Thus one may speak of an episode in any great narrative. If the events, through logical, psychological, or poetic structure, form a unity, the resulting work of art, though containing episodes, is not regarded as *episodic.* A major work of art, because of its characteristic ability to unite many diverse forces into a whole, is not episodic. Certain minor forms of art, like the picaresque novel (a tale of a rogue adventurer), maintain a degree of interest through local color and through the disconnected events being related to the one character.

Escapism. Certain works, very rarely regarded highly as literature, are meant purely for entertainment and for helping the reader temporarily to forget his own problems and absorptions. Such material is not meant to provide wisdom and insight into human problems but to create a world in which they are suspended or do not exist. James Thurber in "The Secret Life of Walter Mitty" gives an amusing satire of the type of personality who would make the ideal escapist reader.

Euphuism comes from a Greek word meaning graceful or well bred. The term "euphuism" has been popularized from John Lyly's *Euphues: The Anatomy of Wit* (1579). This was one of the highly decorative and rhetorical styles that found favor in aristocratic circles during the renaissance. It was characterized by perfectly balanced sentences which, in order to achieve such balance, had to make frequent use of allusions to history, to the herbaries (books dealing with plants) and bestiaries (natural history). Rhyme was sometimes employed, but a chief technical feature was the use of transferred alliteration. Word *A* alliterated with word *C,* word *B* with word *D,* and so on. Shakespeare parodies this style in Henry IV (II, iv, 436ff): "Peace, good pintpot. Peace, good tickle brain."

Exegesis. See *criticism, types of.

Existentialism denying traditional idealism (as in Plato) and materialism (as exemplified in Karl Marx), stresses the value of individual decision in a universe that is often supposed to be without purpose. The pessimistic side of existentialism has been most fully exemplified in the work of Jean-Paul Sartre. We exist; things exist. But the things have no meaning for us except in so far as we create meaning through acting upon them ("commitment" or "engagement"). By personal commitment of some sort we make the world at least temporarily bearable; we at least have the illusion of meaning. Since among the more pessimistic existentialists, the world itself is supposed to be meaningless and absurd, personal commitment eventually leads to loneliness and despair. But something is achieved through commitment—man has had the satisfaction of an illusion. Man should cherish such illusions, for they are the only things he has. As far as literature is concerned, the existentialists have an antipathy for all generalized concepts; they want to *show* through concrete act. The artist should not be seen in his work. Sartre has illustrated such assumptions in his novels, and the Theater of the Absurd owes some of its assumptions to the impact of the more pessimistic side of existentialism. It should be observed, however, that existentialism is a term used in a rather different sense, as in "Christian existentialism" and "affirmative existentialism." Man has freedom and actuality, it is argued, analogous to what God possesses outside of time and space, only in the present moment. A man cannot recover the past—he cannot act yesterday; the future is unborn or, through the possibility of death, unattainable. Such existentialists stress the need for man to give his present moment meaning; and he must *create* such meaning, and not merely be a passive recipient of what happens. This dramatization of the present moment owes a good deal to certain philosophical developments in the works of the Danish Soren Kierkegaard and the German Martin Heidegger. Among affirmative existentialists are Martin Buber and Gabriel Marcel.

Explication de texte. See criticism, types of.

Exposition is that part of a play in which the characters are identified, and their relationships to one another established, so that the ensuing conflict can be understood.

Expressionism. See page 176.

Fable. See *theme.

Fallacy, affective. A term used in W. K. Wimsatt, Jr., and Monroe C. Beardsley, *The Verbal Icon* (1954). The affective fallacy is a confusion between the poem and *its results* (what it *is* and what it *does*). . . ." These critics argue that the affective fallacy derives its standard of criticism from the psychological effects of the poem and ends in impressionism and relativism. The audience's response to a work of art, these critics maintain, is not in itself a guarantee of value.

Fallacy, intentional. See page 93.

Fallacy, pathetic. See *pathetic fallacy.

Falling action. See page 164.

Fantasy makes use of imagery in a different way and for a different purpose than does the imagination. Where the imaginative symbol points to intellectual meaning—the blood on Macbeth's hands, for example, becomes a symbol of a transcendent guilt that no water can wash away—fantasy employs images for their charm and decorative value. Intellectual meaning, if present, is only indirect. Thus *Alice in Wonderland* presents a series of fantasies, in which intellectual meaning is illusive, although the work in its totality has much meaning. Fantasy is the writing that most closely resembles the structure of the actual dream. We can remember in our dreams experiences of most precisely visualized imagery. The images of fantasy have such precision, especially emphasizing physical measurements (Alice growing so tall or so short—Gulliver among the Lilliputians or the Brobdingnagian giants). Shakespeare's diminutive fairies hang pearls in cowslips' ears, war with bats to get material for their coats, and disappear in a third part of a minute. In the fairy tale, the giant's strides are exactly so much; the hero uses such and such specific objects of such and such a size. Often he goes through a set of repeated experiences—generally three times—before he is triumphant. As in a dream, events happen without logical causality. Jack's beanstalk gets bigger and bigger and takes Jack into another land. We can derive many meanings from a dream—psychological, emotional, medical; but the thing that eludes us is the answer to what a dream means in an intellectual and logical sense. A fantasy presents a moving picture of scenes and happenings to which we can respond emotionally. We are, for example, deeply concerned with the fate of Alice, even with those of the White Rabbit and the sleepy Dormouse. But we are concerned in a different way than with Hamlet or Anna Karenina. We are deeply involved in imaginative literature; in the literature of fantasy we have less of a sense of responsibility, more the sense of play, of relaxation. Actually, the fairy tale is the form of writing nearest in form and content to the course of the actual dream. In this sense, this type of fantasy is close to the primitive archetype (see page 36).

Farce. See page 176.

Flashback is a representation, in the course of a narrative, of some event that has occurred before the "actual" time being presented in the story. The chronological arrangement of the story is interrupted for an artistic purpose. The account of the war in Heaven between the loyal and rebellious angels in Book VI of *Paradise Lost,* an event that occurred before the time that the epic action begins, is such a flashback. Raphael, in recounting these events, is serving to warn Adam of his potential danger and the problems he will face. The flashback makes information dramatic and relevant to immediate events and is a way of avoiding a flat chronological order. It is more or less a necessary device in a story beginning in the middle of an action (see **in medias res*).

Flat characters. See *characterization.

Foreshadowing in the drama (or narrative) is a statement or act which later in the work is paralleled by a similar statement or act, then possessing much more serious or tragic meaning. Romeo attempts suicide before Friar Laurence and the Nurse, a foreshadowing of his later actual suicide. At their final parting, Juliet looks down upon Romeo from the balcony and says:

O God, I have an ill divining soul!
Methinks I see thee, now thou art below,
As one dead in the bottom of a tomb . . .

(III, v, 53–55)

This is an unconscious and ironic verbal foreshadowing, for when Juliet sees Romeo again, he is indeed as one dead in the bottom of a tomb.

Form. See page 91.

Free verse avoids both a regular rhythmical pattern and the use of rhyme. It is the verse nearest to the natural rhythms of the language. Lines are long or short depending upon the emphasis that the writer wishes to give. A long line demands faster, more impetuous delivery. A short line demands correspondingly shorter, heavier emphasis.

Genre refers to the classification of a form of art, distinguished by special modes and forms, such as novel, epic, lyric.

Hamartia. See *tragic flaw.

History of ideas, or intellectual history, has become an increasingly important approach to literature. A dominant theme, as in A. O. Lovejoy's *The Great Chain of Being* (1936), is examined with reference to a series of major works that may also include relevant material from history, philosophy, and science, in order to clarify the idea and various interpretations of it. The emphasis here is not on the efficacy of the individual work as art but on the meaning and influence of a universal idea.

History plays. Shakespeare's plays are divided into tragedies, comedies, and histories. The history play was a classification of drama with which the contemporary theater is no longer familiar. In so far as such a play follows the course of historical events, while it may be selective, it may not have the tighter forms of traditional comedy or tragedy. It may contain comic and tragic elements, but it may be episodic and like a series of tableaux ("living scenes" not continuous, except in the sense that the material has a common bond, in this case that of history). Shakespeare's plays dealing with Henry IV fall into this category, as does Marlowe's *Tamburlaine.* All plays dealing with historical material were not necessarily histories. Both Marlowe and Shakespeare wrote tragedies rather than histories in *Edward II* and in *Richard II.*

Homeric simile is a method of adornment in Homer's poetry in which a simile is extended in terms of its setting. "A man runs like a deer" is an ordinary simile. But if we drew an extensive picture of the deer bounding through the autumn woods, fearful of his pursuers, we would add a picture to the comparison in the Homeric manner. Thus Milton compares Satan in size to Leviathan, the fabled sea serpent, and supplements the comparison with a completed picture:

Leviathan, which God of all his works
Created hugest that swim th' ocean stream:
Him haply slumb'ring on the Norway foam
The pilot of some small night-founder'd skiff,
Deeming some Island, oft, as Seamen tell,
With fixed Anchor in his scaly rind
Moors by his side under the Lee, while Night
Invests the Sea, and wished Morn delays.

(*Paradise Lost*, I, 201–208)

Humanism, Christian. See *Christian humanism.

Humanism, the New. A group of American humanists, including Irving Babbitt, Paul Elmer More, Norman Foerster, Louis J. A. Mercier, Robert Shafer, and others, affirmed the conception that man is unique in nature, that he is essentially both spirit and matter and cannot therefore be the product of purely material evolution. These humanists opposed all idealistic doctrines that would make men and nature, together with concepts of God, aspects of one substance only. Babbitt in *Rousseau and Romanticism* (1919) affirmed the classical stress on moderation, the sense of fitness and decorum, the necessity of the "inner check," in contrast to the idea of freedom as unlimited, in contrast to the image of the individual as capable of infinite extension in a ceaseless quest. Man's will is free; his experience is ethical rather than natural. Man should be concerned with what is universal and permanent and should be aware of his relationship to what is essentially and eternally human. The individual should seek a balanced personality, harmoniously developed according to a hierarchy of values. He is to cultivate reason in the Hellenic sense, but he is to be sensitive to the intuitive and imaginative as well. Above all, he is to develop an inner law of proportion which will prevent extravagance and anarchy. Basically the New Humanism was a reaction against naturalism, in the sense that naturalism did not grant man a special place in the universe, and against the ideology of romanticism which was thought both to distort the image of man by neglecting to realize his proper limitations and to degrade man's true value by insisting that he be something he could not properly be—a transcendent spirit, a Byronic wanderer, one outside space and time like Shelley "borne darkly, fearfully, afar." Many of these views are reflected in the work of the late English critic, C. S. Lewis, especially in *The Abolition of Man* (1947). A good account of the New Humanism is given by Louis J. A. Mercier in *American Humanism and the New Age* (1948)

Humor. See page 124.

Iamb. See *metrical feet.

Icon is a word derived from the Greek, meaning likeness or image. For John Crowe Ransom the icon is a particularized image which is contingent and unpredictable. It is an original image born from the unique perception of the artist, as distinct from a well-established image already in existence possessing a number of fixed associations.

Idiom refers to the distinct style of language, the individual imagistic formulation in a work of art. The problem of the artist is to create a fresh impact through his work. This means that his own idiom must not be identifiable with the idiom of previous art to the degree that he seems to be imitating another rather than speaking in his own right.

Image is generally contrasted with concept and idea, which are intellectual and abstract. Image implies some kind of pictorial or audial sensory impression in the mind. A *symbolic* image goes beyond the point of being a sign, an identification, of an object and points to intellectual meaning beyond what is overtly stated (see page 56).

Imagination. See page 58.

In medias res is a convention of the classical epic. By beginning "in the middle of the action," the narrator creates suspense by having chosen a definite time and place in which to start things rolling. By flashbacks he can work in the required background information as the story unfolds. See *epic, *flashback.

Instress and inscape. See page 14.

Intentional fallacy. See page 93.

Intuition. See page 56.

Irony in a broad sense refers to the human condition in which man finds himself. The most basic irony in this sense is that while man strives to live he knows he must die. Unless this fact is viewed against some greater truth, we have the irony of certain forms of *existentialism where man is considered an alien intruder in a meaningless universe. Irony in this sense implies a chasm between man's hopes and desires and an unalterable situation. Implicit in all irony is an opposition between a supposition and a reality. It is ironic when Oedipus in *Oedipus the King* sets out to find the man responsible for the gods' visitation of the plague upon the city of Thebes only to discover that the man is himself. The supposition was that he should do his duty and act as an admirable ruler. The reality was that he had only to look as far as himself. Irony arises from a man's assuming one state of affairs to exist when conditions are quite of a different kind. It is ironical when Capulet tries to relieve Juliet's supposed grief over the death of her cousin Tybalt by arranging a hasty marriage to Paris, when Juliet is, in fact, already married and grieving over Romeo's sentence of banishment. In drama we also speak of irony in the sense that an audience is in possession of special knowledge that is not possessed by the stage character. Thus it is ironical that we know that Juliet is really alive although Romeo thinks she is dead. It has been said that irony is distinguished by emotional detachment. But this is often merely an illusory surface matter. Comic relief as used in a Shakespearean play involves only a temporary detachment, as in the porter scene in *Macbeth*. The porter is clowning at the mouth of Hell, and, after the temporary illusion of detachment, the image of Hell comes with even greater emotional impact. We sometimes speak of conscious and of unconscious irony in literature. Irony is conscious when the character himself realizes his inadequacy or absurdity in a situation, unconscious when he has no idea of the figure he is cutting. Farinata, seated bolt upright in a coffin burning to white heat, will not speak to Dante in the *Inferno* until he is assured that Dante comes from a good family. He maintains his social principles with absurd earnestness under impossible conditions and never suspects that he is a fool whose pride has brought him to such a situation.

Levels of meaning. The poetic art, in particular, because it synthesizes or unites, implies much more than it states directly. In examining levels of meaning we explore and discover, make overt, such implications, and thus become conscious of the full range of the literary statement.

Literal. The literal meaning of a statement is to be distinguished from the figurative or metaphorical. The literal meaning of "serpent" in *Genesis* is the reptile of that name. The figurative meaning is Satan or evil. If a figurative statement is read as a literal one, a complete loss of meaning may result. Manfred says in Byron's play that his actions have made one desert, barren and cold,

. . . on which the wild waves break,
But nothing rests, save carcasses and wrecks,
Rocks, and the salt sea-surf weeds of bitterness.

(*Manfred*, II, i, 56–58)

Restricted to its literal meaning, this statement would be absurd. Manfred made a desert (who would want to make a desert in the first place?). He has supplied carcasses and an unusual vegetation, "sea-surf weeds of bitterness," which are probably rare specimens. Literal meaning has little place here in this intensely moving imagery of the spirit's interior loneliness.

Local color refers to the kind of particularized detail which gives the reader the illusion of being in a specific region. This particularization may be necessary for the writer in order to create plausibility for a character or a situation. In fact, the plot may be dependent on a localized situation for its acceptance. Thus, Melville's *Moby Dick* is essentially united to the local color in which it is set. All the details of New Bedford, the facts about the whaling industry, the routine of the ship, the colors and moods of the sea are an essential part of this suspenseful and symbolic novel.

Lost metaphors is a term used in modern scholarship in reference to metaphors which once had traditional meanings with which the contemporary reader is likely to be unacquainted. Thus Samson in Milton's *Samson Agonistes* is a traditional prototype of Christ, and the play has, as one of its themes, the Passion of Christ. The Orpheus image in "Lycidas" symbolizes the decay of civilization in one country and its rebirth elsewhere. The Thracian women killed Orpheus because his melancholy music bewailing the loss of his beloved Eurydice drove them frantic. They threw his head into the Hebrus and it was borne to Lesbos, the land of the new culture which received it reverently:

His goary visage down the stream was sent,
Down the swift Hebrus to the Lesbian shore.

(62–63)

Lyric derives from the Greek word for lyre. It was a poem sung to the accompaniment of a lyre. It therefore suggests something spontaneous, ardent, emphasizing personal feeling. The lyric poem, as, for example, Herrick's "To Daffodils," is distinct from the epic poem, a narrative, or the dramatic poem. It is also quite distinct from what has been called didactic verse, verse that teaches or makes expositions and arguments as in Pope's *Essay on Man*.

Masque. While the masque is similar to drama, it differs in one essential respect. In a drama, everything must be subordinated to the needs of dramatic *action*. In the masque form, particularly popular in court circles in the sixteenth and seventeenth centuries, action is frankly peripheral to the allegorical theme, the dance, music, and song. Highly conventionalized, the masque has three main movements: the first is the masque movement proper, in which there is a dance featuring the forces of good; the second movement is that of the antimasque, the evil forces, Milton's "rout of monsters" in *Comus;* the third movement represents the victory of the good forces over the evil. The masque, enormously expensive to produce, using expensive stage sets (Inigo Jones is particularly famous as a designer), was privately performed, and members of the audience were invited to participate in certain of the formal dances. Fashioned to the occasion for which it was presented, the masque gave an allegorical interpretation of established myths and legends. The famous speech of Oberon in *A Midsummer Night's Dream* (II, i) describing the bolt of Cupid and the mermaid on a dolphin's back is thought to refer to an elaborate masque previously presented at court.

Melodrama. See page 176.

Mental association refers to the fact that we do a great deal of thinking in terms of images, suggestions, or stream of consciousness. Logical thinking is only one part of the work of the mind. Mental association is *not* illogical thinking but thinking of a different order. Mental association does not operate haphazardly. It is based upon experience and emotional factors. By mental association is meant the habitual way in which ideas and images go together in our mind through our personal experience, which touches more forces in us than the purely logical or deliberate. When we speak of the denotation of a word, we mean its specific, permanent, intellectual meaning. The connotation of a word indicates the range of mental associations we have in regard to it. Mental association also refers to the way in which ideas and images go together in our mind as a result of some external suggestion, frequently verbal, which touches more forces in us than the purely logical or deliberate. Some associations are the result of custom and convention such as "black" with "death" or "night." Other associations result from the unique experience of an individual, conscious or unconscious. Thus "black" develops an unpredictable but aptly communicable mental association in the phrase, "helpless retrospect of black veils."

Metaphor has been defined as "a figure of speech in which a term is applied to something to which it is not literally applicable in order to suggest a resemblance." John Unterecker says that the distinction between a metaphor and a symbol is one between assigned and unassigned meaning. "A metaphor always has at least two assigned meanings (its own sign value and the sign value of the object or idea it stands for). But a symbol stands on one leg only; the other kicks at the stars." Northrop Frye comments: "Thus if we say 'the hero was a lion' we identify the hero *with* the lion, while at the same time both the hero and the lion are identified *as* themselves. A work of literary art owes its unity to this process of identification *with,* and its variety, clarity, and intensity to identification *as.*" See *simile.

Metaphor, mixed. A mixed metaphor implies a combination of two metaphors which, on the literal level, contradict one another or are otherwise incongruous. "General Rommel won his laurels in the African sands." Once we think of laurels (symbolic of victory) in a literal sense, we find the desert an incongruous place for them. On the other hand, some mixed metaphors are so effective that it is an unnatural strain to think of the literal meaning of either one of them. Samuel Johnson adversely criticized Milton's reference to the clergy in "Lycidas" as "blind mouths." But to many readers this would seem to be a very effective compression. "Blind" refers to intellectual and spiritual blindness, and "mouths" is a symbol of hungry greed. The phrase is used in the context with such overwhelming indignation that no one asks *literally* whether mouths can be blind.

Meter is basically a rhythmic arrangement of words. It differs from the great rhythms inherent in normally good prose (determined by the logical and musical construction of language itself), and from those in free verse (determined by the length of the units of vocal delivery), in its having fixed or permanent patterns.

Metonymy and synecdoche. *Metonymy* uses the name of one thing for another to which it has some logical relationship. Thus the Cross is a metonymy for Christianity, the Star of David for Judaism. The image of *synecdoche* uses a part for the whole, the whole for the part, the particular for the general, the general for the particular. Thus Yeats's image of an old man, "a tattered coat upon a stick," would be considered a synecdoche.

Metrical feet. The terminology for English prosody comes from classical sources. In Greek or Latin, metrical measure is determined by long and short syllables. English, however, is a heavily stressed language and we determine metrical feet by stressed and unstressed syllables.

The common metrical feet in English are the *iamb,* an unstressed syllable followed by a stressed one (x/), and the *trochee,* a stressed syllable followed by the unstressed (/x).

Dactyl (from a Greek word, meaning "finger," which has a long joint followed by two short ones) consists of one stressed syllable followed by two unstressed ones (/xx).

Anapest, the reverse of the dactyl, consists of two unstressed syllables followed by a stressed syllable (xx/).

Metrical lines are the dimeter (two feet), trimeter (three feet), tetrameter (four feet), pentameter (five feet), hexameter (six feet). A hexameter in iambics is called an Alexandrine.

Mimesis is a general Aristotelian term that describes the function of art as *imitation.* Art is a heightened or selective imitation of experience, to paraphrase Aristotle's thought. In reference to drama, the mimesis or mimetic action refers to what is actually "acted out" on the stage as distinct from what is referred to through conversation as having taken place or is said to take place off stage. See *aesthetic distance.

Miracle play is a term applied to medieval religious drama. The medieval dramatist adhered to the content of the scriptures, giving them a realistic interpretation, but allowing himself a certain independence in the direction of humor and pathos. Miracle plays were eventually organized into *cycles,* produced yearly in certain towns under the patronage of the guilds. They comprised the whole religious history of man, from the Fall to Christ's Passion and Redemption.

Monologue, interior, grew out of the efforts to express the subconscious part of man's mind. The French writer Edouard Dujardin thus defined it: "The interior monologue is the discourse without auditor, unspoken, by which a person expresses his inmost thought, the thought nearest the unconscious, anterior to any logical organization, by means of sentences with a minimum of syntax. It is done so as to give the impression that it is poured out, and is a slice of the interior life without explanation or commentary." Exponents of this device include Virginia Woolf and James Joyce. See *stream of consciousness.

Morality play is a play in the form of an *allegory, popular from the fourteenth to the sixteenth centuries. It is distinct from the problem play, which is seldom an obvious allegory, in that the answer to the problem raised is fixed and overt rather than ambiguous or inferred. *Everyman,* which depicts the human condition in the face of death, outlines the Christian solution to the problem of facing death, dramatically stating what steps have to be consecutively taken. The morality play does not hesitate to present a whole cast of personified abstractions, as in the case of *Everyman.* Frequently it also mingles real persons with abstractions.

Motif, motive. *Motif* (French) is often anglicized into *motive.* In the broadest sense, motif can be considered roughly equivalent to the leading theme or idea in a work of art. In a narrower sense, a motif is a repeated pattern in a work, especially in a narrative, in which, as developments unfold, more meaning, especially emotional, accrues. An example is the repeated reference to the jingling bells of the fool's cap in Poe's "A Cask of Amontillado."

Negative capability. John Keats in a letter to Richard Woodhouse, October 27, 1818, pictures the poet as one who loses consciousness of self, his sense of identity, and is open to all impressions. "As to the poetical character itself . . . it is not itself—it has no self—it is everything and nothing. It has no character—it enjoys light and shade; it lives in gusto, be it foul or fair, high or low, rich or poor, mean or elevated. It has as much delight in conceiving an Iago as an Imogen. . . . A poet is the most unpoetical of anything in existence, because he has no identity. . . ." Keats called this openness to impression, before conscious selection intervenes, "negative capability."

Neoclassicism is a term applied in particular to the social and aesthetic views prevalent in eighteenth-century England, which were given their most popular and generalized expression in Alexander Pope's *Essay on Man* and in his *Essay on Criticism*. Pope assumes a universal established order in which he identifies the philosopher's ontology or being with the *status quo* (the actual existing state of affairs). Providence has provided man with the best of all possible worlds, and if man finds something seriously the matter with it, this attitude is due to the fact that man has not been able to grasp the entire cosmic picture. Earthquakes do not disturb the natural order, and a Borgia or a Catiline do not disturb the human order. "Whatever is, is right," Pope affirms, implicitly doing away with the age-long problem of evil. The traditional view going back to St. Thomas Aquinas was that everything is good *in so far* as it is. Evil consists in the absence or perversion of being. From this point of view a slum would not be bad in so far as it provided human habitation; a slum would be bad in so far as the habitation available was *deficient,* lacking in the fullness of being. Pope's acceptance of the *status quo* was confirmed in other ways in the eighteenth-century culture. Popular religious instruction maintained that it was a man's duty to fulfill his station in life, but it also frequently assumed that the station in life a person actually had (for example, a woman working twelve to fourteen hours a day in a coal mine) was the actual station *designed* by an almighty Providence—a failure again to note the difference between a universal value and a *status quo*. On the scientific level, Thomas Malthus maintained that without poverty, disease, and even war, the world's population would outrun the food supply. He implicitly discouraged social movements on the basis that social amelioration would make things worse rather than better. Because of the eighteenth-century social structure, such views, alleged with justice to be complacent, did not meet with any forceful opposition until the advent of the Romantic revolution. In regard to art, Pope again assumed a settled order; the canons of art, he believed, had been established in the times of Homer and of Virgil, and to imitate nature was to imitate them. *Nature* was thus interpreted in the light of a universal reasoning man—in other words, according to the view of life commonly held by the eighteenth-century educated class. The neoclassical view differs considerably from the classical view, which thought of nature in terms of a living reality that art imitated according to its own special modes of being. Classicism did not think of art in terms of imitation of previous works of art (see page 187). The eighteenth-century aesthetic removed the unpredictable from the creation of art. It even assumed a settled poetic language, insisted on clarity of expression, in the sense of universally accepted *signs, and was psychologically in opposition to highly individualistic metaphoric language. William Wordsworth, in the preface to the second edition of *Lyrical Ballads* (1800) rejected the conventional eighteenth-century epithets and personifications that characterized the "elevated" language of poetry in favor of what he considered naturalness, sincerity, and spontaneity.

Novel is a term originally derived from the Italian *novella,* a probable abbreviation of the Latin *novella narratio* (new narration). A novel is rather fluidly defined, but certain characteristics can be assumed. It is a long form of fiction (in contrast to the short story); it is meant to represent what is thought to be real life, whether historical (as in the novels of Sir Walter Scott) or contemporary with the author's life (as generally in Charles Dickens). The characters frequently develop or evolve in some way (not necessarily for the better), though in a novel of pure adventure they may remain fairly static. The novel may have a great variety of emphases—humorous, satiric, tragic, psychological, socially critical, didactic, escapist.

Novel, naturalistic, is the type of novel furthest removed from artistic selectivity and convention. Claiming scientific accuracy, it presents a slice of life. Stemming from certain movements in French literature, in particular from Émile Zola, who said that "naturalism is a formula of modern science applied to literature," naturalism allies the novel with practical sociology. The naturalistic novel, as distinct from the realistic novel, has a definite ideological background. Man does not have free will but is determined by his background and environment. He is part of an evolving nature and is inseparable from it.

Novel, realistic, is the type of novel that attempts an accurate observation of everyday life. Artistically, realism presents a problem. How realistic can a realistic novel be without endangering *aesthetic distance? The major realistic novels (including those of Flaubert) indicate a great degree of selectivity in their choice of detail. They are by no means a slice of life. Realism does not necessarily imply an unselective recording of details. As in all great art, irrelevant details must be omitted. But the realistic novelist aims for probability and normality. In that sense he is not fanciful, not romantic. Realism, as a literary doctrine, accompanied the acceleration of scientific growth in the nineteenth century. "Facts, which began by being the master of science, proceeded to become the matter of literature." When the realistic method ceases to be associated with major values and critical perceptions, we have the so-called "human document," which artistically is sometimes on the same level as the clinical report. It may be informing, but it may lack the tension (see page 20) necessary for art.

Objective correlative. According to T. S. Eliot, "the only way of expressing emotion in the form of art is by finding an 'objective correlative'; in other words, a set of objects, a situation, a chain of events which shall be the formula of that *particular* emotion; such that when the external facts, which terminate in sensory experience, are given, the emotion is immediately evoked. . . . ("Hamlet," *Selected Essays*, 1932, pp. 124-125.) A brief illustration of an objective correlative can be found in these lines of Shakespeare:

That time of year thou mayst in me behold
When yellow leaves, or none, or few, do hang
Upon those boughs which shake against the cold,
Bare ruined choirs where late the sweet birds sang.

(Sonnet LXXIII)

Shakespeare wants us to get his sense of loneliness and abandonment. We have the external facts in the picture of an autumn tree, denuded of its last leaf, of the choir, abandoned by its last singer.

These images create in us, as readers, a sense of the sad and the transitory; we have emotions corresponding to those that Shakespeare felt in regard to his own situation in life.

Objective criticism. See *criticism, objective.

Objective and subjective. Any work of art is objective in the sense that it is a created object having its own being. In this sense, if an author makes himself, his own feelings and impressions, the central theme of his work, his writing, as *a work of art,* is just as objective as if he were to write about someone else. These terms are often used relatively in the sense of how far the author's own personality is made evident in a work of art. In a broad sense all art can be termed subjective since it reflects experience as seen by a particular person, the artist. A work of art cannot be created by a committee or by a scientific laboratory; it is the creation of an individual. But, in so far as the artist draws attention to himself in his creation, he may be called subjective; in the degree to which attention is drawn to his theme, as distinct from himself, as in modern nonrhetorical art, he can be said to be objective. Shakespeare, who says nothing directly about himself in his plays, could be called objective. Byron, who is constantly talking about himself under various disguises, could be called subjective. Friedrich Schlegel, who introduced the distinction between classic and romantic, thinks of the classical artist as objective, without reference to private interests, revealing "nothing more of the individual writer than his capacity to achieve the one uniform excellence according to the universal laws of beauty." Romantic art, on the other hand, emphasizes the personal sensibility of the artist.

Ode is a special division of lyric poetry. It is not light and delicate, as is frequently the case in the lyric, but solemn and dignified. It constitutes a very public statement, as distinct from the personal message frequently characteristic of the lyric. It is often commemorative or laudatory, as Marvell's "Upon Cromwell's Return from Ireland" or Dryden's "St. Cecilia's Day." Its tie to the lyric lies not so much in its subject matter as in the fact that originally both the ode and the lyric were closely allied to music. The ode, in particular, is suitable for setting to music and frequently for being chanted by a chorus. The most formal type of ode is the Pindaric (Pindar was a Greek poet, 522–443 2.3.). Each section consists of a strophe and antistrophe (choral song and response) of identical form and an epode (the choral section following the strophe and antistrophe) of contrasting form. The *Horatian ode* has uniform lyric stanzas.

Onomatopoeia from a Greek word meaning the "making of words" refers to the use of words so that the sound itself suggests the meaning, as in the word "whippoorwill."

Ottava rima. See *stanza.

Overtone. The meaning of *overtone* in acoustics indicates its meaning in literature; "any frequency emitted by an acoustical instrument that is higher in frequency than the fundamental." The overtone is the higher range of suggested or implied but not explicitly stated meaning, particularly in poetry.

Oxymoron is a rhetorical figure, particularly popular in the renaissance, which is a form of *paradox. Two apparently contradictory terms are put together in the same epithet, both having valid relationships to the subject named. Thus Shakespeare refers to love as "heavy lightness, serious vanity."

Parable is a short story illustrating by analogy some truth or moral precept. The climax lies in the fullness of interpretation that is given to it. Thus the parable of the sower (*Matthew:* 13:1–28) illustrates the various kinds of receptivity, fruitful and unfruitful, to the prophet's message. "And the one sown upon good ground, that is he who hears the word and understands it. . . ."

Paradox is a statement that appears to be self-contradictory, as in the gospel statement that he who seeks to save his life shall lose it, and that he who loses his life shall save it. In a paradox, the writer is speaking on more than one level at a time. The gospel is thinking of life in a literal sense and also of life in the sense of value—generosity is life, selfishness is death. When Juliet says that her bounty is as boundless as the sea and her love as deep,

. . . the more I give to thee
The more I have, for both are infinite.

(II, ii, 134–135)

she has in mind the assumption that goodness consists in *giving*, so that the more one gives, the more goodness one has. This deeper meaning conflicts with the surface and immediate impression that giving something away implies that one has less. "Paradox" is a word used frequently in the New Criticism in relation to the multiple meanings that may exist in a poetic statement.

Paraphrase attempts to put the meaning of a text in simpler, clearer, or more popular language. This effort is fraught with less dangers of misrepresentation in dealing with denotative prose than in handling highly symbolic and multidimensional meaning as in many kinds of poetry. In the latter case, a paraphrase may capture only a minor aspect of the meaning.

Parody is the application of a humorous method, that of deliberate distortion, in imitation of another artist's method and style. It may operate through exaggerating certain obvious characteristics, deliberately employing *bathos and *anticlimax. It may apply an imitated sublime style of a writer to a trivial content; it may recall the overtones of a work in a deliberately meaningless content. Parody is generally most successful in imitation of work in which a perfect accord between form and content is lacking, especially where the writer's way of saying something becomes more prominent than what he says. William Wordsworth's deliberately simple style, when it became too mannered, as in "The Idiot Boy," became a favorite subject of parody. Wordsworth himself had been aware of the dangers of that poetry in which the language "closely resembles that of life and nature." Wordsworth points out in his preface to *Lyrical Ballads* that verses of this kind can be easily parodied, and he quotes Samuel Johnson's stanza as a specimen:

I put my hat upon my head
And walked into the Strand,
And there I met another man
Whose hat was in his hand.

Lewis Carroll manages in "Jabberwocky" to parody a whole genre rather than a specific work. He gives the essential impression of a medieval ballad, with some romantic rehandling, as it might be recalled by one who was possibly once overexposed to it but whose memory now has become slightly deficient. Using words of his own invention, Carroll captures the mood of such a piece, with its suggestions of marvelous and wondrous creatures, and of the dangers of frumious and whiffling monsters:

'Twas brillig, and the slithy toves
Did gyre and gimble in the wabe;
All mimsy were the borogoves,
And the mome raths outgrabe.

The artistic limitation of parody arises from the fact that it is a derivative literature. It depends for its effect upon the reader's being already well acquainted with the work parodied.

Pastoral. See *eclogue.

Pathetic fallacy is a term invented by John Ruskin in a famous essay of that name. Ruskin was interested in classifying poets. Of the first rank were those who both thought and felt truly. Then came the poets who thought more truly than they felt; then the poets who felt more truly than they thought. Ruskin allowed for a further class—prophets like Isaiah—who had intuitions and visions beyond the limitations of language and even their own intellectual understanding. The very highest vision tended to be expressed confusedly. The phrase itself is composed of one word meaning "affecting the feelings" and the other meaning "intellectually untrue." A poet may write of the "cruel, crawling foam" in which a girl was drowned. The suggestion of cruelty touches our emotions, but in actual fact the foam cannot be cruel or have any other human possibilities. Whenever a writer attributes human qualities to nonhuman nature, he uses the pathetic fallacy. It is often emotionally effective but can easily become sentimental. The reverse procedure, that of stressing the lack of correspondence between human and nonhuman nature, makes for stark and ironic effects.

Pathos. See page 123.

Peripety is a term indicating reversal of fortune for the protagonist in a drama. In *Romeo and Juliet* the peripety may be said to occur when Romeo, who has tried to stop the fight between Mercutio and Tybalt, inadvertently gives Tybalt the opportunity to wound Mercutio lethally. In anger, Romeo then kills Tybalt. Romeo's reversal of fortune starts from that point.

Plot. See *theme.

Poetic justice applies to a situation in which all the participants are rewarded according to their deserts within the story or drama. What this in effect means is a one-level view of the moral world. Tragedy, in which there is disproportionate suffering, or any kind of vicarious sacrifice, would be outside of this mechanical moral measurement. Poetic justice in this sense leaves nothing to a sense of wonder or mystery outside of time and space. Nahum Tate gave a revised ending for *King Lear* in the eighteenth century in which Cordelia married Edgar. Other considerations aside, such an ending removes the deep sense of pity that Shakespeare created, an emotion that great tragedy attempts to arouse. The term is also used ironically to indicate a situation in which the villain through overreaching himself brings upon himself his own punishment inadvertently and unconsciously.

Poetics, a work by Aristotle (composed about 330 B.C.), presents a standard theory of art, in particular about the epic and drama, that has remained constantly influential. Common terms such as "mimesis" and "catharsis" derive from this work.

Point of view is a term applied to narrative. The story can be told in the first person by a character who figures in the story. This is the point of view of a first-person observer. A story is more frequently told in the third person, in the *omniscient* point of view. Here the writer can tell everything about everybody, because the storyteller is assumed to be present everywhere. Another technique is that of the *objective* point of view, where the storyteller presents what actually is said to happen without entering into the thinking processes of the characters. See page 113.

Polarities is a term used with particular reference to the *tension* of art. It refers to the fact that art often succeeds in reconciling discordant or opposed elements. In this sense, it is related to *paradox. The image in the phrase is that of two poles attracting in opposite directions, but yet, paradoxically, going together and reinforcing one another. Thus Andrew Marvell addresses his Coy Mistress:

The grave's a fine and private place,
But none, I think, do there embrace.

Marvell has surprisingly praised the grave (one polarity); he has then disabused us of this notion because of a surprising disadvantage (the other polarity). The two polarities unite in one effective statement, antithetical and witty (see pages 68 and 125).

Problem play deals with a special type of problem either of individual conscience or of civic responsibility. All plays present problems, but against a background of accepted values. In a problem play, the value itself is questioned and its ambiguities dramatically examined. Thus in Galsworthy's *Escape,* the question is raised whether a minister should betray the confidence of an escaped criminal or not. Should his duty to religion take precedence over his duty to the community? In Ibsen's *A Doll's House* the question is raised whether a wife has the right to leave a husband who violates his wife's personality, refusing to allow her the status and maturity of an adult. The accepted conventions were, of course, that a minister should not violate a confidence and that a wife should not disregard her marriage bonds.

Prologue refers to that part of a play that often gives information helpful to understanding what follows. In Plautus's *Menaechmi,* for example, the playwright has to bridge over the unlikelihood of there being twins with exactly the same name in the same town. So we have a long explanation of how this came about. But since the prologue is not generally essential to a play, Plautus's device is a little unusual. Frequently the prologue, like the epilogue, states a theme, makes a social commentary, and eases the audience into the play.

Proscenium. See *apron stage.

Protagonist is derived from a Greek word meaning one actively fighting or struggling on behalf of something. It is a phrase generally applied to the principal character in a tragedy.

Prototype is the original after which a model is formed. It has a narrower meaning than archetype (see page 36), in which the original cannot always be defined. By extension of usage, a prototype does not always mean a model which is consciously imitated. The mere presence of an important resemblance may be sufficient to call a person or a thing a prototype. Thus Prometheus, the ancient Titan who, in his compassion for men, taught them the arts of healing and of fire, was punished by Zeus by being chained to a mountain rock in the Caucasus, where a vulture fed on his daily renewed liver. Because of his sacrificial love, Prometheus has sometimes been called a prototype of Christ.

Psychic distance. See *aesthetic distance.

Pure poetry, while used as a theoretical absolute, is in actual practice a relative term. Though the critics employing this term are by no means in agreement among themselves, poetry is generally regarded as approaching purity when it is removed from rhetoric (see page 94), when it can be detached from context and stand by itself, when it is imagistic and symbolic rather than analytical and assertive. Since uniform agreement is lacking, and some critics do not believe pure poetry exists as distinct from poetry, some consider the use of the term unwise. Can dramatic poetry, for example, be potentially pure poetry under any circumstances? "After life's fitful fever he sleeps well," Macbeth says. Detached and by itself this line (*Macbeth,* III, ii, 23) might even be considered rhetorical. But in the play it expresses a poignant and overwhelming dramatic fact—that Macbeth is envious of the man he murdered, Duncan. It is magnificent dramatic poetry. It could be argued that pure poetry is not necessarily any better than poetry dependent on context and even combined with nonimagistic assertive statement. The term tends in practice to be restricted to special types of imagistic poetry such as that of Paul Verlaine and Arthur Rimbaud in France. As M. H. Abrams has pointed out, the tradition stemming from Longinus thinks of a poetry that is suggestive and hypnotic, leaving the reader in a state of mind resembling a dream. This effect is undoubtedly a resource of poetry, but poetry has a wide range of resources. A critic who believes that the interpretation of a poem should be restricted to its own intrinsic structure does not necessarily believe in the principle of pure poetry.

Radical image. The term has been applied to certain types of images (as in the seventeenth-century metaphysical school) in which the less-emphasized terms of the image may be technical or learned and in which there may be a strong element of prose analysis. George Herbert's emotionally warm religious poem, "The

Collar," presents the underlying analytic (radical) image of a dog with a collar and a rope, barking from a doghouse.

Rhetoric. The modern problem of rhetoric is discussed on pages 94 and 114. Rhetoric as the art of the literary uses of language has had a distinguished history. Shakespeare was thoroughly trained in its devices (see Sr. Miriam Joseph, *Shakespeare's Use of the Arts of Language,* 1947). The renaissance stressed the idea of *decorum and the adjustment of certain types of style to certain subject matters. Milton sought the highest "answerable" style for his epic, whereas Edmund Spenser sought the "second tenor" (*The Faerie Queene,* I, xi, vii). Joseph Scaliger in his *Poetics* (1561) makes very precise definitions of the requirements for the three divisions of style: high, middle, low. They are worth quoting to note that the renaissance had its own new criticism of precision:

> We recognize three kinds of style, the grand or lofty *(altiloqua),* the humble *(infima),* and the mean of the two, which I please to call the moderate *(aequabilis).* Some properties are common to all of these, some are particular. Common properties are perspicuity *(perspicuitas),* refinement *(cultus),* propriety *(proprietas),* elegance or grace *(venustas),* and rhythm *(numerositas).* These qualities should inhere in every poem. Of the other common properties some are not invariably used, but subject to occasion, as smoothness *(mollitia),* winsomeness *(suavitas),* rapidity or spirit *(incitatio),* purity or unadornedness *(puritas),* acumen *(acutum),* sharpness or raillery *(acre),* fulness *(plenum),* and ornateness *(floridum).* As of the common properties, so of the particular, some should be employed always, others only on occasion. In the grand style those to be observed always are dignity *(dignitas)* and sonorousness *(sonus);* those to be used on occasion, ponderousness *(gravitas)* and fervency *(vehementis).* In the lowly style that to be observed always is plainness or artless purity *(tenuitas);* on occasion, simplicity *(simplicitas)* and negligence *(securitas).* Those to be invariably observed in the moderate style are roundness *(rotunditas)* and fluency *(volubilitas).* Such is our classification, and it is complete and invariable. [*Poetics* (1561), IV, ii, in James Harry Smith and Edd Winfield Parks, *The Great Critics* (New York: 1951), p. 160.]

Rhyme royal. See *stanza.

Rhythm, sprung, consists of metrical feet, having one stressed syllable beginning the foot and any number of unstressed syllables.

Rising action. See page 164.

Ritual and magic. The important fact about ritual is that it consists in *set* ceremonies. The exact words, the exact gestures must be observed to produce the desired effect such as rainfall and fertility. Any deviation, however slight, may destroy the desired effect of the ceremony. In so far as ritual affects art, it helps to inspire certain solemn dignified themes, religious in origin, for which the artist may avail himself of traditional emotional response on the part of the audience. Francis Fergusson in *The Idea of a Theater* (1949) has particularly stressed the impact of ritual on the earlier forms of drama. Ritual differs from magic, in that ritual is supported by religious tradition and is designed to have effects which a whole community supports. Magic is ritualistic in manner but may be employed by an individual for individual ends, without reference to the health and well-being of the community as a whole. Ritual is related to what has been always predicated; magic can be related to the unpredictable and the original. Ritual will control the floods; magic will turn the head of Bottom into that of an ass (*A Midsummer Night's Dream*). Ritual restates what is established; magic is experimental and empiric.

Rococo is the word applied to certain developments in decoration and architecture evolving from the *baroque. It is sometimes used loosely for baroque.

Romance suggests etymologically the origin of this type of story in the vernacular language, *Romanica,* as distinct from Latin itself. "Romance" and "romance languages" derive from the same root association. We habitually think of the old romances as tales of the wondrous, the exotic, the heroic, frequently comprising supernatural as well as chivalric elements. Milton has caught the spirit of the old romance in "Il Penseroso":

The story of Cambuscan bold,
of Camball, and of Algarsife,
And who had Canacee to wife,
That owned the vertuous Ring and Glass
And of the wondrous Horse of Brass,
On which the Tartar king did ride:

And if aught else great Bards beside
In sage and solemn tunes have sung,
Of tourneys and of trophies hung,
Of forests, and enchantments drear,
Where more is meant than meets the ear.

(110–120)

Its setting was normally one of knighthood and chivalry. Even when the stories came from an older period, such stories tended, as in the medieval romance of *Sir Gawain and the Green Knight,* to be rewoven in medieval settings. Many of the stories connected with the Arthurian legend could be thus classified. They differed from the epic in that the epic was centrally organized. *Romance* embraced a variety of themes, and was basically more realistic. Whether medieval or not, the romance generally presents travel in strange places, the separation and eventual union of lovers. In later usage, "romance" is often used for a narrative in which the central theme is that of love between man and woman, its generosity, bravery, and impediments. Generally but not always the type of romance ends happily; it need not present the marvelous and the exotic.

Romantic comedy. See page 173.

Romanticism and classicism. Romanticism is a term that may apply to a complex of ideas, an intellectual movement important in the history of culture. It is in this sense that we speak of the Romanticism of the early nineteenth century (see *Romanticism, ideology of). It may also apply to a specific technique in the field of art. It is in this second sense that we shall consider it here. In this sense we may distinguish Romanticism from classicism purely in regard to artistic methodology. The adjective "classical" is used *broadly* in reference to any established work of art. We are not using the word in this broad sense.

Walter Pater says: "The romantic or classical character of a picture, a poem, a literary work, depends then on the balance of certain qualities in it; and in this sense, a very real distinction may be drawn between good classical and good romantic work." Herbert Read states: "The *predominance* which is given on the one hand to order or judgment and on the other hand to emotion or feeling determines those opposed types of expression which are given to the historical terms 'classical' or 'romantic.'" As H. W. Garrod states, it is in the "emphasis which it lays upon the unity of a work of art that the classical conception seems primarily opposed to the romantic."

Examples help to illustrate the two types of expression. A Greek temple is classical; a Gothic cathedral is romantic. Simplicity and proportion are the two qualities that immediately impress one in a Greek temple. One is conscious of the structure as a whole before one notes the details. A Gothic cathedral, on the other hand, is not easily understood *as a whole* at first. One may be captivated by the intricate carvings over the main door; one may be amused by the grin of a gargoyle; one may be absorbed by a fan tracery or the soft clotted colors of ancient stained glass. Only after subjecting the mind to these details does one become aware of the totality (the *summum)* of the cathedral itself, the underlying unity that it blends all this intricacy of detail. The Greek temple possesses perfect balance, adequacy, calm. Its lines are self-bound, gracefully controlled. It has dignity, poise. The Gothic cathedral has magnificence and restlessness with its tireless spires surging toward infinity. The triangle and the circle (dome) of classical architecture in themselves assure control, whereas the unspecified spire of the Gothic suggests the quest of the infinite.

We may say that a classical work of art is a work of art accomplished by an artist who chooses to handle material that is adequately within his control. The classical artist does not deny mystery in experience, but he chooses to explore it only within the terms of soundly established philosophy and principles known to tradition. A classical artist might, for example, handle the subject of death. Theologically men know something of the meaning of death, but, on the level of experience, death is a mystery, a book sealed presumably to all except to those who have actually died. A classical artist would not seek to explore this subject beyond the warrant of traditional theology and philosophy:

Dear, beauteous Death! the jewel of the Just,
Shining nowhere but in the dark,
What mysteries do lie beyond thy dust,
Could man outlook that mark!

(Henry Vaughan, "They Are All Gone into the World of Light!" 16–19)

Unfamiliar to the classical method is the bold and sometimes naïve questing of the unknown in highly individualistic and untraditional terms, as in Fitzgerald's *The Rubáiyát of Omar Khayyám:*

Ah, make the most of what we yet may spend,
Before we too into the dust descend;
  Dust into Dust, and under Dust, to lie,
Sans Wine, sans Song, sans Singer, and—sans End!

(93–96)

Into this Universe, and Why *not knowing*
Nor Whence, *like Water willy-nilly flowing;*
  And out of it, as Wind along the Waste,
I know not Whither, *willy-nilly blowing.*

(113–116)

Walter Pater thinks of classicism in terms of "order in beauty" and of Romanticism in terms of "the addition of strangeness" to beauty. In his seeking for "strangeness" the Romantic artist is particularly interested in questioning and exploring those very mysteries which cannot be entirely penetrated by the human intellect. He does not use these mysteries as established in philosophy and theology as a means of reference for other material in the foreground of his art, but rather inclines to use them as the actual subject matter of his work. Partly for this reason, the Romantic artist inclines to question the attitudes of contemporary society and often finds that contemporary society is in conflict with his own desire to be released from traditional social and ideological controls. The Romantic artist is interested primarily in the technical handling of subject matter that can only be partially glimpsed or understood. He does not wish to impress the spectator with an immediate sense of unity, but rather tends to accent the curious and the unusual before he allows the underlying unity of his work of art to become apparent.

The contrast between Romantic and classical preoccupations and their corresponding artistic procedures is evident in their inferior and degenerate forms. Walter Pater says: "The charm, therefore, of what is classical, in art and literature, is that of a well-known tale, to which we can listen over and over again because it is told so well." It should be noted, however, that in periods of rationalism and comparative self-satisfaction, as for example, in eighteenth-century England, a spurious kind of classicism tends to replace a true classicism. Pseudoclassical art often pays great lip service to the classics but often succeeds magnificently in misunderstanding them. Where genuine classical art constitutes, as all great art does, a *mimesis* of life, pseudoclassical art becomes an imitation of previous works of art undertaken in a narrow and cautious spirit. Classical art, when it degenerates, becomes merely a routine repetition of a pattern. Romantic art, when it degenerates, becomes a mere exploration of the curious, the bizarre, the rococo, the extreme baroque. It loses the necessary underlying organic unity which is at the basis of all great art, Romantic or classical.

Romanticism, ideology of. *Romanticism* as an ideology, while it embraces many differing and even discordant features through its eclecticism (choosing from various sources) and its syncretism (attempted union of opposing principles), has certain general characteristics. Following Immanuel Kant, other Romantic philosophers stress primary understanding (intuition) above secondary reason. (Thus Wordsworth writes, "Our meddling intellect/Misshapes the beauteous form of things.") Intuition tends to be directly related by some Romantics to sense experience. Wordsworth emphasizes the prime and unique importance of "the mighty world of eye and ear" and recognizes in "nature and the language of the sense the anchor of his purest thought." From Jean Jacques Rousseau are derived the Romantic concepts of freedom and of natural law. Institutionalism is the enemy of the naturally good man, and Romantic work frequently rejects state and church. William Blake anticipated the main lines of Romantic ideology. "The cistern contains; the fountain overflows." "Exuberance is beauty." "Prisons are built with stones of law; brothels with bricks of religion." He also anticipated the approach toward mystical experience of the later Romantics. He seeks unity amid diversity, correspondence between all things. "A skylark wounded in the wing;/A cherubim does cease to sing;" "How the chimney-sweeper's cry/Every black'ning church appals." He rejects boundaries, limitations, "the mind-forg'd manacles." The naturally good man, emancipated from institutionalism, should be able to develop an ecstatic vision through freedom and union with nature. The Romantics are deeply sensitive to the actual possibilities of ennui that may follow ecstasy, to the dangers of "dejection." A good deal of their attention is given to the problem of how to maintain an ecstatic and poetic vision (see Books XII and XIII of Wordsworth's *The Prelude,* "Imagination and Taste, How Impaired and Restored"; Shelley's *Alastor;* Keats's *Endymion).* The Romantics stress transcendence, the going beyond of human limitations toward a spiritual absolutism which rejects "the common light of day," though sympathy is constantly expressed for the simple and pastoral life. For Shelley, the Platonic universal is the true reality manifesting itself in the transitory forms fleetingly touched by its beauty. Accompanying this concept are Shelley's distrust for existential experience—birth is an "eclipsing curse" (cf. Wordsworth's "Our birth is but a sleep and a forgetting")—and his love of the death symbol—he is "lured toward sweet death." Both Wordsworth and Shelley glorify childhood and the "antenatal dream." The fullness of adult life is "common day" or "dark reality." Rejecting the narrow world of neoclassicism, some Romantics make quest an end in itself. As Robert Heilman says, "The worth of life lies in pursuit, not in attainment; therefore, everything is worth pursuing, and nothing brings satisfaction—save this endless destiny itself. Goethe's Faust, unlike Marlowe's, has no faith and no fear" ("The Tragedy of Knowledge: Marlowe's Treatment of Faustus," *Quarterly Review of Literature,* II, 1946). Byron maintained that the object of life was sensation—to feel, even if we feel in pain. Though one aspect of Romanticism tends towards multiplicity by gathering all experience (in the beginning was the Act, rather than the Word, Faust said), the Wordsworthian doctrine made man one with nature. This aspect of Romanticism—"monistic naturalism"—was in particular rejected by the New Humanist Irving Babbitt (*Rousseau and Romanticism,* 1919). The New Humanism also rejected the Romantic tendency to make emotion a substitute for moral value, of which the final arbiter was the Romantic individual himself rather than a supposedly universal law. The New Humanism could not accept the Byronic image of the "eternal spirit of the chainless mind." Mind must operate in terms of an inner check founded on universal principle. In so far as Romanticism developed a pessimistic direction, it has affinities with certain kinds of contemporary existentialism, for, on its extreme side, Romanticism sees the external world as nothing in itself; it is merely something that has to be given meaning, be molded by the ego (see existentialism).

Round characters. See *characterization.

Satire. See page 131.

Sensibility. See *dissociation of sensibility.

Sentimentality as applied in literature constitutes an adverse criticism. It suggests the arousing of emotions to which a reader is over-susceptible and for which there is not sufficient artistic cause. In other words, a reader comes not to see the work of art as it is, but simply to use the work as an immediate prompting of emotions he wants to enjoy anyhow. "Let's have a good cry" or "Let's have a good laugh" is the idea in such a reader's mind rather than "Let us see what this work is." Certain writers tailor material for such stock responses. Some works are sentimental, even though the writer is eminently sincere, because of some emotional exaggeration in the presentation of the material, as in Harriet Beecher Stowe's *Uncle Tom's Cabin.*

Sign is a term which in literature is applied to the basic denotation of a word, its basic identification of an idea or an object. The sign is *arbitrary* in the sense that a quite different word could have been created for the referent. *Arbitrary* implies the making of choice for which there is no precedent or law—a pure decision of the will. "Cat" from the point of denotation simply names an animal. An equivalent arbitrary sign for cat could be the French *chat.* In connotation where the *mental associations and *overtones of words play a major role, "cat" will retain its sign value, but what it suggests through mental association and overtone becomes increasingly important. The *sign* value of cat (the identifying name) is retained in a subordinate position. Thus, while "cat," from the point of view of denotation, identifies the animal (and this identification remains always definite), "cat," from the point of view of connotation, might stand at different times or simultaneously for beauty, sleekness, nocturnal stealth, mystery, menace, playfulness. "Cats eat rats" illustrates a statement in which "cats" as *sign* is predominant. "Guns recoil with the wild delicateness of cats' paws" illustrates a statement in which "cats" as connotation and mental association is predominant.

Simile expresses a resemblance, in one way or more, between one thing and another (see *analogy). The difference between a simile and a *metaphor is that in a simile the resemblance is overtly and rhetorically stated by such words as "like" and "as." "Sudden a thought comes like a full-blown rose" is a simile. Keats sees a resemblance between the impact of a sudden emotion-packed thought and the impression that sudden concentration on the form and color of the flower would give. The point of the resemblance lies in the *suddenness* of impression, though the rose is also a metaphor for maturity of beauty. Milton speaks of music creating "a soul under the ribs of death." The comparisons are here implicit and submerged (a metaphor). Music is so powerful spiritually that it can create life in a very skeleton.

Sonnet. See *stanza.

Spenserian stanza. See *stanza.

Stanza. Lines of poetry are gathered together into large patterns, known as *stanzas.* Each stanza usually develops a single thought; stanzas are, roughly, the equivalents of paragraphs in prose.

A frequent error is to call a stanza a verse; a verse is a single line. The most common stanza patterns in English poetry are the following:

(1) The rhymed couplet is composed of two lines which have identical rhymes.

(2) The *tercet* is a short stanza of three lines, with any rhyme scheme (sometimes identical, sometimes rhyming the first and third lines), and in any meter (generally iambic tetrameter).

Example:

The wrinkled sea beneath him crawls;
He watches from his mountain walls,
And like a thunderbolt he falls.

(Tennyson, "The Eagle")

(3) The *quatrain* is a stanza of four lines in which the rhyme scheme may be quite varied. In some quatrains the first and third lines rhyme, and the second and fourth; in others the first and

fourth and the second and third; in still others the second and fourth rhyme and the others do not. Such patterns are usually indicated by letters: the first rhyme by *a;* the second by *b*.

Examples:

Can storied urn or animated bust (a)
    Back to its mansion call the fleeting breath? (b)
Can honor's voice provoke the silent dust, (a)
    Or flattery soothe the dull cold ear of death? (b)

(Thomas Gray, "Elegy in a Country Church-yard")

Who trusted God was love indeed (a)
    And love creation's final law—(b)
Though nature, red in tooth and claw (b)
    With ravine, shrieked against his creed—(a)

(Tennyson, "In Memoriam")

The king sits in Dumfermline town (a)
    Drinking the blood-red wine (b)
"O where will I get good sailor (c)
    To sail this ship of mine?" (b)

(Anonymous, "Sir Patrick Spens")

The ballad stanza, the last illustrated, is also indicated as *abcb*. The lines may be of any length, and may use any meter. The typical *ballad quatrain* is the last, with the first and third lines in iambic tetrameter and the second and fourth in iambic trimeter.

(4) The *quintet* is a five-line stanza. It is not used very often by poets.

Example:

We look before and after
    And pine for what is not:
Our sincerest laughter
    With some pain is fraught;
Our sweetest songs are those which tell of saddest thought.

(Shelley, "The Cloud")

(5) The *sestet* is a six-line stanza, often composed of three sets of couplets. The second half of many sonnets employs the sestet form.

Example:

She walks in beauty, like the night
Of cloudless climes and starry skies;
And all that's best of dark and bright
Meet in her aspect and her eyes;
Thus mellow'd to that tender light
Which heaven to gaudy day denies.

(Byron, "She Walks in Beauty")

(6) The most popular seven-line stanza is the *rime royal,* used as early as Chaucer and as late as John Masefield. It consists of seven iambic pentameter lines, rhyming *ababbcc.*

(7) The *octave* is an eight-line stanza, in which the rhyme scheme may be twice as varied as in the quatrain. Many of Burns's songs are written in octaves.

(8) The *ottava rima* is an eight-line stanza of iambic pentameter lines, rhyming *abababcc.* "Isabella" by Keats is in *ottava rima.*

(9) The *Spenserian stanza,* named after Edmund Spenser, who used it in *The Faerie Queene,* is a stanza of eight verses of iambic pentameter, followed by a ninth line of iambic hexameter, rhyming *ababbcbcc.*

(10) The *sonnet* is a complete poem of fourteen lines of iambic pentameter. There are at least two forms. In one, the poem consists of three quatrains followed by a couplet. The rhyme scheme is often different from quatrain to quatrain, thus, *abab cdcd efef gg.* In another form the sonnet is composed of two parts, one of eight lines (an octave) and one of six (a sestet). The octet may rhyme *abbaabba;* the sestet may rhyme *cdecde* or may end in a couplet *(cdcdee).*

Stichomythia is a form of stylized dialogue in which two speakers in a drama express contrasting views of an idea or a problem in alternative one-sentence lines. While artificial, stichomythia serves the purpose of dramatic compression and emphasis, as in these lines between Helena and Hermia in *A Midsummer Night's Dream:*

HERMIA: The more I hate, the more he follows me.
HELENA: The more I love, the more he hateth me.

(I, i, 198–199)

Stock characters are standard, highly conventionalized types in the drama or narrative, as, for example, the figure of the parasite in plays deriving from the tradition of Plautus.

Stock epithets are conventionalized, much-repeated phrases, as in the eighteenth century's "the fair" for womankind. A stock epithet can serve an artistic purpose in symbolizing the permanent and unchanging aspects of nature as in Homer's "wine-dark sea." A stock epithet differs from a cliché in that the cliché, also a stereotyped expression, has been overused to the point of ceasing to communicate, as in such phrases as "veritable gold mine," "eternal feminine," "ship of state." Clichés can be made to serve a purpose in narrative, either for humorous or ironic use or for indicating a character's commonplace reflections.

Stream of consciousness is the effort to present in writing what Henry James called "the subliminal self—that is, a self below the threshold of consciousness, which may at any time make an eruption into our ordinary life. At its lowest, this is only a deposit of forgotten memories, at its highest, we do not know what it is at all." James used the metaphor of an iceberg. The conscious mind is comparable to the small part above the water, the unconscious to the much greater part that is submerged. The normal narrative technique for presenting the stream of consciousness is the interior *monologue. In using the stream of consciousness technique, the writer is attempting to indicate the way in which the mind really works, outside of conscious formalized expression. It has been argued that the real life of the mind contains no forms, but the writer has to create a form to reflect such formlessness—hence the stream of consciousness technique. It is, in fact, a formal and rhetorical device to suggest formlessness, to suggest the unconscious mind at work before will and consciousness impose form. What the writer attempts to convey through this technique is an imagined process of *mental association before a mental selectivity has discriminated regarding the value and disposition of such associations (as in the case of a poet imposing the line and structure of art upon his associations or of a moralist rejecting images of appetites and actions of which he disapproves).

Structure. See *texture.

Subjective. See *objective and subjective.

Symbolism. See page 29.

Synecdoche. See metonymy and synecdoche.

Synthesis. See page 59.

Tension. See page 20.

Texture is a word sometimes used by critics to refer to the artistry of a work in contrast to *structure,* which consists of the plot, fable, or that basic material of which we can make a *paraphrase.

Theater of the Absurd. See page 178.

Theme is a term used broadly as the total meaning of an artistic whole. It sometimes refers to the symbolic significance of the work. Since a literary work may be productive of a wide range of meanings, critics sometimes speak of the *essential* theme of the work, its basic pattern of meaning and structure which must be presumed even in a wide variety of interpretations. Theme is to be distinguished from *fable* and *plot.* Fable was employed formally as an alternative word for the plot of an epic, a dramatic poem, or play, as in Pope's lines:

> *Know well each ancient's proper character;*
> *His fable, subject, scope, in every page. . .*
>
> (*An Essay on Criticism,* 119–120)

Plot is the machinery of a theme, rather than the theme itself. It is the story line of a play, short story, or novel. Some great works of art present incidents, as in Joyce's "The Dead," rather than the arranged interactions of incidents we call plots.

Tragedy. See page 167.

Tragic flaw refers to the Aristotelian prescript for the tragic hero. He must win our compassion. A person portrayed as completely evil would not win our pity in the event of his meeting disaster. He would be quite indifferent. An entirely good person's meeting disaster would lead not to pity but to indignation with the world at large. The hero, as Aristotle sees him, must be a person who on the whole is good and noble, but who contributes to his own disaster, helps to bring it about, by some contributing failure or weakness on his own part.

Tragicomedy. See page 174.

Trochee. See *metrical feet.

Trope is a term signifying an elaborated figure of speech. It has been a term long employed in reference to the drama. The medieval drama had its origin in the tropes, passages inserted into the liturgy, or rites of worship, of the church by way of embellishment or amplification, as in the *Quem Quaeritis* trope of the Easter Mass.

Tropological is used, particularly in reference to the Scriptures, to indicate a moral interpretation of the text in terms beyond what the text directly says. Thus the tropological interpretation of the story of Abraham and Isaac would stress the need for unquestioning obedience to the will of God. Shylock in *The Merchant of Venice* (I, iii) interprets the story of Jacob and Laban to justify the principle that "thrift is blessing, if men steal it not."

Wit. See page 125.

Zeitgeist. This word meaning spirit of the time is sometimes used by critics to denote what is thought to be a prevailing mood, line of thought, and value to be found through a number of writers contemporary with one another and supposedly reflecting the spirit of a particular society. Thus the writing of the "lost generation" after World War I expresses a *zeitgeist* of restlessness and the loss of traditional roots.

Notes

PART ONE WHAT IS LITERATURE?

The Matthew Arnold quotation on page 1 is from "Literature and Science," in *Discourses in America,* 1885. The Sir Philip Sidney quotation is from *An Apology for Poetry,* 1595.

1 *The Poetics,* I, ii.

2 "Epic poetry and Tragedy, Comedy also and Dithyrambic poetry, and the music of the flute and of the lyre in most of their forms, are all in their general conception modes of imitation. They differ, however, from one another in three respects—the medium, the objects, the manner or mode of imitation, being in each case distinct," *The Poetics,* I, ii–iii, trans. S. H. Butcher, Aristotle's *Theory of Poetry and Fine Art* (New York: 1951), p. 7.

Aristotle observes of imitation generally: "Poetry in general seems to have sprung from two causes, each of them lying deep in our nature. First, the instinct of imitation is implanted in man from childhood, one difference between him and the other animals being that he is the most imitative of living creatures, and through imitation learns his earliest lessons . . . ," *Poetics,* IV, i–iii, trans. S. H. Butcher, p. 15.

3 Mortimer Adler, *How to Read a Book* (New York: 1949), p. 39.

4 In regard to the overall purpose of *The Faerie Queene,* Spenser says in a letter to Sir Walter Raleigh (1589): "The general end therefore of all the books is to fashion a gentleman or noble person in virtuous and gentle discipline. . . In which I have followed all the antique poets historical, first Homere, who in the Persons of Agamemnon and Ulysses hath ensampled a good governour and a vertuous

man, the one in his *Ilias,* the other in his *Odysseis;* then Virgil, whose like intention was to doe in the person of Aeneas. . ."

[5] Eric Gill from the religious point of view expresses a parallel idea in "The Value of the Creative Faculty of Man" in *The American Review,* November, 1935. "Now one of the main springs of energy among animals and among human beings (for humans are also animals) is the sexual appetite. A consequence of the sexual appetite is the increase and multiplication of species. There is no escape from this at present. Males and females we are, and we have an insatiable appetite for one another. But this appetite can be disciplined and dammed up energy can be allowed to flow into other spheres. Normally it overflows into the sphere of necessary work. There could never under any circumstances be full sexual satisfaction; by no arrangement of society could you arrive at sexual satiety, and this seems to be the clear arrangement of the Creator. There is the imagination; but the imagination by itself does not act materially. It must be stirred to action. The energy is provided by the exuberance of the sexual appetite. It is, so to say, an economical arrangement. Nature is full of such contrivances. For example, the domestic hen's ability to lay more eggs than could possibly survive as birds provides innumerable tables with one of the most perfect foods. There is no room for all the oaks which could be grown from all the acorns, but acorns make an admirable poached egg for pigs."

[6] S. T. Coleridge, *Biographia Literaria,* chap. XIV.

[7] Aristotle, *The Poetics,* IX, ii–iii.

[8] *Hamlet,* III, ii, 24–27.

[9] Northrop Frye, *Anatomy of Criticism* (Princeton: 1957), p. 84.

[10] *Johnson on Shakespeare,* ed. Sir Walter Raleigh (Oxford: 1931), pp. 11–12.

[11] M. H. Abrams, *The Mirror and the Lamp: Romantic Theory and the Critical Tradition* (New York: 1958), p. 35.

[12] Courtesy LIFE Magazine © 1963 Time Inc. ALL RIGHTS RESERVED.

[13] Jacques Maritain, *Art and Scholasticism* (New York: 1949), p. 80.

[14] W. H. Gardner, *Gerard Manley Hopkins* (New Haven: 1948), p. 11.

[15] *Ibid.,* p. 11.

[16] Ellsworth Cory, *The Significance of Beauty in Nature and Art* (Milwaukee: 1948), p. 27.

[17] *The Iliad,* trans. Andrew Lang, Walter Leaf, Ernest Meyers (New York: 1929), p. 105.

[18] John Ruskin, *Modern Painters,* vol. III, chap. xii. See *Ruskin as Literary Critic,* ed. A. H. R. Ball (Cambridge, England: 1928), p. 147.

[19] A short but tightly packed essay that indicates some of the main problems of the beautiful in relationship to Thomism is Dr. Emmanuel Chapman's "The Perennial Theme of Beauty and Art," *Essays in*

Thomism (New York: 1942) edited by Robert E. Brennan, O.P. A doctoral thesis by the same author is *St. Augustine's Philosophy of Beauty* (New York: 1939). A book of interest exploring the literature in this field and indebted to Dr. Chapman is Dr. Ellsworth Cory's *The Significance of Beauty in Nature and Art* (Milwaukee: 1948).

20 Dr. Chapman, in analyzing James Joyce's concept of the beautiful in his essay "The Perennial Theme of Beauty and Art," states: "Joyce was right in rejecting an idealist and symbolist interpretation and insisting that radiance refers to the quidditas or whatness of a thing. He, too, might have been surprised by the realistic emphasis given by St. Thomas that not only form but matter is an integral part of the essence of material things, and enters into its very definition."

21 Aristotle argues in *The Poetics* that beauty consists in "magnitude and order." He says a small animal cannot be beautiful, because the vision becomes confused when it is applied to an object so small as to be almost invisible. Nor can a very large animal—such as one a thousand miles long—for the eye does not take it in at once. It presents no unity and completeness of view to those who can look at it. The beautiful for Aristotle must be embraced in one view. Aristotle wrote before the microscope and the satellite carrying a high-speed camera. He also begs the question of whether the animal a thousand miles long might still be beautiful *in itself*.

22 Samuel Taylor Coleridge, "Shakespeare's Judgment Equal to His Genius," in *Shakespeare Criticism: A Selection*, ed. D. Nichol Smith (London: 1936), p. 262.

23 Samuel Taylor Coleridge, *Biographia Literaria*, chap. XIV.

24 In Book II of *The Republic* Plato points out how the fictions of the poets have contributed to a false and misleading theology. The renaissance Francis Bacon, for example, in his essay, "Of Truth," indicates a popular interpretation of Plato in his probable reference to St. Augustine's *Confessions*, I, xvi, 26: "One of the Fathers, in great severity, called poesy *vinum daemonum* (devils' wine), because it filleth the imagination, and yet it is but the shadow of a lie." Sir Philip Sidney in *An Apologie for Poetry* tries to put forward the thesis that Plato banishes poets from the commonwealth because of the abuse, not the use of poetry: "S. Paule himselfe, (who yet for the credite of poets alledgeth twice two poets, and one of them by the name of a prophet) setteth a watch-word upon philosophy, indeede upon the abuse. So dooth Plato, upon the abuse, not upon poetrie. Plato found fault that the poets of his time filled the worlde with wrong opinions of the Gods, making light tales of that unspotted essence; and therefore would not have the youth depraved with such opinions. Herein may such be said; let this suffice; the poets did not induce such opinions, but did imitate those opinions already induced." Sir Arthur Quiller-Couch echoes Sidney in refusing to take Plato seriously on this point: "So men take Plato's conception that poets should be banished from a model republic and take it seriously because it is Plato's. Without looking under the

skirts of the hobby on which Plato arrived at this: without examining, for instance, his demonstration that art is false because the thing it copies is itself a copy of the divine idea, and bad because it aims at pleasure which is no less unknown to the gods than pain." *The Poet as a Citizen* (Cambridge: 1935), p. 4.

[25] *The Basic Works of Aristotle,* trans. Richard McKeon (New York: 1941), p. 1460.

[26] *The Confessions of St. Augustine,* trans. Frank Sheed (New York: 1943), p. 42.

[27] *Ibid.,* p. 43.

[28] Mortimer Adler, *Art and Prudence* (New York: 1937), p. 79.

[29] *Ibid.,* p. 47.

[30] Jacques Maritain, *Art and Scholasticism* (New York: 1949), p. 171.

[31] John Milton, *Complete Poems and Major Prose,* ed. Merritt Y. Hughes (New York: 1957), p. 730.

[32] Joyce makes a point about the beautiful that also bears upon the problem of morality in art. For Joyce the beautiful creates a contemplative experience—a *stasis* (literally, "a standing still"), rather than a *kinesis* (literally, "a movement"). When art produces a stimulation in the kinetic sense, rather than a stasis in the contemplative sense, for Joyce it is not pure nor moral. "The feelings excited by improper art are kinetic—desire or loathing. Desire urges us to possess, to go to something. Loathing urges us to abandon, to go from something. The arts which excite them, pornographical or didactic, are therefore improper arts." *A Portrait of the Artist as a Young Man* (Penguin edition, New York: 1948), p. 159.

The judgment handed down by Judge John M. Woolsey (prefixed to the Modern Library edition of Joyce's *Ulysses*) which removed the ban against the book could not have pleased Joyce altogether. The book, in the judge's opinion, is an emetic rather than an aphrodisiac. Neither term would fit Joyce's concept of a work of art.

[33] "Pollyanna, a blindly optimistic person, from the name of the heroine in a novel by Eleanor Porter, 1868–1920," *The American College Dictionary*. Horatio Alger, 1834–1899, was the author of novels, especially for boys.

[34] Preface to André Gide's *Paludes,* quoted in William York Tindall, *The Literary Symbol* (New York: 1955), p. 14.

[35] Cyril Connolly, *Enemies of Promise* (New York: 1948).

[36] Ralph Waldo Emerson, "The Poet," *Essays: Second Series* (Boston: 1903), p. 16.

[37] Thomas Carlyle, *Sartor Resartus: The Life and Opinions of Herr Teufelsdröck* (London: 1927), p. 187.

[38] D. H. Lawrence, "Dragon of the Apocalypse," in Maurice Beebe, *Literary Symbolism* (San Francisco: 1960), p. 32.

[39] *Anatomy of Criticism,* p. 121.

[40] *Ibid.*

[41] *Ibid.,* p. 88.

[42] John Unterecker, *A Reader's Guide to William Butler Yeats* (New York: 1959), p. 34.

[43] I. A. Richards, "The Analysis of a Poem," *Principles of Literary Criticism* (London: 1924), p. 119.

[44] *Anatomy of Criticism,* p. 99.

[45] D. H. Lawrence, "Dragon of the Apocalypse," in Maurice Beebe, *Literary Symbolism* (San Francisco: 1960), p. 31.

[46] *Anatomy of Criticism,* p. 241.

[47] René Wellek and Austin Warren, *Theory of Literature* (New York: 1956), p. 235.

[48] Thomas Love Peacock, "The Four Ages of Poetry," 1820.

[49] Matthew Arnold, "Literature and Science," in *Discourses in America,* 1885.

[50] Walter Pater, *The Renaissance: Studies in Art and Poetry* (London: 1928), p. 252. This is the concluding statement of the book.

[51] Lecomte du Noüy, *Human Destiny* (New York: 1947), introduction, pp. xviii–xix.

[52] This and the following quotations are from W. H. D. Rouse's translation of *The Iliad* (New York: 1950), p. 291ff.

PART TWO RESPONSE TO POETRY

The Garrod quotation on page 51 is from *The Study of Poetry,* 1936, p. 54.

[1] Edgar Allan Poe, "The Philosophy of Composition," 1846.

[2] *Ibid.*

[3] John Livingstone Lowes, *Convention and Revolt in Poetry* (Boston: 1919), p. 45.

[4] Quoted in Bliss Perry's *A Study of Poetry* (Boston: 1920), p. 106.

[5] Lowes, *op. cit.,* p. 183.

[6] This is Read's basic definition and theme in *English Prose Style* (London: 1947), *passim.*

[7] Dante Alighieri, "Paradise," *The Divine Comedy,* Canto 3.

[8] In a letter to John Taylor, Hampstead, February 27, 1818.

[9] From "The World," *Silex Scintillans,* 1650.

[10] Herbert Read, *English Prose Style* (London: 1947), p. 155.

[11] Eric Gill, "The Creative Faculty in Man," *The American Review* (November, 1935), p. 42.

12 Cleanth Brooks, *The Well Wrought Urn* (New York: 1947), p. 74.

13 Matthew Arnold, "Literature and Science," from *Discourses in America* (London: 1885).

14 John Ruskin, "Of the Pathetic Fallacy," *Modern Painters,* vol. III (London, 1843).

15 In a letter to John Taylor, Hampstead, February 27, 1818.

16 John Milton, *Complete Poems and Major Prose,* ed. Merritt Y. Hughes (New York: 1957), p. 637.

17 George O'Neill, S.J., *Essays in Poetry* (Dublin: 1919), p. 21.

18 Sir Edmund Gosse, "The Milton Manuscripts at Trinity," quoting Charles Lamb, *The Atlantic Monthly* (May, 1900), p. 586.

19 Roy Ridley, *Keats's Craftsmanship* (Oxford: 1933).

20 W. P. Ker, *Form and Style in Poetry* (London: 1928), p. 164.

21 Chard Powers Smith, *Annals of the Poets* (New York: 1935), p. 221.

22 *Ibid.*

23 Lowes, *op. cit.,* p. 128.

24 Poe, *op. cit.*

25 This anecdote is quoted from Rudolf Besier, *The Barretts of Wimpole Street.*

26 *The Dialogues of Plato,* ed. Irwin Edman (New York: 1928), p. 65. Maritain argues in *Art and Faith* (New York: 1948) that our minds can be moved by God in the *natural order* through a "special inspiration" such as is to be found in poetry or philosophy. This view does not go so far as to present the artist as a passive agent for supernatural truth (cf. Brémond, *Prayer and Poetry*). We quote at length: "Yet poetry is from on high—not like grace, which is essentially supernatural, and which makes us participants in what belongs to God only, but like the highest natural resemblance to God's activity. Our art, Dante used to say, *is the grandchild of God.* And not only does it derive, as from its pure archetype, from that art that made the world, but in order to have some idea of its nobility one must call to mind the mystery of the procession of the Word: for intelligence as such is prolific, and there where it cannot produce another self as in God, it wants at least to beget a work, made in our image and where our heart would survive" (pp. 88–89). Maritain continues to stress natural inspiration in these words: "But in the natural order also there is a special inspiration which, too, is above the deliberation of reason, and which proceeds, as Aristotle observed, from God present in us. Such is the inspiration of the poet." Maritain, in establishing a certain legitimacy for the use of "inspiration," does not subscribe to the exaggerations of the Romantics, for the artist remains entirely responsible for what he creates.

27 Francis Thompson, "Sister Songs, Part the Second," *Complete Poems of Francis Thompson* (New York: 1918), p. 42.

28 Sir Arthur Quiller-Couch, *The Poet as Citizen and Other Papers* (London: 1935), p. 100.

29 *Comus,* 1019.

30 Milton, *Areopagitica.*

31 Roger Ascham, *The Schoolmaster,* Book I, 1570.

32 John Milton, Prefatory note to the second edition of *Paradise Lost,* 1674.

33 Cf. Ridley, *op. cit.*

34 Cf. Smith, *op. cit.,* p. 14.

35 Aldous Huxley, *Vulgarity in Literature* (New York: 1940), pp. 26–31.

36 René Wellek and Austin Warren, *Theory of Literature* (New York: 1956), p. 235.

37 Wayne Booth, *The Rhetoric of Fiction* (Chicago, 1961), pp. 35–36. Cf. M. H. Abrams, *The Mirror and the Lamp* (New York: 1958), pp. 21–29.

38 W. K. Wimsatt, Jr., and Monroe C. Beardsley present this argument in "The Intentional Fallacy," in *The Verbal Icon* (New York: 1958), pp. 4–18.

39 Thomas Carlyle, "Goethe," in *Essays: Collected and Republished (First Time, 1839; Final, 1869)* (Boston, no date), p. 251.

40 William Butler Yeats, "The Symbolism of Poetry," in *Essays and Introductions* (London: 1961), p. 159.

41 *Anatomy of Criticism,* p. 88.

42 *Ibid.,* p. 89.

43 M. H. Abrams, *The Mirror and the Lamp* (New York: 1958), p. 133.

44 C. S. Lewis, *A Preface to Paradise Lost* (Oxford: 1942), p. 59.

45 *Ibid.,* p. 59.

46 Rosamond Tuve, *Images and Themes in Five Poems by John Milton* (Cambridge, Mass.: 1957), p. 188.

PART THREE RESPONSE TO PROSE

The Hemingway quotation on page 99 is from *Death in the Afternoon* (New York: 1932), p. 191.

1 Rachel L. Carson, *The Sea around Us* (New York: 1950), p. 89.

2 Anne Morrow Lindbergh, *Gift from the Sea* (New York: 1957), pp. 39–40.

3 Daniel J. Sullivan, *Introduction to Philosophy* (Milwaukee: 1957), p. 105.

4 Shakespeare, Sonnet CXVI.

5 William York Tindall, *A Reader's Guide to James Joyce* (New York: 1950), p. 188.

6 *The Poetics,* XXVI, iv–v. Tragedy, Aristotle argues, is superior to Epic, because it has everything the epic has; also it has power *both* when read and when acted, the purpose of the imitation is attained in less space, and the more concentrated form is more pleasing than that which is made thin by occupying a long time.

7 Mary M. Colum, *From These Roots* (New York: 1944), p. 171.

8 Matthew Arnold, Preface to first edition of *Poems* (London: 1853).

9 Colum, *op. cit.,* p. 162.

10 *Ibid.,* p. 164.

11 *Ibid.,* p. 354.

12 René Wellek and Austin Warren, *Theory of Literature* (New York: 1956), p. 204.

13 Joseph Warren Beach, *The Method of Henry James* (Philadelphia: 1954), revised introduction (1954), p. lxxix.

14 Gotthold Lessing, *Laokoön,* ed. W. G. Howard (New York: 1910), p. 42.

15 Wayne C. Booth, *The Rhetoric of Fiction* (Chicago: 1961), p. 19.

16 *Ibid.,* p. 112.

17 *Ibid.,* pp. 140–141.

18 Anne Davidson Ferry, *Milton's Epic Voice: The Narrator in Paradise Lost* (Cambridge, Mass.: 1963), p. 15.

19 Sean O'Faolain, *The Short Story* (New York: 1931), p. 148.

20 Northrop Frye observes: "When Milton sat down to write a poem about Edward King, he did not ask himself: 'What can I find to say about King?' but 'How does poetry require that such a subject should be treated?' The notion that convention shows a lack of feeling, and that a poet attains 'sincerity' (which usually means articulate emotion) by disregarding it, is opposed to all the facts of literary experience and history." *Anatomy of Criticism,* p. 97.

21 This and the following quotations are from *Anna Karenina,* trans. Rochelle S. Townsend (New York: 1958), vol. II, chap. XXX, XXXI.

22 From Sir Thomas Malory, *Morte D'Arthur,* XXI, v.

23 *The School for Scandal,* I, i.

24 *Critical Works of John Dennis,* ed. E. M. Hooker (Baltimore: 1939), vol. I, p. 375.

25 This and the following quotations are from Bernard Guilbert Guerney's translation of Gogol's *Dead Souls* (New York: 1961).

26 This and the following quotations are from Lytton Strachey, *Queen Victoria* (New York: 1921), pp. 234–236.

27 This and the following quotations are from Dostoievski's *Notes from Underground,* trans. Constance Garnett, in Bernard Guilbert Guerney's *A Treasury of Russian Literature* (New York: 1943), pp. 442–537.

28 This and other quotations from Zamiatin's *We* are based on *An Anthology of Russian Literature in the Soviet Period from Gorki to Pasternak,* ed. Bernard Guilbert Guerney (New York: 1960), pp. 168–353.

29 Joseph Wood Krutch, "No Essays—Please!" *Saturday Review,* Mar. 10, 1951.

30 "Mrs. Battle's Opinions on Whist," first published in *The London Magazine,* February, 1821.

31 G. K. Chesterton, *Stories, Essays, and Poems* (London: 1935), pp. 129–130.

32 D. H. Lawrence, "Two Blue Birds," in *The Woman Who Rode Away and Other Stories* (New York: 1928), pp. 3–20.

33 James Joyce, "The Dead," in *Dubliners* (New York: 1962), pp. 175–224.

34 Caroline Gordon and Allan Tate, *The House of Fiction* (New York: 1950), p. 280.

PART FOUR RESPONSE TO DRAMA

The James Joyce quotation on page 155 is from *A Portrait of the Artist as a Young Man* (New York: 1948), pp. 167–168.

1 Cf. the concluding remarks of the chorus in *Oedipus the King.*

2 Quoted from the translation by R. C. Jebb in *Seven Famous Greek Plays,* ed. Whitney J. Oates and Eugene O'Neill, Jr. (New York: 1938), p. 187. The subsequent quotations from *Antigone* are based on the Jebb translation.

3 *The Poetics,* XXVI, iv–v.

4 See above, p. 22.

5 *The Poetics,* XIII, iii.

6 *Preface to Shakespeare,* 1765.

7 Aristophanes (448?–383? B.C.) is the first great exemplar of this type of satiric comedy.

8 Martin Esslin, "The Theatre of the Absurd," in *Theatre in the Twentieth Century,* ed. Robert W. Corrigan (New York: 1963), p. 243.

[9] *Ibid.*, pp. 232–233.

[10] Robert W. Corrigan, "The Theatre in Search of a Fix," in *Theatre in the Twentieth Century*, p. 14.

PART FIVE THE CRITICISM OF LITERATURE

The Emerson quotation on page 183 is from *Blotting Book*, no. II, p. 251, indexed in Kenneth Walter Cameron, *An Emerson Index*, Hartford: Transcendental Books, 1958.

[1] M. H. Abrams, *The Mirror and the Lamp* (New York: 1958), p. 4.

[2] Alexander Pope, *An Essay on Criticism* (1711), II, 69–70.

[3] *Ibid.*, I, 173.

[4] Matthew Arnold, "The Function of Criticism at the Present Time," in *Essays in Criticism*, 1865.

[5] Samuel Taylor Coleridge, "Shakespeare's Judgment Equal to His Genius," in *Shakespeare Criticism: A Selection*, ed. D. Nichol Smith (London: 1936).

[6] George E. Saintsbury, *A History of Criticism* (London: 1929), vol. I, pp. 226–227.

[7] Walter Pater, *The Renaissance: Studies in Art and Poetry* (London: 1928), introduction, p. x.

[8] Northrop Frye, *Anatomy of Criticism* (Princeton: 1957), p. 85.

EPILOGUE THE POWER OF THE IMAGINATION

The Tolstoi quotation on page 203 is from *What Is Art?* (see note 3), p. 228.

[1] Thomas De Quincey, "The Poetry of Pope," *The North British Review*, August, 1848.

[2] Eric Gill, "The Value of the Creative Faculty in Man," *The American Review*, November, 1935.

[3] Leo Tolstoi, *What Is Art?* trans. Aylmer Maude (Fair Lawn, N.J.: Oxford University Press, 1959), p. 143.

[4] Cf. Tolstoi, *What Is Art?*, chap. XV.

[5] Herbert Read, *Education through Art* (New York: 1945), p. 69.

[6] *Ibid.*, p. 60.

[7] The *American College Dictionary* defines catalysis: "The causing or accelerating of a chemical change by the addition of a substance (catalyst) which is not permanently affected by the reaction."

Bibliography

Abrams, M. H.: *The Mirror and the Lamp: Romantic Theory and the Critical Tradition,* W. W. Norton & Company, Inc., New York, 1958.

Adler, Mortimer: *Art and Prudence,* Longmans, Green & Co., Inc., New York, 1937.

———: *How to Read a Book,* Simon and Schuster, Inc., New York, 1940.

Aristotle: *The Basic Works of Aristotle,* ed. Richard McKeon, Random House, Inc., New York, 1941.

Arnold, Matthew: *Discourses in America,* Macmillan & Co., Ltd., London, 1885.

———: "Preface," *Poems,* Macmillan & Co., Ltd., London, 1853.

Auerbach, Erich: *Mimesis,* trans. Willard Trask, Princeton University Press, Princeton, N.J., 1953.

Babbitt, Irving: *Rousseau and Romanticism,* Houghton Mifflin Company, Boston, 1919.

Beach, Joseph Warren: *The Method of Henry James,* Albert Saifer, Philadelphia, 1954.

———: *The Twentieth Century Novel,* Century Company, New York, 1932.

Beebe, Maurice: *Literary Symbolism: An Introduction to the Interpretation of Literature,* Wadsworth Publishing Company, San Francisco, 1960.

Bodkin, Maud: *Archetypal Patterns in Poetry: Psychological Studies of Imagination,* Oxford University Press, Fair Lawn, N.J., 1963.

Booth, Wayne C.: *The Rhetoric of Fiction,* The University of Chicago Press, Chicago, 1961.

BROOKS, CLEANTH: *The Well Wrought Urn: Studies in the Structure of Poetry,* Reynal & Hitchcock, Inc., New York, 1947.

BRÉMOND, HENRI, ABBÉ: *Prayer and Poetry,* Burns & Oates Ltd., London, 1927.

CHAPMAN, EMMANUEL: "The Perennial Theme of Beauty and Art," *Essays in Thomism,* ed. Robert E. Brennan, Sheed & Ward, Inc., New York, 1939. Out of print.

COLUM, MARY D.: *From These Roots: The Ideas That Have Made Modern Literature,* Columbia University Press, New York, 1944.

CORRIGAN, ROBERT W.: *The Modern Theatre,* New York, The Macmillan Company, 1964.

———: *Theatre in the Twentieth Century,* Grove Press, Inc., New York, 1963.

CORY, HERBERT ELLSWORTH: *The Significance of Beauty in Nature and Art,* The Bruce Publishing Company, Milwaukee, 1947.

ELIOT, T. S.: *Selected Essays,* Harcourt, Brace & World, Inc., New York, 1932.

EMPSON, WILLIAM: *Seven Types of Ambiguity,* New Directions, Norfolk, Conn., 1947.

FERRY, ANNE DAVIDSON: *Milton's Epic Voice: The Narrator in Paradise Lost,* Harvard University Press, Cambridge, Mass., 1963.

FRYE, NORTHROP: *Anatomy of Criticism: Four Essays,* Princeton University Press, Princeton, N.J., 1957.

GARDNER, W. H.: *Gerard Manley Hopkins, 1884–1889,* Yale University Press, New Haven, Conn., 1948, 2 vols.

GILBERT, ALLAN H.: *Literary Criticism, Plato to Dryden,* American Book Company, New York, 1940.

GILL, ERIC: "The Value of the Creative Faculty in Man," *American Review,* November, 1935.

GOSSE, SIR EDMUND: "The Milton Manuscripts at Trinity," *Atlantic Monthly,* **85**:586–93, May, 1900.

GUERNEY, BERNARD GUILBERT: *An Anthology of Russian Literature in the Soviet Period from Gorki to Pasternak,* New York, Random House, Inc., 1960.

———: *A Treasury of Russian Literature,* Vanguard Press, Inc., New York, 1943.

GOGOL, NIKOLAI: *Dead Souls,* trans. Bernard Guilbert Guerney, Holt, Rinehart and Winston, New York, 1961.

HAMILTON, EDITH: *The Greek Way to Western Civilization,* New American Library of World Literature, Inc., New York, 1959.

HOMER: *Iliad,* trans. W. H. D. Rouse, New American Library of World Literature, Inc., New York, 1960.

———: *Odyssey,* trans. W. H. D. Rouse, New American Library of World Literature, Inc., New York, 1960.

HOFFMAN, FREDERICK: *Freudianism and the Literary Mind,* Louisiana University Press, Baton Rouge, 1945.

HOY, CYRUS: *The Hyacinth Room: An Investigation into the Nature of Comedy, Tragedy, and Tragicomedy,* New York, Alfred A. Knopf, Inc., New York, 1964.

HUXLEY, ALDOUS: *Vulgarity in Literature,* Harper & Row, Publishers, Incorporated, New York, 1940.

JOYCE, JAMES: *Dubliners,* Viking Press, Inc., New York, 1962.

———: *A Portrait of the Artist as a Young Man,* New American Library of World Literature, Inc., New York, 1944.

———: *Ulysses,* Modern Library, Inc., New York, 1942.

KER, W. P.: *Form and Style in Poetry,* Macmillan & Co., Ltd., London, 1928.

LAWRENCE, D. H.: *Apocalypse,* Viking Press, Inc., New York, 1932.

LECOMTE DU NOÜY: *Human Destiny,* Longmans, Green & Co., Inc., New York, 1947.

LEWIS, C. DAY: *The Poet's Way of Knowledge,* Cambridge University Press, New York, 1957.

LOWES, JOHN LIVINGSTON: *Convention and Revolt in Poetry,* Houghton Mifflin Company, Boston, 1919.

MARITAIN, JACQUES: *Art and Faith,* trans. E. de P. Matthews, Philosophical Library, Inc., New York, 1943.

———: *Art and Scholasticism,* Sheed & Ward, Inc., New York, 1949.

———: *Creative Intuition in Art and Poetry,* Pantheon Books, New York, 1953.

———: *La Situation de la poésie,* Paris, Desclée de Brouwer et cie, 1938.

MERCIER, LOUIS A. J.: *American Humanism and the New Age,* The Bruce Publishing Company, Milwaukee, 1948.

MILTON, JOHN: *Complete Poems and Major Prose,* ed. Merritt Y. Hughes, The Odyssey Press, Inc., New York, 1957.

MIZENER, ARTHUR: *The Sense of Life in the Modern Novel,* Houghton Mifflin Company, Boston, 1964.

NICOLL, ALLARDYCE: *The World of Harlequin: A Critical Study of the Commedia dell' Arte,* Cambridge University Press, New York, 1963.

O'FAOLAIN, SEAN: *The Short Story,* The Devin-Adair Company, Inc., New York, 1951.

O'NEILL, GEORGE: *Essays in Poetry,* Talbot Press, Dublin, 1919.

PATER, WALTER: *Appreciation,* Macmillan & Co., Ltd., London, 1890.

———: *The Renaissance,* Macmillan & Co., Ltd., London, 1913.

PERRY, BLISS: *A Study of Poetry,* Houghton Mifflin Company, Boston, 1920.

PLATO, *The Philosophy of,* ed. Irwin Edman, Random House, Inc., New York, 1928.

POE, EDGAR ALLAN: *The Philosophy of Composition,* 1846.

QUILLER-COUCH, SIR ARTHUR: *The Poet as Citizen and Other Papers,* Cambridge University Press, New York, 1935.

RANSOM, JOHN CROWE: *The New Criticism,* New Directions, Norfolk, Conn., 1941.

READ, HERBERT: *English Prose Style,* Holt, Rinehart and Winston, Inc., New York, 1928.

———: *Education through Art,* Pantheon Books, New York, 1945.

RICHARDS, I. A.: *Principles of Literary Criticism,* Routledge & Kegan Paul, Ltd., London, 1924.

RIDLEY, MAURICE ROY: *Keats's Craftsmanship,* Oxford University Press, Fair Lawn, N.J., 1933.

RUSKIN, JOHN: *Modern Painters,* London, 1843, 3 vols.

ST. AUGUSTINE: *Confessions,* trans. Frank Sheed, Sheed & Ward, Inc., New York, 1943.

SAINTSBURY, GEORGE E.: *A History of Criticism and Literary Taste from the Earliest Texts to the Present Day,* William Blackwood & Sons, Ltd., London, 1929–1934, 3 vols.

SCOTT, WILBUR: *Five Approaches of Literary Criticism,* The Macmillan Company, New York, 1962.

SIDNEY, SIR PHILIP: *An Apology for Poetry,* 1578.

SMITH, CHARD POWERS: *Annals of the Poets,* Charles Scribner's Sons, New York, 1935.

SMITH, JAMES HARRY, AND EDD WINFIELD PARK: *The Great Critics,* W. W. Norton & Company, Inc., New York, 1951.

SOPHOCLES: *Antigone,* trans. R. C. Jebb, in *Seven Famous Greek Plays,* ed. Whitney J. Oates and Eugene O'Neill, Jr., Modern Library, Inc., New York, 1950.

SYNGE, JOHN MILLINGTON: *Riders to the Sea and the Playboy of the Western World,* intro. E. R. Wood, William Heineman, Ltd., London, 1961.

TATE, ALLAN, AND CAROLINE GORDON: *The House of Fiction,* Charles Scribner's Sons, New York, 1950.

TINDALL, WILLIAM YORK: *The Literary Symbol,* Columbia University Press, New York, 1955.

TOLSTOI, LEO: *Anna Karenina,* trans. Rochelle S. Townsend, E. P. Dutton & Co., New York, 1958, 2 vols.

———: *What Is Art?,* trans. Aylmer Maude, Oxford University Press, Fair Lawn, N.J., 1959.

UNTERECKER, JOHN: *A Reader's Guide to William Butler Yeats,* The Noonday Press, New York, 1959.

VIRGIL: *Works: The Aeneid, Eclogues, Georgics,* ed. J. W. Mackail, Random House, Inc., New York, 1934.

WELLEK, RENÉ, AND AUSTIN WARREN: *Theory of Literature,* Harcourt, Brace & World, Inc., New York, 1956.

WESTON, JESSIE L.: *From Ritual to Romance,* Doubleday & Company, Inc., Garden City, N.Y., 1957.

WIMSATT, WILLIAM K., JR., AND CLEANTH BROOKS: *Literary Criticism: A Short History,* Alfred A. Knopf, Inc., New York, 1957.

———, AND MONROE C. BEARDSLEY: *The Verbal Icon: Studies in the Meaning of Poetry,* The Noonday Press, New York, 1958.

YEATS, WILLIAM BUTLER: *Essays and Introductions,* The Macmillan Company, New York, 1961.

Index

The Abolition of Man, 243
Abrams, M. H., on analogy, 217
  on Longinus, 260
  on shift of critical emphasis from poem to poet, 92
Abstract and concrete, meaning of, 211
Action, meaning of, 212
  (*See also* Drama; Literature)
Adamanov, Arthur, in Theater of the Absurd, 179
The Adding Machine, 177–178
Adler, Mortimer, *Art and Prudence*, 25
  on book as information, 6
  on catharsis, 24
Aeneas, journey to Hades, 103
  as noble gentleman, 235
  as symbolic of Roman history, 236
Aeneid, court poet in, 235
  as secondary epic, 236
Aesthetic distance, defined, 212
  and presentation of evil, 18, 26
  in realistic novel, 253
Agamemnon, 12
"The Age of Anxiety," 117
Alastor, 267
Alger, Horatio, 28
Alice in Wonderland, as fantasy, 239
  as literary art, 112
"Alive-Alive, Oh," analyzed, 143–144
Allegory, meaning of, 213–215
Alliteration, defined, 215
Allusion, defined, 215
Ambiguity, defined, 215
  as multiple meaning, 70
Ambivalence, and artistic tension, 70
  meaning of, 216
American Humanism and the New Age, 243
Anagogic meaning, 216
Anapest foot, 249
Anna Karenina, analyzed, 119–123
  as great canvas, 138
  irony and tension in, 46–47
  symbolic suggestion in, 29
  tragic emotion in, 123
Antaeus, 103
Antigone, analyzed, 157–162
  conclusion of, 167
  different levels in, 43
  irony of decision in, 47
  tensions in, 21
Antithesis, meaning of, 217
Apology for Poetry, decorum emphasized in, 231
  quoted, 1
Apostrophe, meaning of, 217
Archetype, defined and illustrated, in relation to myth, 36–41
  The Waste Land as, 39–41
Areopagitica, view of censorship in, 27
Ariosto, Lodovico, concept of hero in, 8
Aristotle, on action, 107, 162
  on art, 6, 187
  catharsis in *Poetics*, 222, 258

Aristotle, on distinction between poet and philosopher, 10
on drama, 162–163
on emotional release, 27
on material world, 22
on tragic flaw, 78, 168, 176, 274
(*See also* Catharsis; Mimesis; *Poetics*)
Arnold, Matthew, on action, 107
as a classical critic, 185
on critical power, 187
"Literature and Science," 60
on literature as public statement, 41
on need for humane letters, 1
Ars Poetica, of Horace, 195
"Ars Poetica," of Archibald Macleish, 96
Art, and action, 107
as catalytic agency, 208
of conflict, 12, 18, 25, 218
and contemplation, 14
as criticism of life, 6
function and being in, 16
as imitation and mimesis, 6, 26
presenting evil in, 26
psychological health and, 8, 22
responsibility to truth, 9
sublimation through, 8, 23
theory of art for art's sake, 67
as willing suspension of disbelief, 9
(*See also* Literature)
Art and Prudence, 24–25
Artist's intention, 93–94, 189
As You Like It, 173
Ascham, Roger, 79
Assonance, meaning of, 218
Ate, 53, 161
Atreus, House of, as illustration of violence in literature, 12–13
Auden, W. H., 117
Auerbach, Erich, 92
Autobiography, 138
Autotelic, meaning of, 218

Babbitt, Irving, view of humanism, 242–243
view of Romanticism, 267
Ballad, form of, 270
genre of, 219
Balzac, Honoré de, 109, 114
Baroque, meaning of, 219
Bathos, meaning of, 220
Beardsley, Monroe C., 239
Beaumont, Francis, 174
Beauty, and art, 14
of conflict, 18
and contemplation, 5, 8, 13
integrity, harmony, and individuation in, 17–20
perception of, 16
Beckett, Samuel, in Theater of the Absurd, 156, 179–180
Bedivere, Sir, 123–124
Benét, Stephen Vincent, 142
Bennett, Arnold, 109
Beowulf, as epic, 235
Bernanos, Georges, 151
Bernini, Giovanni, 219
"The Bishop's Beggar," 142
Blackmur, Richard P., 229
Blake, William, as inspired writer, 65
on Milton, 73, 93
and Romantic ideology, 226
Boccaccio, Giovanni, 114
Boileau-Despréaux, Nicolas, as neoclassical critic, 185–186
Booth, Wayne, 116
Boswell, James, 139
Brave New World, 132, 135
Brooks, Cleanth, on meaning of poem, 60
as new critic, 229
The Brothers Karamazov, beauty in, 19
extraneous material in, 115
Browning, Robert, 66
Buber, Martin, 239
Byron, George Gordon, Lord, figurative meaning in *Manfred,* 245–246
life as sensation, 267
as a subjective artist, 254

Caesura, meaning of, 222
Callida junctura, in Horace, 195
Canto, meaning of, 222
Carlyle, Thomas, on artist's intention, 93
on symbolism, 32
Carroll, Lewis, 112, 256
Carson, Rachel L., 100
"A Cask of Amontillado," repetition of pattern in, 140, 250
The Castle, 179
Catachresis, meaning of, 222
Catharsis, and emotion, 8, 222
as purgation, natural and artificial, 24
in Poetics, 222, 258
relation to morality in art, 23–25
(*See also* Aesthetic distance)
Centrifugal meaning, as outward, 33–34
Centripetal meaning, defined, 223
as inward, 33–34
structure of, in myth, 39
Chaplin, Charlie, 176
Chapman, George, 4
Characterization, modes of, 223

Chaucer, Geoffrey, as direct narrator, 113–114
as humorist, 125
Roman de la Rose, interpreted, 214
tension in *The Knight's Tale,* 21
Chekhov, Anton, 151, 176
Chesterton, G. K., "A Defence of China Shepherdesses," as example of essay, 137–138
as detective story writer, 148
epigrammatic statement in, 125
"The Yellow Bird," analyzed, 145–146
Chorus, meaning of, 223
Christian humanism, 223–224
Cicero, Marcus Tullius, use of rhetoric by, 94
Classicism, meaning of, 263–266
Climax, defined, 225
as part of dramatic action, 164
Coleridge, Samuel Taylor, on mechanic and organic form, 19, 91, 187
on the reconciliation of opposites in art, 20, 22
"Rime of the Ancient Mariner," 10, 219
as Romantic critic, 185
"The Collar," 261
Comedy, of humors, 173
of ideas, 173
and intellectual detachment, 171
of manners, 173
Comedy of Errors, 172
Comic relief, in Dante and Shakespeare, 245
defined, 225
in *Macbeth,* De Quincey on, 174, 225
in *Riders to the Sea,* 69
Commedia dell'Arte, 225
Comparative literature, defined, 226
Complication in drama, 226
Comus, as masque, 247
symbolism in, 31, 35–36
virtue in, 76
Conceit, literary, defined, 226–227
Confessions of St. Augustine, 24
Congreve, William, 173
Content and form, 91–93
Context, defined, 227
Convention, defined, 227
and illusion, 9
role in art, 116–118
Coriolanus, decorum in, 231
Crashaw, Richard, 233
Criticism, approach to, 184
archetypal, 230
decorum and, 231
Freudian, 228
as judgment and interpretation, 185–186
Criticism, literary labels in, 191
as mimesis, 188
moral criticism, 190–191
neoclassical criticism, 185–187
the new criticism, 33, 68, 185, 229
objective criticism, 230
of poem, 194–200
the reader as critic, 192–193
as science and art, 188–190
types of, 193–194, 230
vividness in, 191
Cronos, myth of, 37–38
Culture, as embodiment of thought, 7–8
and literature, 7

Dactyl foot, 249
"The Daffodils," 210
Dante Alighieri, the beautiful in, 18
direct narrator, 113
The Divine Comedy, 18, 43, 106
imagery in, 15
integrating principle in, 43
intuition in, 56
irony in, 245
the mystic rose in, 35
Paradise, 35
sin in, 27–28
as transcending his time, 46
understanding his work, 111
vision of heaven in, 106
David, King, 83
"The Dead," 114, 273
analysis of, 149–152
Defence of Poetry, Shelley's view of poetic function in, 66
Demosthenes, use of rhetoric by, 94
Dennis, John, 126
Denouement, meaning of, 174, 232
De Quincey, Thomas, on literature of power, 204, 209
on *Macbeth,* 174, 225
"The Deserted Village," 232
Deus ex machina, 175, 232
Dialogues of Plato, 3
Dickens, Charles, 115, 252
Didacticism in art, 232–233
didactic poem, 117
Dionysus in Greek theater, 157
Dissociation of sensibility, 233
The Divine Comedy, beauty in, 18
integrating role of, 43
providence in, 106
(See also Dante Alighieri)
A Doll's House, 259
Donatus on Terence, 231
Donne, John, 233
Dostoievski, Fyodor, Henry James's view of, 152

Dostoievski, Fyodor, on man's reason, 132
  as realistic novelist, 110
Drama, action as open question, 163
  Aristotelian principles of, 162–165
  as art of conflict, 164, 218
  deus ex machina, 175, 232
  divisions of dramatic action, 164
    climax, 164
    denouement, 164
    exposition, 164
    falling action, 164
    rising action, 164
  expressionism in, 176–178
  foreshadowing in, 164, 169, 241
  Greek, 12
    analysis of *Antigone,* 157–162
  medieval drama, 171–172
  as mimetic art, 156
  moral evil in, 175
  recognition scene in, 172
  Theater of the Absurd, 178–180
  theater of Plautus, 172–173
Dreiser, Theodore, 109
Dryden, John, 233, 254
Dubliners, 145
Dujardin, Edouard, 250

"The Eagle," 269
Eclogue, defined, 233–234
"Edward," 219
Edward II, 242
Eisenhower, Dwight D., General, 139
El Greco, 220
Elegy, defined, 234
"Elegy in a Country Churchyard," 234
Eliot, T. S., on dissociation of sensibility, 233
  "Love Song of J. Alfred Prufrock," 31
  on objective correlative, 253
  as symbolist, 95
  The Waste Land analyzed, 39–41
Elizabeth I, 79
Emblem, defined, 234
Emerson, Ralph Waldo, on criticism, 183
  on symbolism, 31–32
Émile, 43
Empathy, defined, 234
The Emperor Jones, 177
Empson, William, on ambiguity, 215–216
  as new critic, 229
Endymion, 267
Epic, 105–107, 235–236
Epilogue, defined, 236–237
Epiphany, defined, 237
  negation of, in anticlimax, 221
Epiphany, as revelation, 209
  as used by Joyce, 32
Episode, defined, 237
Escape, 259
Escapism in literature, 237
Essay, meaning of, 135–136
Essay Concerning Human Understanding, 136
Essay on Criticism, 251
Essay on Goethe, 93
Essay on Man, 247, 251
Euphuism, defined, 237
"Eve of St. Agnes," critical analysis, 197–200
  redrafting of, 88
Everyman, 250
Exegesis, meaning of, 231
Existentialism, meaning of, 238
Explication de texte, 231
Exposition in drama, 164, 239
Expressionism in the theater, 176–178

Fable, meaning of, 237
The Faerie Queene, allegory in, 213
  purpose of, 235
  renaissance middle style in, 261
  rose symbol in, 35
Fail-Safe, 42
Fallacy, affective, 239
  intentional, 93
  pathetic, 257
Fantasy, defined, 239
Farce, 176
Fatal flaw *(see* Tragic flaw)
Fergusson, Francis, 262
Ferry, Anne Davidson, 116
Fielding, Henry, 115
Finnegans Wake, 111
Flashback, defined, 240
Flaubert, Gustave, belief in action, 107
  emphasis on showing rather than telling, 114
  selectivity of detail in, 253
Fletcher, John, 174
Foerster, Norman, 242
Foreshadowing, defined, 241
  in *Romeo and Juliet,* 169
Form, organic and mechanical, 19, 187
  in poetry, 65–66
  in relation to content, 91–93
  value of traditional, 88
Form and Style in Poetry, 65
Free verse, 85–87, 241
Freud, Sigmund, emotional release according to, 27
  influence on modern novel, 110
  inhibition, 228
  psychological criticism, 230

Freud, Sigmund, on sublimation, 8, 23
  theory of unconscious, 69, 228
Freudian criticism, 228–229
From Ritual to Romance, 39
Frye, Northrop, on centripetal structure, 39
  on criticism of poetry, 194
  on involuntary writing, 94
  on metaphor, 248
  on moving body of imagery, 36
  on poem as microcosm, 32

Galsworthy, John, 259
"The Garden," 195
Garrod, H. W., on associations of words, 51
  on classicism, 264
Genesis, literal meaning in, 254
  relationship to myth, 38–39
Genre, meaning of, 241
Georgics, 233
Gettysburg Address, 94
Gift from the Sea, 100
Gilbert, William S., 173
Gill, Eric, on creative image, 59
Giradoux, Jean, 156
Goethe, Johann Wolfgang von, Carlyle's essay on, 93
  concept of Faust, 267
  on inspiration, 65
Gogol, Nikolai, *Dead Souls,* 126–129
Goldsmith, Oliver, didactic poem, 117, 232–233
  Samuel Johnson on, 139
Gorboduc, 231
Gordon, Catherine, 152
Gorki, Maxim, 177
Gray, Thomas, 234, 270
The Great Chain of Being, 241
Gulliver's Travels, 131–132

Hamartia *(see* Tragic flaw)
Hamlet, comic relief in, 225
  conventions in, 227
  drama of synthesis and harmony, 21
  interior state of mind in, 11
  open-ended art in, 3
  pity and sorrow aroused in, 24
  suggestion in the language of, 29
  violence in, 12
Harmony, in art of conflict, 18
  as constituent of the beautiful, 17–18
Harte, Bret, 149
Hazlitt, William, 185
Hebraic-Christian tradition, 9
Heidegger, Martin, 239
Heilman, Robert, 267
Hemingway, Ernest, 103, 149
Henley, William Ernest, 86, 207
Henry IV, 238
Herbert, George, 260
Hero, concept of, 8
  as moral exemplar, 110
  public and private heroes, 102–107
  in realistic novel, 107
Herrick, Robert, 19, 111, 247
Heterocosm, poem as, 11
Heyerdahl, Thor, 103
History of ideas, defined, 241
History plays, special genre of, 242
Hitler, Adolf, 22
Holmes, Oliver Wendell, 63
Homer, and canons of art, 252
  Chapman's translation of, 4
  compared with James Joyce, 104–105
  concept of hero, 8
  as epic poet, 235
  human values in, exemplified, 44–46
  standardized epithets in, 102, 272
  union of universal and individuated in, 15
Homeric simile, defined, 242
Hopkins, Gerard Manley, 14, 32
Horace, as ancestor of Boileau and Pope, 187
  meaning of *callida junctura* in, 195
"The Hound of Heaven," 196
Hubris, 53, 161
Humanism *(see* Christian humanism; New Humanism)
Humanities, meaning of, 42
Humor, meaning of, 124–126
    distinguished from wit, 125–126
    illustrated, in Gogol's *Dead Souls,* 126–128
      in Lytton Strachey's *Queen Victoria,* 129–130
      in medieval drama, 171
Huxley, Aldous, satiric method, 135
  on vulgarity in literature, 89–91

Iambic foot, 249
Ibsen, Henrik, 163, 176, 259
Icon, meaning of, 243
The Idea of a Theater, 262
Identification, explained, 113
"The Idiot Boy," 256
Idylls of the King, 39
Iliad, analysis of scene, 45–46
  Helen of Troy, 3
"Il Penseroso," auditory imagery, 35
  baroque element, 220
  romantic element, 262
Imagery, auditory, 35
  creative, Eric Gill on, 59

Imagery, defined, 244
as mental event, 36
poet as maker of, 59
radical, 260
suggestive power, 68
as symbolism, 58
Imagination, in poetry, 58–59
power of, 204–210
Imagistic means of knowing, 54, 58–61, 208
In medias res, defined, 244
Individuation, meaning of, 18–19
relation to transcendence, 14
Inferno, 18, 245
Inscape, 14, 32
Inspiration, theory of, 64–67
Instress, 14
Integrity as constituent of the beautiful, 17
Intentional fallacy, 93
Interior monologue, defined, 250
as late development in novel, 110
in *Ulysses,* 105
Intuition, in poetry, 56–58
in relation to material world, 15
Ionesco, Eugene, 179
Irony, defined, 244–245
and levels of meaning, 68–69
"Isabella," 196
Isaiah, 64, 257

"Jabberwocky," 256
James, Henry, as critic of Dostoievski and Tolstoi, 152
and stream of consciousness, 272
theory of fiction, 113–115
Job, Book of, 80
Jones, Inigo, 247
Johnson, Dr. Samuel, on art as mirror of nature, 11
James Boswell on, 139
on mixed metaphors in "Lycidas," 59, 248
on Shakespeare's plays, 248
Wordsworth's parody of, 256
Jonson, Ben, 173, 176, 223
Joyce, James, art form in "The Dead," 149–152
concept of epiphany, 32, 237
Dubliners, 145
Finnegans Wake, 111
stream of consciousness in, 105, 250
theory of beauty in *A Portrait of the Artist as a Young Man,* 17–18
Ulysses, analyzed, 104–105
Jung, Carl, influence, on criticism, 230
on modern novel, 110
Jung, Carl, symbol as unitive of the conscious and unconscious mind, 29
theory of collective unconscious, 37

Kafka, Franz, as anti-rationalist, 111, 179
Kant, Immanuel, 266
Keats, John, *Endymion,* 267
"The Eve of St. Agnes," analysis of, 197–200
redrafting of, 88
on negative capability, 250
on neoclassicism, 185–186
on poetry, as highest thought, 57
as religious vocation, 67
as state of vision, 267
Sleep and Poetry, 67, 185–186
syntheses in "Isabella," 196–197
use of simile, 269
Keats's Craftsmanship, 65
Ker, W. P., 65
Khayyám, Omar, 44
Kierkegaard, Sören, 239
King Lear, 33, 258
The Knight's Tale, 21
Kon-Tiki, 103
Krutch, Joseph Wood, on the modern essay, 135, 137

"La Belle Dame Sans Merci," 219
Lamb, Charles, 64, 136–137
Laurel and Hardy, 176
Lawrence, D. H., on myth of Cronos, 37–38
on symbolism, 32
"Two Blue Birds," analyzed, 146–148
Lessing, Gotthold, 115
Levels of meaning, ambiguity and ambivalence in, 68–73
in Henry Vaughan, 57, 70–72
in *Paradise Lost,* 73–79
purpose of, 245
Lewis, C. S., the New Humanism and, 243
on primary and secondary epic, 236
ritual in *Paradise Lost,* 95
Lewis, Sinclair, 108, 109
Life of John Milton, 139
Life of Dr. Samuel Johnson, 139
Lincoln, Abraham, 94
Lindbergh, Anne Morrow, 100
Literal meaning, 245–246
Literature, contemplation and, 5, 8
as criticism of life, 6–7
culture and, 7
as focal point, 6–7, 42
human values and, 41–44
as imitating action, 107

Literature, as imitating nature, 11–12, 103
(*See also* Mimesis)
integrating role of, 43–44
levels of meaning in, 68–73
morality and, 22–28
obscenity in, 112
organic truth in, 10
psychological growth and, 8
responses to, 52
scientific truth and, 9
symbolism in, 29
tension in, 20, 70
the unconscious in, 29, 105, 110
values in, 47
violence in, 12–13
Local color, meaning of, 246
Locke, John, 136
Longinus, 95, 260
Lost metaphors, meaning of, 246
"Love Song of J. Alfred Prufrock," 31
Lovejoy, A. O., 241
The Lower Depths, 177
"Lycidas," baroque element in, 219
Charles Lamb on manuscript, 64
pastoral (eclogue) conventions, 116, 233–234
struggle with material, 65
theme of fame in, 74
use of, metaphors, 59, 246, 248
syntheses, 59
Lyly, John, 237
Lyrical Ballads, Preface to, definition of poetry, 66
rejection of neoclassicism, 252
simple style and parody, 256

Macbeth, De Quincey on, 174, 225
as dramatic poetry, 260
imagistic intuition in, 58
irony in, 245
as revelation, 33
Machiavelli, Niccolò, 16
Macleish, Archibald, 96
Madame Bovary, 107
The Madwoman of Chaillot, 156
Magic in relation to ritual, 262
Mallarmé, Stéphane, 95
Malthus, Thomas, 251
Man of the Renaissance, 39
Manfred, 246
Marceau, Marcel, 156
Marcel, Gabriel, 239
"Margaritae Sorori," 86–87
Maritain, Jacques, on Christian Humanism, 224
presenting evil in art, 26
Marlowe, Christopher, concept of sin in, 78
image of Helen of Troy, 3–4
Tamburlaine, bathos in, 221
as history play, 242
The Tragical History of Doctor Faustus, 4, 78–79
Marvell, Andrew, 195, 233, 254, 258
Marx, Karl, 238
Masque, defined, 247
Masson, David, 139
Medea, 161
Melodrama, 176
Melville, Herman, 246
(See also Moby Dick)
Menaechmi, 172, 259
Mental association, defined, 247–248
relation to poetry, 61–64
in stream of consciousness, 272
Merchant of Venice, 54, 274
Mercier, Louis J. A., 242–243
Metaphor, defined, 248
lost, 246
mixed, 248
Metaphysical poetry, 35
Meter, 93, 248
Metonymy, defined, 249
Metrical feet, 249
Metrical lines, 249
Michelangelo, 25
A Midsummer Night's Dream, 215, 220–221, 226, 247, 262, 271
Milton, John, the baroque in, 219
concept of romance, 262
Homeric simile in, 242
use, of blank verse, 222
of convention, 116–117
of decorum, 95
views on poetry, 63
(See also Comus; Paradise Lost; Samson Agonistes)
Mimesis, 11, 12
and aesthetic distance, 26, 212
criticism of literature as, 188
defined, 6, 249
in *Poetics,* 258
true and false, 187
Mimesis (Auerbach), 92
Miracle play, 249
The Misanthrope, 175
Moby Dick, 103, 118, 246
Molière (Jean Baptiste Poquelin), and comedy of ideas, 163, 173
influence of Plautus on, 172–173
tragic element in comedy of, 174
use of *deus ex machina,* 175
Monologue, interior (*see* Interior monologue)
Montaigne, Michel de, 135

Montgomery, Bernard, General, 139
Moore, George, 109
More, Paul Elmer, 242
More, Sir Thomas, 175
Motif, defined, 250
  use in "A Cask of Amontillado," 140
"Mrs. Battle's Opinions on Whist," 136
Myth, 36–38

Narrative, great scene in, 118–123
  identification in, 113
  as short story, 139–143
  as showing rather than telling, 114
Naturalistic novel, 108, 252–253
Negative capability, defined, 250
Neoclassicism, in criticism, 185–188
  meaning of, 251–252
New Criticism, emphasis of, 229
  likeness to Romantic criticism, 185
  paradox in, 256
  stress on multiple meaning, 33
  terminology of, 70
New Humanism, attitude toward Romanticism, 267
  meaning of, 242–243
Nicoll, Allardyce, 226
1984, 132, 135
Notes from Underground, 132, 134
Noüy, Lecomte du, 44
Novel, defined, 252
  naturalistic, 108–110, 252–253
  realistic, 107–108, 253

Objective correlative, meaning of, 253
Objective and subjective, distinction between, 254
Obscenity, defined, 112
Ode, defined, 254
Odyssey, compared with Joyce's *Ulysses,* 104–105
  epic hero in, 235
  as primary epic, 236
Of Education, 63
"Of the Pathetic Fallacy," 15
O'Faolain, Sean, on convention, 117–118
  on realism, 213
The Old Man and the Sea, 103
"On First Looking into Chapman's Homer," 5
"On the Knocking at the Gate in *Macbeth,*" 174, 225
O'Neill, Eugene, 177
Onomatopoeia, defined, 255
  in "The Passing of Arthur," 81
Othello, 27, 177, 236
Ottava rima, 271
"Out of the Cradle Endlessly Rocking," 84
Overtone, defined, 255
  relation to symbol, 30
  use in short story, 140
Oxymoron, meaning of, 255

Parable, defined, 255
Paradise (Dante), 35
Paradise Lost, ambivalence of Satan in, 216
  baroque element in, 219
  Edgar Allan Poe's view of, 56, 91
  fusion of images in, 15
  levels of meaning in, 73–79
  Logan Pearsall Smith's view of, 91
  Milton's intention in, 93, 189
  Milton's judgment on, and on *Paradise Regained,* 189
  need of rhetoric in, 116
  as public statement, 95
  as secondary epic, 240
  syntheses in, 196
  T. S. Eliot's view of, 233
  theme of glory in, 73–79
  Virgilian tradition in, 107
  the war in heaven as flashback, 240
Paradise Regained, 189
Paradox, defined, 255–256
Paraphrase, defined, 256
"The Passing of Arthur," 39, 81
  analysis of passage in *Morte D'Arthur,* 123–124
Pastoral, defined, 234
Pater, Walter, on objective or criticism, 189
  on purpose of art, 42
  on romantic, as distinguished from classical, 263–266
Pathetic fallacy, meaning of, 196, 257
Pathos, defined and illustrated, 123–124
Peacock, Thomas Love, on poets, 41
Peripety, defined, 257
"The Philosophy of Composition," 91
Pindaric ode, defined, 254
Pinero, Arthur Wing, 163
Plato, art of measurement in, 53
  the mirror-reflector and, 11
  moral philosophers and, 42
  on poetic inspiration in the *Apology,* 67
  The Republic, 22, 29
  views, of art contrasted with Aristotle's, 23
    of artist in society, 22
    of reality, 29–30
Plautus, conventions in, 227
  elements of his theater, 172–173

Plautus, stock characters in, 272
use of prologue, 259
Plot, meaning of, 273
probability of, 141–142
relation to theme, 212
Poe, Edgar Allan, ironic motif in "A Cask of Amontillado," 140, 250
on long poem, 56
the objective of a poem, 54
poetry, as "musical thought," 89
as technique, 66
"Ulalume" criticized as vulgar and parodied by Aldous Huxley, 89–91
The Poet and the Lunatics, 144–145
Poetic justice, meaning of, 258
Poetics (Aristotle), date of, 258
definition of art in, 6
theory of catharsis, 222
tragedy as highest form of art, 106
(*See also* Aristotle; Catharsis; Mimesis)
Poetics (Scaliger) renaissance rhetoric in, 261
Poetry, centrifugal meaning in, 33, 34
centripetal meaning in, 33, 34, 39
climax of mood in, 79
dependent on image, 60
difference, from philosophy, 10
from prose, 53, 100
inscape and instress in, 14
inspiration in, 64–67
problem of pure poetry, 94–97, 260
relation to mental association, 61–64, 100
Romantic view of, 67
synthesis in, 59–61
uniqueness of individual experience in, 62
value of "difficulty overcome" in, 88
word order in, 82
Point of view, importance of, in showing rather than telling, 113–114
in narrative, 258
Polarities, meaning of, 258
Pollyanna, 28
Pope, Alexander, 20, 117, 247, 273
as neoclassicist, 185–186, 251–252
A Portrait of the Artist as a Young Man, 17–18, 237
(*See also* Joyce, James)
Pound, Ezra, 95
The Prelude, 67
The Prince, 16
Problem play, defined, 259
Prologue, defined, 259
Prose, difference between functional and creative, 100–101
as distinct from poetry, 53, 100–102
as personality and reflection, 125–139
Protagonist, meaning of, 259
Prototype, meaning of, 259
Proust, Marcel, theme of time, 11
Psalms, 83, 87
Psalm 137, 84

Quatrain, 269
Quem Quaeritis, trope, 274
Quidditas, meaning of, 19
Quintet, 270

Radical image, 35, 260
Raleigh, Sir Walter, 235
Ralph Roister Doister, 172
Ransom, John Crowe, on the icon, 243
on ontology of poetry, 229
Read, Herbert, definition of poetry, 55
on role of imagination, 59
on synthesis, 195
on training of imagination, 206–207
Realistic novel, 107–108
"Release" in works of art, 27
Republic, 22, 29
Rhetoric, in narrative, 115–116
and pure poetry, 94–97
traditional rhetoric, defined, 261
The Rhetoric of Fiction, 116
Rhythm, 83–91
sprung, 261
Rice, Elmer, 177
Richard II, 242
Richards, I. A., on imagery as mental event, 36
Riders to the Sea, 69, 175
analysis of, 165–167
Rilke, Rainer Maria, 95
Rimbaud, Arthur, 95, 260
"The Rime of the Ancient Mariner," 10, 229
Rime royal, 270
Ritual in relation to magic, 262
Rococo art, 262
Roeder, Ralph, 139
Roman de la Rose, 214
Romance, meaning of, 262
Romantic comedy, 173
Romanticism, as artistic method, 233–266
as ideology, 266–267
Romeo and Juliet, 226, 241, 257
analyzed as tragedy, 168–171
Rousseau, Jean Jacques, 43, 266
Rousseau and Romanticism, 243, 267
The Rubáiyát of Omar Khayyám, 265
Ruskin, John, classification of poets in "Of the Pathetic Fallacy," 257
combining levels in poetry, 15
on Oliver Wendell Holmes, 63

St. Augustine, view of tragedy, 24
"St. Cecilia's Day," 254
St. Ignatius Loyola, 220
St. John of the Cross, 220
St. Theresa of Avila, 220
St. Thomas Aquinas, 251
Sainte-Beuve, Charles Augustin, 185
Saintsbury, George, 187
Samson Agonistes, approach to free verse in, 85
  lost metaphors in, 246
  use of chorus in, 223
Sartre, Jean-Paul, as antirhetorician, 115
  as existentialist, 238
Satire, illustration of, in Zamiatin's *We,* 132–135
  meaning of, 130–131
Saturn (Cronos), myth of, 37
Scaliger, Joseph, 261
Schlegel, Friedrich, 254
The School for Scandal, 125, 172, 173, 236
Science and literary truth, 8
Scott, Sir Walter, 115, 252
"The Secret Life of Walter Mitty," 237
Selected Essays (T. S. Eliot), 253
Sensibility, defined, 233
Sentimentality, defined, 268
  in writing, 109
Sestet, 270
Shafer, Robert, 242
Shakespeare, William, ambivalence in, 70
  blank verse in, 222
  catharsis in *Hamlet,* 22–23
  conventions in, 227
  euphuism in, 237
  idea of harmony in *The Merchant of Venice,* 54
  inconclusiveness in, 47
  intuition in drama of, 57–58
  multidimensional characterization, 223
  as objective artist, 254
  objective correlative in *Sonnet* LXXIII, 253
  regarded as barbarian, 187
  romantic comedy in, 173
  Samuel Johnson's views on themes of plays, 174
  as tragic artist, 168–171
  unities in, 163
  (See also Hamlet; Macbeth; A Midsummer Night's Dream; Romeo and Juliet)
Shakespeare's Use of the Arts of Language, 261
Shaw, George Bernard, comedy of ideas in, 173
  Major Barbara and Antigone, 160
  state of the question as drama, 163
She Stoops to Conquer, 172
Shelley, Percy Bysshe, art as mirror of the artist's mind, 11
  maintaining poetic vision, 267
  theory of inspiration, 66
Sheridan, Richard Brinsley, 125, 236
Short story, characterization in, 142
  distinction between stories with and without plot, 139–141
  new art form in, 149–152
  probability of plot in, 141–142
  range and versatility, 143–148
  suspense in, 142–143
Sidney, Sir Philip, *Gorboduc* commended for decorum, 231
  on poet, historian, philosopher, 41
  quoted, 1
Sign, meaning of, 238
  relation to symbol, 34
Simile, defined, 269
Sir Gawain and the Green Knight, 263
"Sir Patrick Spens," 219, 270
Sister Miriam Joseph, 261
Sitwell, Osbert, 143–144, 148
"Sleep and Poetry," 67, 186
Smith, Logan Pearsall, 91
Sonnet form, 271
"Song at the Feast of Brougham Castle," 21
Spenser, Edmund, concept of hero in, 8
  glory of national epic, 74
  method of allegory, 213
  middle style in, 261
  objective of *The Faerie Queene,* 235
  use of rose symbol, 34
Spenserian stanza, 271
Spillane, Mickey, 27
Spiritual Exercises of St. Ignatius, 220
Stanza, types of, 270–271
Stevenson, Robert Louis, 223
Stichomythia, meaning of, 271
Stock characters, 271
Stock epithets, 272
Stoll, Elmer Edgar, 193
Stowe, Harriet Beecher, 268
Strachey, Lytton, 129–130, 139
Stream of consciousness, defined, 272
  in Joyce, 105, 250
Structure, centripetal, 39
  defined, 273
Subjective, distinguished from objective, 254
Sublimation, Freud on, 8, 23
Sullivan, Sir Arthur, 173

Symbol, centripetal, 33
multiplicity of meaning in, 31
origin of word, 32
relation to overtones, 30
role of intelligence in, 30
unitive of conscious and unconscious, 29
Symbolism, and the new criticism, 33
and poetry, 100
Synecdoche, defined, 249
Synge, John Millington, 65, 165
Synthesis, applied in literary criticism, 195–201
defined, 59, 195–196

Tableaux, meaning of, 242
Tamburlaine, bathos in, 221
as history play, 242
Tartuffe, 172, 174, 175
Tasso, Torquato, 8
Tate, Allen, on James Joyce's "The Dead," 152
as new critic, 229
Tate, Nahum, 258
Tennyson, Alfred, Lord, 39, 81, 269, 270
Tension in work of art, 20–22, 70
Tercet, 269
Texture, defined, 273
Thackeray, William Makepeace, 114
Theater, of the Absurd, 148, 178–180, 238
of Plautus, 172–173
Theme, defined, 212, 273
Theocritus, 233
"They Are All Gone into the World of Light," 264
discussed in terms of the new criticism, 70–72
Thompson, Francis, 67, 106
Thurber, James, 237
Tindall, William York, 105
"To Daffodils," 111, 247
"To Helen," 4
"To His Coy Mistress," 258
"To the Rose upon the Rood of Time," 35
"To a Skylark," 11
Tolstoi, Leo, analysis of *Anna Karenina,* 119–123
Henry James on, 152
"infectiousness" in art, 206
integrating principle in, 43
on purpose of art, 203, 206
as realist, 143
symbolism in, 29
unitive force in art, 203
Tom Jones, 115
Tradition, Christian humanism, 223–224
Judaic-Christian, 9, 45–46, 175
meaning of, 3
Platonic, 67
renaissance humanism, 42
Romantic, 67, 226–267
Virgilian, 107
Tragedy, emotional power of, 167–171
as highest form of art, 106
Tragic flaw, meaning of, 167–168, 273–274
The Tragical History of Doctor Faustus, 4, 78–79
Tragicomedy, 174–175
A Tree Grows in Brooklyn, 10
Trochee, 249
Trope, defined, 274
Tropological, meaning of, 274
"The Twa Corbies," 219
Twelfth Night, 173
"Two Blue Birds," 146–148

"Ulalume," 89
Ulysses, 104–105, 112, 117
The Uncelestial City, 195, 208
Uncle Tom's Cabin, 268
Under the Sun of Satan, 151
Undset, Sigrid, 148
Unterecker, John, metaphor and symbol distinguished, 248
on sign value of symbol, 33
"Upon Cromwell's Return from Ireland," 254

"The Value of the Creative Faculty in Man," 59
Vaughan, Henry, 47, 233, 264
analysis of poetic statement in, 57, 70–72
The Verbal Icon, 239
Verlaine, Paul, 260
Victoria, Queen, 129–130, 139
Virgil, concept of hero in, 8, 106–107
eclogue form in, 233
epic form in, 235
model for neoclassicism, 252
Volpone, 172, 176
Voltaire, 231

Waiting for Godot, 156, 180
War and Peace, 43
Warren, Robert Penn, 239
The Waste Land, 39–41
Watteau, Jean Antoine, 234
We, analyzed as satire, 132–135

Wells, H. G., 114
Weston, Jessie L., 39
What Is Art?, 206
"When Lilacs Last in the Dooryard Bloom'd," 84
Whitman, Walt, 20, 82–84
Wilde, Oscar, 125
Wimsatt, W. K., Jr., 229, 239
The Winter's Tale, 173
Wodehouse, P. G., 172
Wolfe, Humbert, 195, 208
Woodhouse, Richard, 250
Word order in poetry, 82
Wordsworth, Dorothy, 89
Wordsworth, William, exemplifying exercise of imagination, 209–210
  parody illustrated by, 256
  on poetic inspiration, 66
Wordsworth, William, principle of tension illustrated by, 21
  rejection of neoclassicism, 252
  Romantic ideology in, 267
The World of Harlequin, 226
Wycherley, William, 173

Yeats, W. B., on poetry as state of trance, 94
  symbolism in, 35
"The Yellow Bird," analyzed, 145–146

Zamiatin, Eugenii Ivanovich, 43 132–135
Zeitgeist, defined, 274
Zola, Émile, 109